I WAS THERE
ON PQ17
THE CONVOY
TO HELL

Through the Icy Russian Waters
of World War II

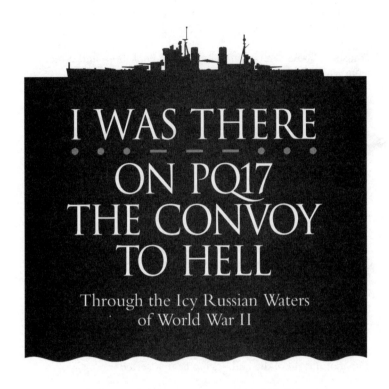

I WAS THERE

ON PQ17 THE CONVOY TO HELL

Through the Icy Russian Waters
of World War II

PAUL LUND & HARRY LUDLAM

foulsham
LONDON • NEW YORK • TORONTO • SYDNEY

foulsham

The Oriel, Thames Valley Court, 183–187 Bath Road, Slough, Berkshire, SL1 4AA, England

Foulsham books can be found in all good bookshops and direct from www.foulsham.com

ISBN: 978-0-572-03542-6

First published in 1968 by W. Foulsham & Co. Ltd © Paul Lund and Harry Ludlam

This edition copyright © 2010 Paul Lund and Harry Ludlam

Front cover photographs © Imperial War Museum (top) and Superstock (bottom)

Back cover photographs © (clockwise, from top left) © Imperial War Museum, Mirrorpix, Mary Evans Picture Library, Mirrorpix (2), Corbis, Imperial War Museum, Mirrorpix (3)
Chapter-head drawings by Hilton Brodie, Chief Cook, the SS *Carsbreck*

A CIP record for this book is available from the British Library

The moral right of the authors has been asserted

All rights reserved

Other books by these authors:
I Was There to Face the Night of the U-boats

The Copyright Act prohibits (subject to certain very limited exceptions) the making of copies of any copyright work or of a substantial part of such a work, including the making of copies by photocopying or any similar process. Written permission to make a copy or copies must therefore normally be obtained from the publisher in advance. It is advisable also to consult the publisher if in any doubt as to the legality of any copying which is to be undertaken.

Printed in Great Britain by Thomson Litho Ltd, East Kilbride

Contents

	Introduction	7
1	The Arctic Convoys	9
2	To Save Stalingrad	15
3	How is the War?	31
4	Scatter!	51
5	Black Sunday	79
6	Flight to Funk Creek	99
7	Bloody Marvellous!	121
8	Snatched from the Sea	147
9	Full Ahead on a Prayer	169
10	The Hungry Wait	185
11	The Final Toll	203
12	Whose Fault?	221
	Abbreviations	247
	Acknowledgements	249
	Maps	254

To all the men who survived PQ 17 and to the memory of those who did not, this book is dedicated. Their bodies are laid, overdosed by fitful wave and swirling tide; No headstone but the gleam of Northern Light; No tears shed here, only rain and spray; No voice of pity, but that of the wheeling gull; Their shroud the long sea grass will be, Their plot the shifting sea-bed sand.

Third Officer Henry W Phillips RFA, the *Aldersdale*

Introduction

I have never been able to rejoice with my American friends on Independence Day, because July 4 is, to me, a day to hang my head in grief for all the men who lost their lives on Convoy PQ 17 and in shame at the recollection of one of the bleakest episodes in Royal Naval history, when the warships deserted the merchant ships and left them to their fate. For that, in simple terms, was what we were obliged to do.

Vice Admiral W D O'Brien CB DSC
Commander Far East Fleet

Chapter 1

The Arctic Convoys

'Hell below zero' they called it, the men who ran the convoys to north Russia. They had choicer descriptions, too, for the desolate Arctic regions that proved one of the most challenging arenas of the Second World War. Here half the battle was fought against the elements, and an icy sea could claim a man within minutes of immersion.

In the winter it was a fight against intense cold and long hours of darkness. Freezing fog was a constant companion until it was blown away by winds that turned sharply to howling gales. Ships heaved and rolled, forging their way through dangerous loose ice and icebergs. Icy spray lashed across them, freezing on decks and gun mountings. It whiplashed the lookouts' faces, turning them the colour of raw steak. With the gales came hail like tiny machine-gun bullets, and snow that piled up on deck and froze if it was not dug away quickly. Crews had to watch out constantly for ice forming: too heavy a build-up could cause a ship to capsize in rough weather.

In midsummer, when PQ 17 sailed, the Arctic could show a very different but still treacherous face. Around the coast of Iceland you encountered heavy seas, biting cold and dull grey skies, but as you headed north-east, passing near Jan Mayen Island, and then due east, steaming north or south of Bear Island, conditions improved. Here was a world where the sun shone brilliantly for 24 hours a day. You could feel it tanning you at 2 a.m., even with the temperature below zero – but the enemy could see you for 24 hours a day.

There was still ice and fog, but in different forms. To the north was the ice barrier, dividing the blue sea from the dazzling expanse of ice that stretched away unbroken to the North Pole; in midsummer the distance from the ice edge to the Pole was about 700 miles. Huge icebergs sailed past majestically, like multi-coloured schooners glinting in the sun. Fog banks rose out of the sea and eerily engulfed you. Generally, however, it was a lighter, softer, friendlier fog than experienced in the grim winter months, and you were soon out of it and back in a world of cobalt blue sky and sea. For this was a part of the Arctic where the Gulf Stream made itself felt, causing great variations in sea temperature and sudden shifting fog banks.

The perpetual daylight made it difficult to remember whether it was 4 a.m. or 4 p.m., whether your next meal was going to be breakfast or supper. This feeling of unreality was increased by the heady thinness of the air and the unusual clarity of the atmosphere, which brought a strange, dream-like quality to everything. Even the dancing, sparkling waves seemed to have a hypnotic effect. Other ships seemed to spread themselves out into the shape of islands or elongate themselves into tall trees, all length and no breadth. Other ships seemed to sail upside down above the horizon on a sea in the sky. Then you remembered that mirages as vivid as any seen in the desert occurred in these regions.

This was the weird, lonely world convoy PQ 17 sailed into.

When Hitler invaded Russia on 22 June 1941, Stalin immediately appealed to Britain and America for war materials and supplies for his hard-pressed armies. A first convoy was sent to Russia in August. In September the long series of PQ convoys began, planned to sail at ten-day intervals. They did not happen, however, though they still kept to a heavy schedule.

On 7 July 1941, only a fortnight after Hitler marched on Russia, Iceland was occupied by American forces, so the PQ convoys sailed from there. They went up the west coast of Iceland, round to the north and east, past Jan Mayen Island and Bear Island, along the northern ice edge, as far as possible from enemy airfields in northern Norway. Then they travelled into the Barents Sea, down to the Kola Inlet and the port of Murmansk: 2,000 miles from Scapa Flow. Most ships went to Murmansk, the only Russian port that remained ice free all year. If the ice permitted, some sailed 400 miles further on, east to Archangel.

PQ 1, ten ships escorted by a cruiser and two destroyers, left Iceland for Archangel on 28 September 1941. In the words of someone who took part in it, the operation was 'a piece of cake'. More convoys followed at roughly fortnightly intervals. None were attacked and by the end of the year more than 50 merchantmen had steamed safely through.

In the early months of 1942, however, as successive convoys fought their way through winter gales and blizzards, enemy resistance slowly built up. Even so, when the 12 ships of PQ 12 sailed on 1 March, only one outward-bound merchantman and a destroyer had been lost.

From then on, losses mounted, though they were still small. PQ 12 lost one ship; the next convoy four ships; and PQ 14 one, though 16 vessels had to turn back because of ice. PQ 15, made up of 25 ships, which sailed in April, lost three merchantmen. The Navy's losses at this time also included two valuable cruisers, the *Trinidad* and the *Edinburgh*, both torpedoed.

Now it was the Arctic summer, with 24 hours of daylight. There was no darkness to give the slow-moving merchantmen and their escorts some protection against enemy attacks. As well as enemy planes and U-boats, the fast, immensely powerful battleship *Tirpitz* and her consorts, lurking in the Norwegian fjords, were a threat. The *Tirpitz* had already made one sortie: PQ 12 had narrowly escaped her.

Stalin was adamant that the convoys should continue without interruption, however, and President Roosevelt also believed they should go on; American merchant ships were now queueing up to join the convoys. Churchill had little option but to comply with the wishes of the other two leaders, so PQ 16 – a total of 35 ships, the largest convoy yet – sailed from Hvalfjord on 21 May. It had 17 close escorts, shadowed by four cruisers and three destroyers, which accompanied it as far as Bear Island. The battle fleet was to the rear, ready to intercept the *Tirpitz* if she put to sea. She did not, but during a very tough run to Murmansk, PQ 16 lost seven ships, six from heavy attacks by enemy aircraft.

Then it was the turn of PQ 17. After PQ 16's bitter experience, the question was: should PQ 17 sail or wait for a return of winter darkness? After the loss of the *Trinidad* and the *Edinburgh* no escorting cruisers could be risked beyond Bear Island, and no aircraft carrier spared for the run. There also remained the threat from the *Tirpitz* and other German heavy ships. Strong information had been received that the enemy intended to make an all-out assault on the next convoy.

Stalin, concerned only with his country's plight, insisted that the convoys should continue whatever the cost. Roosevelt concurred. Churchill was therefore forced to make a political decision, and the Admiralty, which had strongly objected to the convoy sailing in broad daylight, was obliged to follow the Government's wishes.

PQ 17's original sailing date was 11 June 1942, but because of the demands of the Malta run on fleet escorts, it was postponed to 27 June. At Hvalfjord, we in PQ 17 knew nothing of these deliberations, only that it was a long, long wait.

Chapter 2

To Save Stalingrad

In the still, cold waters of Hvalfjord a flotilla of merchant ships lay silently at anchor, each displaying her name on large boards on either side of her bridge. It looked like the prelude to some strange regatta to be held within sight of the fjord's snow-capped hills. There was an air of quiet expectancy.

Suddenly the peace of the June day was disturbed by an urgent blinker message from one of the American ships, the *Christopher Newport*. The signal was received by the battleship USS *Washington*, and soon a contingent of US marines was speeding across the fjord by motor launch to quell a 'mutiny' aboard the merchantman. They found that some of the crew had found a shipment of Scotch whisky for Admiral Stanley, the US *Ambassador* in Moscow, and things had got out of hand. The marines quickly restored order.

     This incident, worthy of a comic opera and the first 'armed action' of PQ 17, was just one symptom of the deep frustration felt by the seamen. They had made the long journey across the Atlantic only to find themselves held up at Hvalfjord for weeks, waiting for PQ 17 to sail. More than two-thirds of the convoy was to be composed of American ships: there were 24 of them, carrying massive aid from the United States for the hard-pressed Russians.

Those of us in the small naval escorts had seen them come in. They included ships like the *Alcoa Ranger* from Philadelphia, loaded with 7,000 tons of steel, armour plate and flour, with 19 tanks lashed to her deck. The *Washington* and the *Honomu*, from the same port, were loaded with ammunition, steel, foodstuffs and TNT. They, too, had tanks and truck chassis stacked on deck. The *Daniel Morgan* from Baltimore also carried tanks, with similar cargoes and deck-loads on the rest of the American ships. By normal standards they were all grossly overladen.

The majority were hard-worked vessels with names as unspectacular as their appearance. There were old Hog Islanders like the *Exford* and the *Hoosier*, with their characteristic humpback profiles, products of the Pennsylvania shipyard, with more than 20 years of nautical miles behind them. And then there was the *Ironclad*, a vessel so small and rusty that we wondered whether the Germans would bother to waste an expensive torpedo on her.

Four vessels carried very proud names – the *Samuel Chase*, the *John Witherspoon*, the *William Hooper* and the *Benjamin Harrison* – men who signed the US Declaration of Independence. But these were the 'ugly ducklings' of the convoy: squat, slow Liberty ships from the moulds of Henry Kaiser, built quickly from prefabricated sections and welded together instead of riveted in the traditional way. The seamen on board the Liberty ships did not like them – their rigid construction made them dangerous in bad seas – but these vessels played an important role in the Atlantic lifeline.

Not all the American ships were crewed by US seamen. *El Capitan* from New York, rows of planes lashed to her decks, flew the Panamanian flag; her ten-strong gun crew were the only Americans aboard. *El Capitan* reached Hvalfjord during the last week of May, as most of the American ships had. The merchant crews found the prolonged delay after their Atlantic crossing almost unbearable. At first it was a tremendous let-down, then tension was mixed with unutterable boredom: they were confined to ship, denied permission to visit Reykjavik, the Icelandic capital, whose tempting lights could be seen not far off. Small wonder Admiral Stanley lost a little of his whisky.

The American ships had made long voyages. The crew of the *Peter Kerr*, from Portland, Oregon, which included Second Mate William Connolly, joined her in a shipyard in New York. There the veteran freighter was fitted out with her scanty arms and armour, loaded, mainly with foodstuffs, and had her decks filled with tanks and planes. It was no secret where she was bound: she had an extra steam radiator installed in each compartment, a sure and obvious sign that she was destined for north Russia.

The *Peter Kerr* had sailed from New York on Easter Sunday 1942, steaming alone to Halifax, Nova Scotia. There she joined a regular North Atlantic convoy and crossed to the Firth of Clyde. Then it was on to Loch Ewe, in western Scotland, where she joined another small convoy bound for Iceland, and on to Hvalfjord. There her crew were confined to ship for 23 days as they waited for PQ 17 to sail. One reason given to Second Mate Connolly and his colleagues for the ban on shore leave was that earlier crews allowed ashore had been found amusing themselves by throwing eider-duck eggs at each other. The eider duck was a valued natural resource, and the Icelanders had taken a poor view of such antics.

There was some truth in this, though there was rather more to it, as men of the Allied forces who did get ashore, or who had the misfortune to be stationed there, could testify. The Icelanders did not welcome them. Until recently they had encountered open hostility: to go out alone after dark was to risk being beaten up. The Icelanders' resentment had now turned to more passive resistance, but it was not uncommon to be spat on when your back was turned.

This frigid reception was hardest to bear when it came from the Icelandic women. We were not worried by the men completely ignoring our presence, but it hurt our pride when beautiful women with magnificent blonde hair cascading down their backs looked through us. These tall, elegant girls never let their eyes meet those of a 'foreigner' for a second. In shops, cafés and hotels, the girls who served you were coldly polite and correct, but froze at the least sign of familiarity. 'Smashing pieces them blondes, but they don't even see a bloke!' was the cry from the British lower deck.

The Icelanders showed exceptional bitterness towards the Americans. Some unfortunate incidents had not helped, including cases of Icelanders, some of them children, being accidentally shot at near American camps. There was 'rum-running' by Icelanders from ships in Reykjavik harbour, resulting in chases and shooting by Allied and Icelandic police. The rum bottle was the only entrée into Icelandic social life, though other opportunities were offered by taxi-riding prostitutes who leaned out of taxi-cab windows soliciting the sex-starved seamen.

The Allied rank and file were bewildered by this hostile attitude, since the Icelanders enjoyed great prosperity as a result of the 'invasion'. The streets of brilliantly lit Reykjavik were full of large American cars, the shops were full of luxury US goods, there were lashings of good food and the women dressed in Bond Street style. Even visits to the quayside had to be kept as short as possible because of the high dues charged by the Icelanders.

So there was only Hvalfjord close by. The British sailor never thought he would describe any place as being 'worse than Scapa Flow', but he did so now. Hvalfjord was a desolate place, often swept by howling gales that tore vessels from their moorings. In winter it was bitterly cold, and in summer, as now, just cold. The shore amenities amounted to one large hut-canteen selling strong Canadian beer, where fights broke out nearly every night.

So, in fact, the American seamen of PQ 17 were missing very little. It did not seem that way, however, to men confined to their ships, especially when on a glorious dawn, with the sun turning the snow-covered mountains a delicate pink, they could glimpse gaily coloured Icelandic fishing boats pulling in their daily catches. These were a people seemingly untouched by Hitler's war.

Some of the eight British merchant ships which, together with a Dutch ship and two Russian tankers, were to complete PQ 17, arrived at Hvalfjord later than the Americans, so escaping part of the frustrating waiting period. Typical among these ships was the *Earlston*, a 6,000-ton 'utility' ship only a year old, crammed with a cargo of field guns, lorries, crated Hurricane fighter planes and hundreds of tons of naval ammunition. On deck aft she carried drums of high-octane fuel and toluene, the chief constituent of TNT; athwartships, just forward of the bridge, a naval steam pinnance or powered launch was secured, destined for the Admiralty base at Archangel.

The British ships were as heavily laden as the American vessels. One of them, the *Empire Tide*, was unique: she was a CAM ship, a catapult aircraft merchantman. She carried a Hurricane fighter that could be launched into action once only: when the pilot returned he had to ditch the plane into the sea after baling out by parachute, trusting that he would be hauled to safety from the freezing sea. The *Empire Tide* had some peculiarities of construction designed to mislead the enemy, and as well as guns and a barrage balloon, she had the advantage of being fitted with an early type of radar for aircraft detection. Despite all the secrecy surrounding her, however, her destination had been made as obvious while loading at Newport, Rhode Island, as had the *Peter Kerr's* at New York, since many of the packages swung aboard were clearly marked: 'Admiral Dolinin – Murmansk' or 'Admiral Dolinin – Archangel'. So much for security.

The *Empire Tide's* radar advantage was shared by the *Ocean Freedom*, a new British ship built quickly in South Portland, Massachusetts, and, like the Liberty ships, more than half welded. The *Ocean Freedom* had made her maiden voyage across the Atlantic with a cargo of steel plates and reloaded in the UK with tanks, Bren-gun carriers and other equipment for Russia. She then led a small convoy from Loch Ewe to Hvalfjord, with her master, Captain William Walker, as Commodore. On this trip she tasted action – of a kind. It was a standing regulation that aircraft should not approach a convoy during fog, but an American aircraft did approach and was shot down by the *Ocean Freedom* and the *Earlston* in mistake for a Focke-Wulf. Its crew were picked up and Capt. Walker told to forget the incident and not let it affect his gunners' trigger-fingers.

The *Earlston's* armament was typical of the merchant ships. She had twin Brownings on the 'monkey island' or gun platform above the bridge, two Oerlikons on the bridge wings, two at the after-end of the boat deck and two more forward of the poop. Also for use against aircraft there were two 'pig troughs' or sets of rockets on the boat deck, and to deter U-boats, an old four-inch surface gun.

Some ships had more, some less. They carried gun crews of anything up to 12 men, with British gunners occasionally seconded to the American ships, as with the *Olopana* from San Francisco. The majority of US ships carried their own armed guard unit, however. The one Dutch ship, the *Paulus Potter*, had British gunners.

Some ships had acquired their armament very hastily. The Hog Islander *Exford* had stayed at Loch Ewe just long enough to take on board two marines and two Royal Navy gunners to man the still crated 30-calibre guns. As for the 'mutinous' *Christopher Newport*, when Lieutenant Daniel Jones, from the USS *Washington*, visited his friend, the armed guard officer aboard her, he was appalled to find an old four-inch gun taken from a park in Baltimore mounted on the fantail, its rifling almost worn smooth and its elevation no more than about 35 degrees. After seeing the other worthless weapons and the inadequate quantity of ammunition the ship had to defend herself with, Lieut. Jones left with a heavy heart and the conviction that only a miracle would allow her to survive what was in store for her.

Only a small number of the American merchant captains had first-hand knowledge of the sort of seas and weather to expect. Captain Julius Holmgrun of the *Hoosier* had come out of retirement from a farm in Maine to answer the call of his adopted country. Born in Stockholm, Sweden, he had gone to America as a young boy. Now in his late seventies, he was again in his childhood waters. Among the British masters with good experience of the Arctic, however, was Captain Stenwick of the *Earlston*, originally a Norwegian baron who was now a naturalised Briton.

The crews of the American ships were not only unfamiliar with northern waters, but for many of them, boys from all parts of the States, it was their first long voyage. For some, it was their first time at sea. There were similar young men among our British merchant crews, too, serving side by side with veterans who had acquired a quiet fatalism serving on ships that had ploughed slowly through enemy waters.

There were also inexperienced boys and older veterans on our naval escort vessels, which shared the long wait at Hvalfjord. There were seven of us: three minesweepers and four anti-submarine trawlers, forming a third of the convoy's escort. By ourselves we could scarcely deter the enemy, but the rest of the fleet escorts would be joining us when we rounded Iceland. If the men of a 10,000-ton merchant vessel found the small minesweepers, such as the 850-ton *Salamander*, hard to accept as warships, they looked askance at our diminutive coal-burning trawlers, whose top speed of around ten knots was well below the flat-out capabilities of most of the merchantmen.

One trawler, the *Northern Gem*, was German-built, from Bremerhaven. One of a number of German fishing vessels given to Britain as part of reparations after the First World War, she was faster and better constructed than the British-built trawlers, of which the *Lord Austin* was typical. Our little 700-ton vessel looked what she was, a deep-sea fishing trawler with single funnel, high bow and low well-deck, which in rough weather was mostly under water. Her black-and-tan colour had been changed to blue and white – Admiralty camouflage – so she merged with the sea and ice. If the merchantmen's armaments were a motley collection, ours were positively awe-inspiring. We carried a single four-inch surface gun, with an Oerlikon abaft the bridge, twin point-fives on a stern platform and two Hotchkiss machine guns on the bridge-wings. On deck, on each side of the bridge, were two depth-charge throwers. Whenever we sent a depth charge over the side, the *Lord Austin's* stern rose up and shuddered.

Two PAC rockets, similar to those carried by the merchantmen, were set on either side of the bridge. Fathoms and fathoms of wire attached to a parachute were fixed to the rockets: the idea was that when the rocket was fired at a diving aircraft, the plane would get entangled in the trailing wire and crash. 'All right on sparrows, perhaps,' one wag remarked.

The most enterprising contraption of all was the Holman projector. This consisted of a stove-like pipe attached to a steam pipe from the engine room. The man firing it built up the steam pressure, then put a tin with a lightly soldered lid containing a hand grenade into the pipe. The idea was that if a plane was diving at the ship, the firer released the steam, which shot up the tin. This twisted round in mid-air, the lid shot off, the solder was melted by the steam, out shot the grenade with its lever released, and the plane – if it was still there – caught some of the shrapnel. No one ever saw a plane hit by one, but they had some near misses on themselves when the hand grenades fell back on the ships. The trawler crews called the Holman projector the 'hot potato cart'. Our ships shot potatoes at one another for fun: it was the contraption's safest use.

The hard core of the trawler crews were naval men, fishermen and tug men of the Northern Patrol, but, like the merchantmen, the trawlers also carried many men who were absolutely raw. On the *Northern Gem*, for instance, more than two-thirds of the crew were boys who had never been to sea, or even seen it before they joined up. All of us, however, were as anxious as the merchantmen to get going. The lot of the *Lord Austin* in the war had so far been mainly fighting heavy weather, gales, bitter cold, discomfort and soul-destroying monotony. During the long months on the Northern Patrol, the long weeks in Iceland and the fogs and ice floes of a recent convoy, we had had neither sight nor sound of the enemy. Now the prospect of meeting him face to face, of seeing some real action, however horrible and bloody, had us keyed up. Some hair-raising stories of what had happened to PQ 16 had filtered back. Seven ships lost. Would it be as terrible as others made out, or were their tales exaggerated for effect? How would each of us stand up to the ordeal? What would it really be like? Would we survive it?

Above all we felt strongly that at last we would be doing a worthwhile job in the war. Nothing, we were told, was more vital than getting these emergency supplies through to Russia – to save Stalingrad. Without them, Russia was likely to be defeated by the Germans and the war could drag on for years.

Suddenly the long wait was over. The cruiser *London* reappeared at Hvalfjord, her enormous bulk dwarfing the merchant vessels and making our tiny trawlers seem like toys. During the long wait the *London* had fussed about like some mammoth nursemaid, holding conferences at Seydisfjord, Hvalfjord and Akureyri in the north; now she was back at Hvalfjord for a final conference, held in a hut ashore. The flagship of Rear Admiral L K H Hamilton, she was to lead a combined British and US cruiser squadron that would shadow PQ 17 to Bear Island.

Merchant gunners and some officers had been briefed earlier about the enemy's tricks in the Arctic: the prowling U-boats went under the ice to escape detection by asdic beam or depth-charge attack, or lay in wait against an iceberg, their blue and white camouflage making them extremely difficult to detect. The convoy procedure was run through for the merchant captains and officers: among them was a Russian woman officer from the *Azerbaijan*, one of the two Russian tankers sailing with us. Her presence caused much surprise.

The naval escort commanders returned to ship after the conference. They were in a positive frame of mind – with some a little the worse for wear. One was collected by his whaleboat crew: 'We're going to shink shubmarines and lay the bastards we capture out on deck and shkin 'em alive!' he said. 'Silly old runt,' one of the crew said. 'I'd rather skin him alive any time.'

But it set the mood. At the conference one of the main speakers had been Commander J E ('Jack') Broome, who, in the destroyer *Keppel*, would lead the naval escorts. He was very optimistic. The Germans, he thought, would be reluctant to attack such a strong escort: 21 warships in all. His destroyers had just spent a short time at sea trying out some moves in case the surface ships came our way: he was sure the timely use of smoke and torpedoes would deter them.

Cdr. Broome was a very experienced convoy escort officer, 40 years old, and a man's man. In action, his crew said, he could look 'dog rough', without teeth or cap; ashore he cut a jaunty figure, wearing a thick jersey, dentures, and with his cap at a natty angle. Everyone respected him for his resolute character and the determined way he ran his ship. He had the unqualified respect and loyalty of the *Keppel's* lower deck. And on his ship the rum was neat.

Nor was there anything of the remote sea commander about the leader of the merchantmen, Commodore John Dowding RNR, on the British *River Afton*. Just into his fifties, he was a forthright man who had spent a lifetime at sea. He had served in cruisers and destroyers in the First World War, and then for nearly 20 years at sea for the Orient Line. In 1940 he had brought his crippled ship back from Dunkirk to win a DSO. He was quietly confident, every inch a convoy man, and the merchant captains, after patiently listening to administrative officers, none of whom were coming with the convoy, were agreeably impressed when Commodore Dowding addressed them as 'Your Commodore for the trip'.

The confidence of these two leaders set the mood for the convoy. Tactics were to be little changed from those of PQ 16. The merchantmen, with the minesweepers and trawlers, would sail up Iceland's west coast and turn north-east, where they would be joined by the balance of the escorts led by the *Keppel*, which were sailing up from Seydisfjord. Then they would begin the long haul past Bear Island into the Barents Sea. The shadowing cruiser force, made up of the *London* and the *Norfolk*, the US cruisers *Wichita* and *Tuscaloosa* and three destroyers, would guard us against surface attack as far as Bear

Island – any attack, that is, which they were capable of handling. That excluded the menacing *Tirpitz*. The cruisers were not to go beyond Bear Island or the longitude of the North Cape (25 degrees E). The safety of the convoy would therefore depend on the close escorts and some British and Russian submarines operating in the area.

A heavy force well to the rear, cruising between Scapa Flow and Spitzbergen, was to give protection on the earlier part of the journey. This force, led by the Commander in Chief Home Fleet, Admiral Sir John Tovey, on the battleship the *Duke of York*, included the USS *Washington*, the aircraft carrier *Victorious*, two cruisers and 14 destroyers. Its main function was to patrol west of Bear Island to guard the convoy against surface attack in that area. The whole operation was under Admiral Tovey's command.

So, on the afternoon of 27 June, PQ 17 began its eventful journey. The sun shone through the thin Icelandic air on to the calm waters of Hvalfjord, which was flanked by jagged peaks. As our small escort vessels circled around waiting for their cue, it looked like a scene from a picture postcard. We waited until the clumsy bulk of the first merchantman broke the entrance to the fjord. She lumbered slowly past, followed by another and then another, as the heavily laden vessels turned from their month-long anchorages and passed in line out to sea. It seemed to take hours for the procession to clear: 33 merchant ships, two Russian tankers and two British fleet oilers, the *Gray Ranger* and the *Aldersdale*, both rigged with a dummy funnel to make them look like merchantmen.

One by one the waiting escorts sailed out of the fjord to take up their stations. The *Lord Austin's* position was right at the stern of the convoy, so we were the last to go. As we glanced back with a touch of envy at the rest of the ships lying serenely at anchor in that desolate haven, we could imagine what their crews' comments were: 'Thank God we're not going with that lot, poor bastards!' We had said the same thing when PQ 16 had sailed. Now it was our turn.

As soon as the *Lord Austin* passed through the mouth of the fjord into the open sea the waves rose, the wind strengthened and our small vessel began to pitch. The sun vanished and a dank greyness descended. We began to feel the cold.

Meanwhile, the *London* returned to Seydisfjord, where the rest of the escorts were making ready to sail. The most important were two anti-aircraft ships, the *Palomares* and the *Pozarica*. They were not dedicated naval warships but converted merchantmen – banana boats – used in peacetime for carrying cargo and a few passengers. Now they were fitted with thousands of tons of armour plating and bristled with guns. The *Pozarica* had twin four-inch anti-aircraft guns and four-barrelled pom-poms; her close-range arms had been newly installed. She was so loaded with shells that they were stacked up on the magazine deck. Deck stowage! This was certainly going to be some party.

The *Pozarica* had been on convoy duties in the western approaches for over a year, and arguments had raged on her mess decks: which was the lesser of the two evils? Malta or Russia? The Malta convoy was a comparatively short run. There was fierce opposition, especially in the air, but aircraft carriers gave some air cover. There was little let-up in the attacks after leaving Gibraltar, but there was a warm swim if you found yourself in 'the drink' and land was never far away. The Russian run, on the other hand, was a very different kettle of fish: a long journey through bleak waters, no aircraft carrier to give cover, and very little hope of survival if it came to a swim in the icy water. Some odds.

The convoy had four corvettes, two brand new and making their maiden voyages, then six destroyers led by Cdr. Broome in the *Keppel*. These included veterans like the *Fury*, with two Russian runs behind her, but apart from the *Offa*, a larger fleet destroyer, all were small Hunt-class destroyers or First World War vessels that were now obsolete. The *Keppel* herself was known to 'leak like a sieve', her steam pipes tied up with spun yarn. There was even an old four-stacker American destroyer from the First World War, the USS *Twiggs*, now named HMS *Leamington*. She was one of 50 such ships given to the Royal Navy by America in return for a chain of bases.

So the convoy was a jumble of warships and conversions. However, the small fleet of 12 vessels, together with two submarines – one sailing with us from Hvalfjord – could combine with our trawlers and minesweepers to enable us to oppose any attacker.

At Seydisfjord there was a welcome yet sobering addition to this force: three 'tail-end Charlies', small merchant ships whose job would be to dog the convoy and rescue survivors of stricken ships. The *Rathlin*, the *Zaafaran* and the *Zamalek* were around 1,500 tons. In peacetime they rarely undertook voyages more than 40 hours long, running from east-coast ports to the Continent, or ploughing down from Glasgow to London. Now, fitted out with guns and medical equipment, and with a naval surgeon, sick-bay attendants and gunners sailing with their merchant crews, they were to make a marathon run in grim waters. The lower holds of all three rescue vessels were fitted with empty casks to give them greater buoyancy.

The little *Rathlin* had been a cattle carrier and general cargo boat on a regular run from Glasgow to Ireland. Now, like the others, she had grown teeth, with a four-inch gun forward, a long, thin-barrelled Bofors hurriedly installed aft, Oerlikons on her bridge and boat deck, and the Blue Ensign hoisted proudly at her stern.

There was a final word among the escorts, and from captains to crew. The message was drummed into everyone: the convoy must get through. It was their duty to protect the merchant ships to their utmost.

Mid-afternoon on Monday 29 June 1942. The escorts, preceded by their submarine, slipped out of Seydisfjord past the guardian *London* and headed north to join us.

That same day 'Force X' sailed from Scapa Flow. This was a dummy convoy of nine colliers and minelayers, accompanied by two cruisers and five destroyers. It was designed to draw the enemy's attention away from Convoy PQ 17. It was the final part of the Admiralty's plan.

Chapter 3

How is the War?

'I've got spurs that jingle, jangle, jingle, As I go riding merr-i-ly along … '

The voice came from the lookout on our bridge, his round, red face just visible from behind balaclavas, scarves and a duffle-hood. The jagged, grey Icelandic coast was just discernible on our starboard side as the convoy wallowed through a heavy swell. A porpoise-shaped submarine rolled a little way astern of us.

'Take good care of your baby!' the senior minesweeper flashed us as she steamed down the lines of ships.

The submarine was the *Lord Austin's* special charge. We were to keep an eye on her, especially in bad weather. If we ran into fog, which was likely on this part of the voyage, perhaps combined with drift ice, ships could easily become separated.

Large merchantmen could be rounded up without much difficulty when it cleared, but the submarine would be hard to spot – and strict wire and radio transmission silence was now in force. When she surfaced, the submarine looked very small and helpless compared with the rest of the convoy, but she had a 'sting in her tail' and would have a say in affairs if any of the German surface fleet showed themselves.

On this first full day at sea, 28 June, the convoy settled to a speed of seven knots to accommodate the slowest vessels. As soon as we left Hvalfjord we had encountered a heavy swell, with grey skies and bitter cold, and our 'baby' had an especially rough time of it. All the merchantmen were rolling and pitching. The seamen looked over to the two large Russian tankers, the *Azerbaijan* and the *Donbass*, wondering how many women they had on board and how they were faring. Nearly all Russian ships carried women crew members.

We had already suffered our first casualty when the American ship, the *Richard Bland*, was grounded on the Icelandic coast as we left harbour. All the way across the Atlantic just for that! For the rest of us it was a cautious journey north. At one point there were only four miles between the coast and the Allied minefield, and the escort vessels could never decide which was more dangerous – hugging the cliffs or skirting the minefields.

All day the convoy wallowed along following the coastline, lashed by biting showers of sleet and snow. As we stared out at the bleak coast many of us wondered whether some Nazi agent was tuning up his transmitter and preparing to tap out a message to the enemy. It was said that spies were scattered all round the coast, giving information on the departure of Russian convoys, and the smoke from the merchant ships and our coal-burning trawlers was very visible. There was a lot of speculation on how soon we would be picked up by a 'Shad', the nickname for an enemy spotter plane. Form told us it should be around the fourth day.

Aboard the *Northern Gem*, on the convoy's starboard quarter, crewmen cleaned and traversed the trawler's main armament, an old four-inch gun from the First World War, then polished the dust off its telescopic sights. Gunners on the other ships were busy doing similar tasks.

All through the third day, 29 June, fog persisted, thick, dark, cold, and accompanied by heavy rain. It made station-keeping a nightmare and lookout duty a freezing, soaking misery. Later we were to welcome fog, even pray for it, but not now. Early on, the *Ocean Freedom* was groping slowly along the inshore side, listening for sound signals, when a grey, ghostly shape appeared out of the murk close on her starboard side. Both ships took hurried action to avoid a collision. The merchantman and the minesweeper, the *Salamander*, glided alongside each other, practically scraping the other's paint. As the bridges drew level an anxious voice rang out from the *Salamander*: 'Where the hell do you think you're going?' From the *Ocean Freedom*, the equally strained voice of Capt. Walker replied, 'Russia, I hope.'

Unknown to us, the decoy Force X, steaming boldly off Norway, had also become blanketed in fog. It shrouded the decoy so completely from German reconnaissance that its attempts to lure the enemy were rendered useless.

Along with the fog there were heavy floes of drift-ice. Though the merchantmen's bows had been specially strengthened, their masters wondered at times whether their vessels would be able to withstand the thunderous, shuddering impact of the floes. Poor visibility and the close proximity of the convoy ships meant avoiding action could not be taken. So, as we neared the northernmost point of Iceland, we suffered our second casualty. The *Exford* ran smack into ice.

It was 4.20 a.m. Oiler Lionel Smith had just made a round and was having coffee when he felt the ship shudder. There was a 'Stop' announcement and a 'Full Astern' – then a

'Stop' again. When no explanation came down from the bridge over the voice pipe, he was sent up to investigate. The fog was thick and the noise of the ships' whistles growing fainter as the rest of the convoy pulled on ahead was a lonely sound. Going forward Smith found the captain and mate looking over the bow, and saw that the *Exford* had hit ice jutting just five feet out of the water, but it had bent the ship's stem and opened the forepeak, badly holing her.

Even so, the *Exford's* bosun wanted the ship to go on, even though he knew it was asking the impossible. They would have to head back to Hvalfjord for repairs.

'This may be lucky ice,' Smith said to him, for they had always called the old *Exford* a 'lucky pile of junk'. Just how fortunate she was on this occasion they would hear later in Iceland, when beached there for repairs.

Against orders, the *Exford's* captain broke the strict radio silence imposed on the convoy and signalled the *River Afton:* 'To Commodore: My bow has been damaged by ice. What are your instructions?'

Naturally, no reply came from Commodore Dowding. The *Exford's* captain repeated his request an incredible eight times, endangering the whole convoy, before finally turning his ship back to Hvalfjord.

On 30 June, our fourth day at sea, we swung round to the far north of Iceland and reached the point where we were to rendezvous with the escorts sailing up from Seydisfjord. Promptly at noon they appeared: six destroyers, a submarine, four corvettes and the two anti-aircraft ships, the *Palomares* and the *Pozarica*. In their peculiar camouflage, the *Palomares* and the *Pozarica* looked like painted cardboard with no breadth to them, but they were solid enough and were heavy with anti-aircraft guns of all kinds.

What a fleet! With the minesweepers and trawlers it was the biggest naval escort old hands had seen on any convoy.

The new arrivals played stirring martial music over their loudspeakers as they met up with the merchantmen, whose crews cheered, waved hats and scarves and danced on deck. An enormous wave of confidence, even cockiness, swept over the vast array of ships. That so many vessels, convoy and escort, could put to sea and Hitler could do nothing to stop them, made all hearts swell with pride. Across the waters you could hear the throaty roars of men on the American merchantmen, their Stars and Stripes flag tattered from the long Atlantic voyage. At last they were seeing evidence that the British Navy meant business.

The destroyers and corvettes quickly positioned themselves on either flank of the columns of merchantmen, with a trawler stationed forward and aft of each line of warships. The *Palomares* took the starboard side of the convoy and the *Pozarica* the port side, enabling the two ships to give anti-aircraft cover over the whole formation, which was nine miles long and five miles wide when spread out in full station. The three rescue vessels were positioned on each side and astern. On the *Lord Austin* we now lost our 'baby'. She joined her sister submarine in the centre of the convoy, and we moved up to take the lead position on the convoy's starboard bow.

We sailed steadily forward, through drifting, rolling banks of thick, impenetrable fog. Up starboard we lost sight of the convoy for several hours, but regained contact when the fog cleared for a time.

The regular pattern of convoy work clicked into action, with men on constant gun watch, a chilling business on exposed gun platforms. It was a common sight to see our heavily muffled gun watch doing physical jerks on the barrel of the four-inch, running round and round the small platform, or practising dance steps with each other, solemnly fox-trotting and waltzing around the gun. Then the ever-welcome cry of 'Rum-o!' rang out, and another muffled figure would appear with mugs of the life-saving spirit. The watch drained their mugs, glowing and tingling from head to toe. Never was the rum issue more appreciated.

The trawlers' main duty was to keep asdic watch for U-boats. The asdic beam was like underwater radar. All day and all night the asdic set went 'PING … ping … ' The second, fainter 'ping' was the echo from the sea-bed: an expert operator knew from the nature of the return signal whether it was sandy or rocky. When the beam hit an underwater object the interval between the two 'pings' indicated how far away the object was. The set also gave its bearing. An expert could tell the difference between a shoal of fish and a submarine. For four long hours at a time the asdic operator sat hunched up in his chair on the bridge listening intently to the eternal pinging note. It was said that all asdic ratings went mad in time.

If a U-boat was traced our drill was to drop depth charges until a destroyer came up to take over the hunt. The trawlers were slow moving, so unless they were going at maximum speed, dropping a pattern of depth charges would probably blow the stern off. Secondly, if they went off U-boat chasing, they might never catch up with the convoy again.

Another chore for the trawlers was to urge on lagging merchantmen or warn them about making too much smoke. A lot of smoke usually meant careless or lazy firing by the stokers: by piling on large heaps of coal instead of just enough at a time, they could go back into the engine room, sit down and watch the wheels go round.

Some of the answers received were colourful, to say the least. One that bears repeating was: 'First we're not going fast enough. Then if we put coal on to get more speed, we're making too much smoke. What the bloody hell do you want us to do? Sprout wings and fly?'

The *Lord Austin* herself drew a blast from the senior escort. We had been belching thick black smoke from our funnel as trawlers do, until a long plume streamed away behind us, hanging like a banner in the still air. The *Keppel* flashed an angry signal: 'Make less smoke.' The bridge passed the rebuke down to the engine room. Back came the Chief's voice, hoarse with indignation: 'Well, what do the bastards want me to do? Whitewash the bloody coal?'

For the lookouts, the eerie silence of these northern waters was broken only by the occasional clicks of Aldis lamps flashing messages between the escorts. The destroyers were always alert for the presence of U-boats: at this stage of the war it was a familiar and wearisome drill. The perpetual shortage of naval escorts meant they were hard stretched, alternating between convoys to north Russia and Malta. Repeated U-boat attacks had bred in them a fatalistic acceptance of losses.

Turning over the watch on the bridge usually went like this: 'Course … speed … Usual station 2,000 yards on the port bow of … I have been zig-zagging about 20 degrees either side. A couple of ships were hit over on the far side of the convoy about two hours ago, and someone over there has been dropping a lot of depth charges. Otherwise nothing much is going on. Bloody cold – as usual!'

The routine continued. The captain of the destroyer *Wilton* practically lived on the bridge. He was only three or four years older than the handful of young and very inexperienced officers he depended upon, but he had a couple of years' war experience. He slept when he could, in a deckchair tucked into the relatively sheltered well at the forward end of the exposed bridge, swathed in sweaters, balaclavas and blankets. He only allowed himself the luxury of a nap in his sea-cabin, one deck below, when visibility was good and things seemed quiet. He was always tired and often bad-tempered, but his officers trusted him implicitly. They also spent long periods at action stations, so sleep was always their most urgent need. You did not undress – things could happen far too suddenly and quickly – but just flopped on to your bunk into oblivion. You seldom got more than an hour or two's sleep.

This constant need for sleep was shared by all the men on every ship in the convoy. Our priorities were to eat, sleep and stay alive. So far, there had been no action stations. How much longer would this peaceful state of affairs continue?

Next morning, 1 July, the first U-boats were sighted. They surfaced on the calm sea, but were driven off by the destroyers. We now all waited for the inevitable.

Just after noon it arrived: the first 'Shad'. The sun was struggling to break through a thin mist. Alarm bells rang as the black shape of the three-engined floatplane, a Blohm and Voss 138, loomed out of the mist, its nose tipped slightly to the water like a bloodhound. We knew that as it zoomed in and out of the fog, just out of range of our guns, it was busily reporting back to base in Norway with details of the convoy's course, configuration and speed.

The first signal sent to the Admiralty, 'Picked up by the "Shad"', was received and answered. We saw in our mind's eye the heavily braided figures in the Operations Room in London now closely following PQ 17's progress on their charts.

Then there was another U-boat alarm. The dull rumble of depth charges being dropped by the escorts was followed by the warning signals of ships blowing off steam to give their positions in the gathering fog. Suddenly on the *Lord Austin*, still well away up starboard, the alarm bell rang again – a surface alarm. Our old four-inch gun was quickly swung round, a shell and cartridge rammed in and the breech slammed. Ahead, the fog had suddenly lifted. On the horizon we could see the shapes of several large ships. The group seemed to include a battleship, cruisers and destroyers. The convoy was out of sight astern; we faced the warships alone. The same thought flashed through every man's mind: could it be the *Tirpitz*, the *Hipper* and others steaming out from their Norwegian lair?

Radio silence had been officially broken when the 'Shad' appeared. Our radio operator was ordered to report the presence of unidentified warships as quickly as possible to the senior escort. Back came the reply: 'Go in and challenge them.'

Our gallant trawler sailed in to challenge the ironclads, her single four-inch gun trained and the signalman flashing furiously on his ten-inch lamp. After some anxious moments an answering flicker was seen. A minute later came the shout of 'Friendly vessels!'

'Lucky we didn't fire first,' one of our crew ironically observed. 'We might have sunk one of our own battleships.'

As the warships steamed away, probably unaware of the consternation they had caused, one of them blinked a message to us. 'Sorry we can't accompany. Good luck to all'. A nice gesture, even if it was all we ever saw of the battle fleet.

During the afternoon the fog cleared and the whole of the convoy was clearly visible. The 'Shad' still flew just above the horizon. These long-range planes were said to have an endurance of 24 hours at a stretch: they were relieved as regularly as clockwork by one of their fellow planes.

Some tentative shots were fired at the 'Shad', all hopelessly wide of the mark. Soon it was joined by other aircraft, this time torpedo-carrying Heinkel seaplanes, until there were nine planes circling the convoy. A formation of them came close to the ships at the rear and we heard the rattle of Bofors guns. The planes dropped their torpedoes but there were no hits. Then a lull: just the 'Shad' continued its menacing course over the horizon. The escorts' watches had now been on duty or at action stations for 18 hours out of the past 24.

All this time the escorts were being refuelled from the fleet oiler, the *Aldersdale*. The other oiler, the *Gray Ranger*, destined to take up duties as station oiler in Archangel, conserved her supply. The *Aldersdale* steamed at the rear of the convoy's central column. This was not a happy position. When she was refuelling ships she had to reduce speed, so by the time she had topped up a vessel she was well astern of the convoy, leaving her company feeling isolated.

Captain Archibald Hobson of the *Aldersdale* decided to alter the routine. At the start of each operation he hoisted the flag 'Disregard My Movements', then increased speed, hauled out of line and steamed up between the columns. When he was in the first line he reduced speed and carried out the job. This meant that when a ship had been refuelled, the tanker was comfortably back in her original position. No one cared to be a straggler.

About 9 p.m. we hit more patches of fog, and the alarm bells rang again. Three torpedo planes came in close to us. Our gunners managed to fire off a few rounds and the planes vanished. Later our skipper, Lieutenant Leslie Wathen RNR, saw through his glasses a U-boat surface way ahead, and one of the torpedo planes land on the water beside it. The plane took off again in a hurry when a destroyer steamed over and sprayed a pattern of depth charges over the spot where the U-boat submerged. Later we passed a large patch of oil and wreckage, so assumed the attack had been successful. However, U-boat crews were wily, often pumping out a quantity of oil to deceive their pursuers.

Near to midnight a loud crash shook the ship, rousing our off-watch company from their dozing. We heard something scrape its metallic way along the bottom of the ship. It must have been a U-boat just below the surface, but we had no time to stop and investigate. We felt cheered by the thought that the crash must certainly have severely damaged its periscope or conning tower.

At midnight all was quiet. The convoy was now in the sea of the midnight sun. Instead of the sun rising and setting normally, it made an irregular arc around us, rather as the 'Shad' had done.

Now it was 2 July. The day began pleasantly, with a calm sea and the sun shining through a slight haze. But the calm was deceptive. U-boats were about all day and the slow boom of depth charges sounded frequently as the outer escorts tried to drive them off. The destroyer *Offa* fired at extreme range on a U-boat that surfaced: she missed and it dived.

The 'Shad' watched it all, swinging along doggedly a foot above the horizon. Close to noon it was joined by five more identical aircraft. They circled the convoy like giant dragonflies. It was frustrating to know that they were reporting our every movement – and we could do nothing about it. Oh for an aircraft carrier – just a little one! In the afternoon the six 'Shads' were joined by ten Heinkel 115 floatplanes, each carrying two torpedoes. They obviously meant business – and at 4.30 p.m. the attack came.

The Heinkels were met by a hail of fire from every ship that sighted them. The German pilots were not very determined and retreated quickly, most of them before they had a chance to drop their torpedoes. A small group of the planes had seemed intent on laying their 'tinfish' at the *Pozarica*, on the port quarter, but they flew off when she exploded into action. First blood, however, was drawn by the destroyer *Fury*: the Heinkel she shot down dropped into the sea on the port side, ahead of the convoy. As the German crew took to their dinghies, another Heinkel flew up and landed close alongside, coolly picking up the survivors. One of the escorts chased after the 'sitting duck', but it managed to take off unscathed. Brave action by the German pilot.

During the afternoon we were treated to the unusual sight of a friendly aircraft flying over. It was a Walrus from the shadowing *London*, come to blink a message to the *Keppel* to alter course more to the north to increase our distance from enemy airfields. Ships waved greetings to the Walrus. Then three more enemy planes arrived. They circled for a time, then made a sudden dash at the merchantmen. They were driven off by more heavy gunfire, the Walrus getting dangerously caught up in the barrage.

A general signal was received from the *Keppel*, complimenting all escorts on their skill and determination in holding off the raiders. It ended: 'Keep it up, chaps!' Meanwhile the constantly shifting cruiser force steamed to within 20 miles of us, awaiting any move by German surface vessels.

The evening brought constant alerts, with the 'Shad' still droning about the sky, a monotonous but ominous sight. It was hard to drive the frightening vision of it from one's closed eyes when trying to sleep. A destroyer called up the plane with her lamp, blinking out in German: 'Can't you go round the other way? You are making us dizzy!' To which the 'Shad' replied, 'Anything to oblige an Englishman,' and immediately began circling in the opposite direction. After this a regular conversation was kept up between some of the escorts and this aircraft: the enemy took the opportunity to describe the dreadful fate in store for us.

At midnight we began to pass majestic icebergs. They were an enchanting sight, lit by the glancing rays of the midnight sun, but they were also highly dangerous. At 3 a.m. the *Gray Ranger* struck a small iceberg and holed her bow. She reduced speed while Chief Engineer David Hood went with Captain Gausden into the forepeak to inspect the damage. It was bad. The hole was far too big to consider temporary repairs and they feared the deep foretank plates would not stand up to the pressure. Even so they did not relish being so far behind the protection of the convoy, which had now drawn well ahead. They contacted the senior escort and hurriedly steamed up to rejoin the convoy.

Instructions finally came: 'Turn back.' So at 6 p.m. the *Gray Ranger* went alongside her companion oiler, the *Aldersdale*, and handed over her special charts. Then she steamed sadly back to North Shields for repairs, unmolested by the enemy. The *Aldersdale*, which was originally to have left us at the North Cape, would now continue to Archangel.

Three casualties now, though as yet none brought about by enemy action. How long before the big attack came? There was an air of foreboding over every ship.

The weather was much colder in this iceberg region. From a distance one of the smaller icebergs looked like an aeroplane covered in ice; as the *Pozarica* passed close by it showed itself to be just another icy floating shape. An inquisitive walrus surfaced close by the *Lord Austin*. Its great head with two long tusks peered at us from a sudden wave that heaved past the ship. Then just as suddenly it was gone.

During the afternoon the escorts were again busy driving off U-boats. Then five Heinkels approached. They fired their torpedoes at us from a distance, but with no result. The *Offa* beat off an attack by another aircraft.

These sporadic raids kept every nerve taut. When the shadowing cruiser force was again glimpsed in the distance, their presence seemed both encouraging and fateful. There was a popular theory that they and the battle fleet, now hundreds of miles to the rear, were awaiting an appearance by the *Tirpitz* – and we were the bait. Unknown to the vast majority of us was the disturbing news – already received via the Admiralty – that the *Tirpitz* and the *Hipper* had left their usual berths at Trondheim. It was not yet known where they were heading: bad weather had hampered air reconnaissance. We pressed on regardless, the time on the clock now almost meaningless in the eternal daylight. Every man aboard just wanted a good, sound, unbroken sleep.

The *Aldersdale* was constantly busy refuelling escorts, and now the cruiser squadron sent in the USS *Rowan*, one of its two American destroyers, to top up. As she steamed over, more torpedoes were sighted, their wake clearly visible in the clear

Arctic water. The destroyer had to dodge them. She approached us as a group of three or four enemy planes manoeuvred to attack the convoy from the port bow. The *Rowan's* appearance in their midst broke up their planned attack and they seemed uncertain whether to attack the destroyer or the convoy. The *Rowan* allowed them no time for a conference. She opened fire and sent one plane scuttling, then another. When a third crossed her bow to starboard she tracked it with her guns. The plane did not turn for a good 20 seconds and the *Rowan* got a shot right under it, setting it ablaze. The smoking plane went over in front of the convoy, followed by another. Both landed. As the damaged plane sank, its survivors got away in the other aircraft before any other ship could race to the spot. It was another daring rescue – and good luck to them – except it meant that more airmen had been saved to inevitably return and harry us later.

When the *Rowan* returned to the cruiser squadron, the *Wichita* signalled her: 'Welcome back. How is the war?' 'Mighty fine,' the *Rowan* answered. 'We claim one German plane.'

Since the convoy was so vast in size, some of the skirmishes with enemy planes, and the torpedoes they succeeded in dropping, occurred without the knowledge of a great number of the other ships. To those involved, however, an encounter with a torpedo was never to be forgotten. The sight of a torpedo heading for your ship was numbing: your stomach was gripped with sheer fright. The fast, zig-zagging destroyers had every chance of skilfully avoiding a torpedo, but for the ponderous merchantmen and the slower escorts like the trawlers it was a hair-raising business.

One example was an incident on the *Northern Gem*, after some enemy planes had dropped their 'tinfish' well outside gun range. Coxswain Sid Kerslake was making his way to the wheelhouse when there was a shout from the point-five platform: 'Torpedo on the starboard quarter!' Kerslake saw the torpedo's track approaching the ship's side at an angle of 15 degrees, heading straight for the engine room over which he was standing, rooted to the spot, heart thumping. He heard the skipper shout 'Hard a port!' and saw with relief that the torpedo was now travelling parallel, on the same course as the trawler – and overtaking.

There were more shouts: 'Steady as she goes' and 'Bring her back.' Then Kerslake saw the track of bubbles sweep under the *Northern Gem*'s bow. She had been making ten knots, her top speed, to close up with the convoy. What wind there was had made her smoke blow 15 degrees over her starboard quarter: one of the planes could have crept in using it as cover, before dropping the torpedo. The enemy was well versed in such cunning tricks.

Lord Haw-Haw was now broadcasting from Germany. He could be heard regularly over the ships' radios, telling PQ 17 of the dire fate that awaited it. He named individual ships and made particular threats about the rescue ships, the *Zaafaran* and the *Zamalek*. They would not get through, he sneered.

These two vessels were both German-built reparation ships, their exotic names – *Zamalek* ('Place of Kings') and *Zaafaran* ('Place of Queens') – given them by the Egyptian Mail Line. The *Zamalek* was exceptionally strongly constructed and no picture-book vessel. She could always be picked out, with her array of rescue rafts on deck and a large black mark amidships where there were overflows of oil on the boat deck every few months. On this trip she was carrying a naval commander, an official observer for the Admiralty briefed to find out why so many warships were being lost on the Russian run. He had an early taste of action on 3 July. During brief raids a marauding 'Shad' accorded the *Zamalek* the doubtful honour of being the first ship in the convoy to be attacked by machine-gun fire. The plane, passing overhead, raked the rescue ship with bullets. One passed through the commander's duffle coat.

As he ducked out of the way of more fire he sprained an ankle. He was lucky. One of the *Zamalek*'s gunners was badly injured by a splinter from a gun casing entering his eye.

Midnight passed, ushering in 4 July. There was a temporary calm as we steamed to the north of Bear Island. Aboard the *Palomares*, Signalman Barron Taylor had just taken over watch and the scene from the bridge was unusual. The convoy was visible in all directions but the sky was blotted out by a mist that hung in the air just above mast height. We thought that protected us against discovery from the air. As Taylor stood scanning the ships sailing quietly on in a smooth sea he heard what he thought was the noise of an aircraft's engines. He reported this to the officer of the watch. Everyone listened intently as they waited for the captain to come up to the bridge. Taylor thought he heard the noise again, very faintly, but no one else did, and he began to fear what the captain would say when he discovered he had been called up for a false alarm. Just as the captain got to the bridge, however, everyone assembled there heard the sound of an aircraft.

They strained to detect which direction it was coming from, hoping it would fail to make contact because of the thick mist, though it was now very close on the starboard beam. Suddenly the plane dived through the mist at the edge of the convoy. Before any guns could be trained on it, it dropped a torpedo, pulled back into the mist and was gone. Taylor ran to the ship's siren and sounded six short blasts to warn the merchantmen, as the *Palomares* took swift action to avoid the torpedo. It passed within yards of the 'ack-ack' on the ship's bows but went straight on for a merchant ship on her port side.

It was 2.30 a.m. The ship being targeted was the luckless *Christopher Newport*. Her seamen gun-loaders and others near the gun pits panicked. Yelling at Seaman Gunner Hugh Wright to run for safety, they scrambled down the ladder on the after end of the flying bridge, heading for the lifeboats on the port side. But Wright stuck to his post. Opening fire in the water just ahead of the torpedo's wake, he continued firing, changing the pans of his 30-calibre gun as fast as he emptied them. He kept up a barrage of cool and accurate fire, screaming oaths at the ineffectiveness of his gun, until the torpedo passed out of sight under the starboard boats that were swung out. It struck the ship. Wright was blown right off the flying bridge down two decks to the boat deck. He was knocked unconscious and also sprained his ankle.

The torpedo had struck the *Christopher Newport* squarely amidships, where the firemen, oilers and a second engineer were on early watch. Thick black smoke rose from the ship, her engines stopped and she swung broadside on to the convoy. The *Empire Tide* had to take swift avoiding action to get clear of her.

It was a pitiful, sobering sight to see the huge vessel fall back, maimed and helpless. Everything had happened so quickly and unexpectedly. The *Zamalek* was quickly on the scene to rescue the crew and the *Zaafaran* also took some survivors aboard, but seamen watching on the *Peter Kerr*, immediately to starboard, saw a scene of smoke and utter chaos as the *Christopher Newport* was swiftly abandoned. In the meantime, the destroyer *Offa* had been contending with another enemy raider.

The captain of the *Christopher Newport* came aboard the *Zamalek* carrying a revolver, He insisted he must keep it, since he had such a mixed crew. *Zamalek's* captain quietly took it away from him.

The crippled *Christopher Newport* was now a danger to navigation and a prize for the enemy. She was torpedoed by one of our submarines. Despite the large explosion, she took 20 minutes to sink to the bottom with her precious war cargo.

The rest of the early morning was ominously quiet. Four enemy planes, seemingly motionless, flew above the horizon, but they were now too familiar a sight to arouse much interest. We were passing far to the north of Bear Island, its stark landscape normally only visited by deep-sea fishermen. Many of us now remembered their tales of incredible hardship. The island, not yet visible in the far distance, was the most dangerous part of the Arctic run: it was the nearest land on a straight flight out from the German air bases. We were keyed up, expecting more action.

Everyone thought even more keenly than usual about their personal safety, particularly the clothes we wore. Should we continue to wear all our thick, heavy gear – or lighten the weight and risk being frozen stiff? Heavy clothing could soon drag a man down in the sea, but on a long watch on an exposed gun platform you had to muffle up or freeze. Many men compromised by leaving off their sea boots but wearing thick stockings and gym shoes. If sunk or blown out to sea they had a fair chance of pulling off their duffle coats, scarves, balaclavas and other clothing so they could fight their way to a rescue net, but sea boots were impossible to remove. They would drag a man down into the icy depths.

In such a tense frame of mind many of us on the British ships were astonished to see all the American vessels hauling down their Stars and Stripes flags from the jackstaff. Had they gone mad? The answer came two minutes later. They hoisted their colours again, this time brand new flags that seemed ten times as big as the old ones, which had been tattered crossing the Atlantic. Of course, it was the Fourth of July: Independence Day. It was a splendidly defiant gesture in the face of the enemy. Loud music came from some of the American ships and their crews could be seen dancing around on deck. This time it was not just exercise to keep warm in the cold.

Over in the cruiser squadron to starboard, the *Tuscaloosa* and the *Wichita* lowered their normal cruising ensigns and hoisted large ceremonial flags. A flutter of messages was exchanged. Admiral Hamilton sent these words to the American cruisers and destroyers in his force:

'On the occasion of your great anniversary it seems most uncivil to make you keep station at all, but even the freedom of the seas can be read in two ways. It is a privilege for us all to have you with us and I wish you all the best of hunting.'

The USS *Wichita* replied:

'It is a great privilege to be here today with you in furtherance of the ideals which July 4th has always represented to us and we are particularly happy to be a portion of your command. Celebration of this holiday always required large firework displays. I trust you will not disappoint us.'

The British cruiser, the *Norfolk*, joined in, sending the *Wichita* this message: 'Many happy returns of the day. The United States is the only country with a known birthday.' To which the *Wichita* answered: 'Thank you. We think you should celebrate Mother's Day.'

Soon there would be celebrations – or at least fireworks.

Scatter!

BRODIE.

The Fourth of July was a cold but glorious morning. The sun shone brilliantly from a clear blue sky on to an equally blue sparkling sea, as calm as a millpond. The cruiser force had moved in closer and could be seen a few miles ahead on our starboard hand, the four cruisers and their three destroyers with a Walrus spotter plane flying lazily above. Our little trawler was the ship nearest to them, steaming up ahead on the convoy's starboard bow. It was from the starboard – the south – that more enemy aircraft would come, flying out from the North Cape. Anxious eyes watched the sky.

The calm of the sea seemed to be reflected in the orderliness of the convoy. The merchant ships were steaming in four long lines abreast with the two 'ack-ack' ships among them. The remainder of the escorts were deployed on either flank, with the little specks of the two submarines lying astern of the freighters.

Hanging low on the horizon ahead and astern, however, were two 'Shads'. After a long, uneasy interval they were joined by Junkers 88 bombers, one or two at a time, like vultures gathering for the kill, until planes were droning menacingly all around us.

The cruisers' Walrus made a hasty landing. Two spotter aircraft from the American cruisers, out on anti-submarine patrol, also returned to ship after a brief encounter with a 'Shad'. They were no match for the enemy's pugnacious and far superior aircraft.

Then, as the afternoon wore on, the Junkers 88s began to make quick tip-and-run attacks. They dropped their bombs without success but kept the convoy's gunners busy. The deep boop-boop-boop of the multiple pom-poms mingled with the staccato crackle of the Bofors and Oerlikons from the merchant ships under attack. A low mist had descended again and the planes could often be heard but not seen.

Other enemy aircraft appeared, among them Heinkels and a Focke-Wulf or two, but there was still no concentrated attack. In the late afternoon when things seemed to have quietened down, the US destroyer *Wainwright* steamed over from the cruiser force to refuel from the *Aldersdale*. Shortly after 5 p.m. she was halfway through the convoy on her way to the tanker when six Heinkels were seen flying in from the port side. The *Wainwright*'s captain, 'Don' Moon, closed in on the planes to see if he could get within firing range – the destroyer's five-inch guns had a maximum range of about 12,000 yards – but when she did fire the splashes fell 500 yards short. Captain Moon moved in still closer and fired a few more rounds. They were still short by about the same distance. The German pilots clearly knew the ship's gun range, but at least she had let them know she was ready for action.

All this time the merchant ships and escorts also blazed away. The *London* joined in the barrage, opening fire at long range with her big guns. Twelve Heinkels made the raid, circling round and dropping torpedoes, but all without success. They continued to circle the convoy for a while, then attacked some of the escorts, but retreated in the face of more heavy gunfire. By the end of the afternoon, however, we were fortunate that all we had suffered in the day's attacks was a little superficial damage to some of the ships – and some of this came from our own over-enthusiastic gunners.

Another lull followed, so at 6 p.m. the USS *Wainwright* finally made contact with the *Aldersdale* and started refuelling. Mist now hung low in the sky on the convoy's starboard side, so that while some ships on the port side, looking north towards the ice barrier, could still see bright sun in a blue sky, many of those to starboard saw only a grey, muffled ceiling. Beneath the mist, however, visibility was remarkably clear and sharp, and the sparkling sea as smooth as glass.

The lull was short-lived. An Admiralty signal was received, warning that an unspecified number of aircraft had left Norway and could be expected within the hour. We all knew a big attack would come – and it came almost on time.

The 'ack-ack' ships' radar picked up approaching aircraft and alerted the convoy. On the *Lord Austin* we received a message that 25 planes were flying in at a distance of 30 miles. These were in addition to the other planes still circling overhead and obviously waiting to join the mass attack. The *River Afton* hoisted signal 'JG', which meant 'Man the guns and prepare for instant action'. The escorts with the greatest anti-aircraft power closed their ranks to give the maximum barrage against the raiders. Every gun on every ship was made ready. It was a formidable array of fire power, with the two 'ack-ack' ships as the spearhead.

It was 6.22 p.m. when the *Wainwright*, still fuelling from the tanker, received her first report of 19 low-flying aircraft heading towards the convoy. Capt. Moon immediately cast off fuelling lines and steamed at emergency full speed to position his ship between the planes and the convoy. As he did so, one of the aircraft circling overhead made an attempt to put the destroyer out of action. Its engines were heard off her starboard quarter, just above the mist. Capt. Moon went to the starboard wing of the bridge, listened for a moment and quickly gave the order to the helmsman for hard right rudder. Seconds later three exploding fountains of water shot up into the air 100 yards off the *Wainwright's* port bow, dead on her former course. The unseen bomber had 'laid its eggs' well, but Capt. Moon's manoeuvre undoubtedly saved his ship. Another plane made a similar swoop on the *Keppel*, but she, too, escaped: the bomb burst in the sea less than 100 yards astern.

Aboard the *Pozarica* William Mayne suddenly spotted from his action station on the after deck a large number of seaplanes, which appeared to have landed on the sea about six miles astern of the convoy. They seemed to be stationary, almost holding a conference. Then one appeared to take off and others followed. Crew on the bridge of the destroyer *Offa* saw the enemy aircraft suddenly lift above the whole arc of the southern horizon like a swarm of mosquitoes.

Tension mounted on the *Palomares* as her radar picked up the mass of planes flying in. 'Ten enemy aircraft approaching' reported the gunnery officer. Almost immediately this was amended to 'Twenty aircraft … thirty … ' On the bridge Sub Lieutenant Leslie Clements, the ship's radar officer, counted an astonishing 42 planes as they came up on the ship's starboard side, the leading plane away on her bow. There may have been one or two more, but at that moment they turned in to attack. Clements stopped counting and hurried below to watch them on the gunnery radar screen. There were clusters of echoes on the screen. He stood with his knees bent, holding on to the transmitter frame, as he waited for a torpedo to hit. He was certain one was sure to hit the ship from all those planes.

At the radar screen on the destroyer *Leamington* Oswald Tranter could scarcely keep pace. 'Twelve aircraft approaching, bearing ... Twenty aircraft approaching, bearing ... Thirty-five aircraft approaching, bearing ... ' The screen was a mass of contacts. Then all hell was let loose on board. He could no longer hear himself shouting his readings up to the bridge.

Up ahead on the convoy's starboard bow we looked back from the *Lord Austin* to see the combined flock of Heinkels and torpedo-carrying Junkers 88s launch their deadly attack. Suddenly there was a shout from our lookout: 'Look, there's one of the bastards!'

A little black dot could be seen racing towards the convoy, skimming the surface of the smooth sea like a water beetle. For a moment there was silence, then a barrage of fire was let loose on the lead plane. It flew straight on through the bursting shells, heading for the convoy from the rear. A spout of water rose near the two submarines as the plane briefly targeted them, then it made for the merchantmen between the lines of warships.

As it banked across the bows of the *Pozarica* the pilot put up his hand, as if to tell them 'You are going up!' In the terrific barrage of close-range anti-aircraft fire, the *Pozarica's* pom-pom shells appeared to burst on the sides of the merchantmen as well as hitting the daring floatplane. As it banked away it was hit by shells from the 'ack-ack' ship's starboard pom-pom and a small fire broke out just in front of the tailplane.

Chief Engineer William Brown of the *Aldersdale* had kept his binoculars trained on the plane as it flew in close. 'I could see right into the perspex-covered cockpit. With tracer bullets ripping the plane from all angles the cockpit was a mass of flames and inside were five men, four of them laid around either dead or dying, and a fifth, the pilot, swaying but still upright. I saw him reach out, touch something, and a moment after I saw the torpedoes fall and the pilot drop.'

The fire spread rapidly as the plane crossed the *Pozarica*'s bows. It dipped, recovered, then dipped again and nose-dived into the sea. There was a splash, followed by a blinding flash of flame shooting high into the air, then a great cloud of smoke, and with the blazing cockpit still burning fiercely, the plane sank slowly below the surface. When the *Pozarica* passed by all that could be seen was a large oily slick on the water, with a flame flickering in the centre. It had been an awe-inspiring display of suicidal courage – and a successful one – for the pilot's resolutely planted torpedoes had skimmed through the water towards the merchant ships, striking the British *Navarino* with a terrific explosion. She reeled from the shock, smoke pouring from her.

More enemy planes were upon the convoy almost immediately. Like their downed leader, they came in so low they seemed to be touching the sea, little winged insects growing bigger and more menacing every second, until suddenly they were blotted out by a black wall of bursting shells.

As the deafening roar of the barrage went up, a tremendous explosion could be heard above it: it seemed to those watching from the merchantmen that the *Wainwright* had been blown up. In fact, the destroyer had opened up with all her five-inch guns; she seemed to leave the water in an eruption of fire as her semi-automatic main battery let loose. Two planes went down quickly, one after the other, before her devastating initial salvoes. They sank quickly with their tailfins high in the air, a large black swastika on the tails. Yellow life rafts quickly appeared in the water beside the downed planes, with at least one man in each.

At close range the *Wainwright*, acrid smoke from burning powder and flying cork filling the air around her, opened up with her 20-millimetre guns, spraying the heavy bullets over the whole area. Her five-inch guns never stopped firing even when the planes were within 100 yards of her. The shells exploded about 25 or 30 feet from the planes. One burst under the port wing of a Heinkel and nearly turned it over, but incredibly the pilot managed to level off and release two small, fat torpedoes. They hit the water, bucked twice and then submerged, on course for the convoy.

By this time the *Wainwright* had steamed right into the centre of the planes' course, They split up, some going astern of the destroyer and some ahead. At least three more planes were downed in the general barrage and some were smoking as they dived by her, one flying across the bow only a few feet away: its pilot could be seen gritting his teeth as the destroyer's 20-millimetre gunner fired directly into the Heinkel's belly as it passed over.

The fact that the German torpedo planes had had to get under the low overhang of cloud to make their attack was an undoubted advantage to us. It left them wide open to the warships' tremendous fire power, with the two 'ack-ack' ships in particular putting up a great curtain of fire. The din was indescribable. It seemed as if nothing could survive that mass of high explosive, yet the remainder of the planes emerged from it, weaving, dodging and turning like a flock of black crows scared by a shotgun. Some made resolutely for their targets; others hesitated, wavered and turned to port and starboard, trying to fly round the intense barrage to attack the convoy from front and rear. They flew up and down the lines of ships so closely that the pilots and navigators could be clearly seen in the cockpits. Amazingly, seamen used to looking *up* at aircraft found themselves actually looking *down* on the planes as they raced in, so low and close that it seemed as if they could be hit with a sling-shot.

The sea was alive with torpedoes; they criss-crossed the water and snaked through the merchantmen. Messages flew to and fro: 'My God, one's coming straight at us!'… 'Look out, *Bellingham*, there are two heading right for you!'

The swooping, swerving planes were coming in from all sides now, often narrowly missing each other. The ear-shattering roar of the guns continued; cockpits glowed red, then turned into incandescent orange balls floating down to the sea or exploding violently in mid-air. As soon as the planes had dropped their two torpedoes they streaked out of the barrage like bats out of hell.

It was inevitable that some torpedoes would find their mark. Three planes swooped close to the brand new Liberty ship the *William Hooper*, heavy in the water with her trucks and tanks stacked on deck. She blasted off with her three-inch and four-inch guns and the machine guns she was able to use, setting the port engine of one plane on fire and registering a direct hit with a three-inch shell on the starboard wing of another. But a third plane, coming to within 800 feet of the ship, coolly released two torpedoes at point-blank range. The *William Hooper* desperately made hard left rudder and avoided one of them, but the second scored a hit on her starboard side, penetrating the engine room before exploding, blowing up the engines and steering gear. Three men in the engine room were killed, fire broke out and the ship started to flood. Three seamen and four of the ship's gun crew jumped overboard immediately. The captain had to prevent the lifeboats being lowered before the ship lost way.

Next a torpedo missed the *Aldersdale*'s stern by less than 20 feet but struck the Russian tanker *Azerbaijan* in the tank just forward of the engine room, blowing a great gaping hole in her. She veered wildly to starboard and once again the *Empire Tide* narrowly escaped a collision. The tanker only just cleared her stern, a fountain of oil shooting up from the stricken vessel as she belched black smoke that towered to the sky and poured from both her sides. A bridge gunner on the destroyer *Ledbury* only had time for a short burst of fire as the torpedo bomber passed over, but he was right on target. In a last split-second glimpse before the *Azerbaijan* dropped back ablaze you could see one of her women crew rushing to the aft machine gun to join in firing furiously at the retreating plane. It crashed to the sea further on down the line of ships.

As the tanker was hit there was a shout down the voice pipe in the minesweeper *Halcyon*: 'Sparks, get yourself on top. It's just like the bloody pictures, there's a tanker standing on end!' The minesweeper's crew did not realise this was an encounter with death. Rushing on deck, Telegraphist J A Hart looked over the minesweeper's side at the blue sea and a strange flashback brought back memories of his mother's 'blue bag' on washing day. Wreckage was already filling the blue, along with lifeboats and seamen struggling to survive in fuel oil.

In the confusion, with the torpedo planes flying so low, the merchantmen had to contend with the added danger of ship sweeping ship with the crossfire from their own guns: the mast of at least one vessel was brought down in this way. The *Silver Sword*, last in one of the lines of ships, took a four-inch shell in her starboard bow fired from another US merchantman. Luckily it failed to explode and remained embedded in her cargo in No. 1 hold.

The American ships on the *Empire Tide*'s port side had begun firing when the planes were well astern of the convoy and kept tracking and depressing their machine guns until they smothered the British ship in a hail of bullets. Her rigging was shot away, her boat decks riddled and the smoke floats under her 12-pounder platform ripped by a stream of lead. If it had been two inches higher, it would have smashed the gun crew's legs. As it was, one of the gunners on the monkey island had just set foot on the ladder to his gun pit when he was cut down by a ricocheting point-five bullet, which shattered his thigh bone. However, in the melée the *Empire Tide*'s gunners helped to shoot down two torpedo bombers, bursting a 12-pound shell right on the nose of one of them.

On the *Ocean Freedom*, Gunner Jimmy Gordon was making a quick run round the different gun pits to see that all was well. Capt. Walker looked up to the top of the wheelhouse where Gordon operated his own pet gun, a twin-barrelled quick-firing Colt nicknamed 'Wimpey', and saw that it was unmanned. With a diving Heinkel apparently picking out the *Ocean Freedom* for a raid, the captain scrambled up to try and bring 'Wimpey' to bear on the menacing aircraft. Just then Gordon came dashing up to take over the gun, and as the captain turned quickly away he caught his foot on the lanyard of one of the PAC rockets – triggering it off. The rocket went 'swoosh,' right alongside him, zooming up with its fathoms of wire attached. The plane was now right overhead and the rocket made straight for it. Off came the Heinkel's port wing as clean as a whistle, then floated gracefully down alongside the ship like a piece of paper. The plane burst into flames and crashed into the sea a few hundred yards ahead. A great cheer went up from all on board. Through the din Gunner Gordon told the captain, 'It's my wedding anniversary today.'

'Count yourself honoured,' Capt. Walker replied, 'you've had more than a 21-gun salute!'

Curses filled the air on the *Dianella* as all her anti-aircraft guns jammed. The corvette's four-inch was brought to its lowest depression and as planes flew past it fired – and blew off the door of the wheelhouse. More curses. The captain ordered a ceasefire: they were unintentionally doing more damage than the Germans.

One of the quietest of dramas was played out on the *Zamalek*. Just as the planes attacked, Surgeon Lieutenant Norman McCallum had begun a difficult operation on the ship's gunner, who had been badly wounded the previous day by a splinter in his temple and eye. As the *Zamalek* ploughed steadily on with her guns roaring overhead, the surgeon worked calmly and methodically amid the barrage as if he was in the quiet of a hospital ashore. Though his medical orderly's hands were trembling, as was the ship, he began to stitch the wound. He was deterred for a moment because of the heaving of the ship and had to steady himself by the belt attached to the operating table. He completed the delicate operation on the gunner as the ship was wheeling round to rescue survivors. As he came up on deck he saw the rigging in tatters from the fire emitted by the forward point-five gun during the attack. The ship's barrage balloon had disappeared.

Over in the cruiser force they watched the battle from less than 10,000 yards away, still keeping to instructions and staying out of range of concentrated attack and the constant U-boat danger: they were waiting for the surface situation to be clarified by the Admiralty. Everyone fretted at their inability to help as they gazed on a sky packed with brown and black blotches of bursting shells. The *London* and the *Norfolk* had set up a long-range barrage, briefly engaging the enemy formations as they flew past, though the aircraft paid little heed to the cruiser squadron and headed straight for their primary target: the convoy. The fact that the *London* managed to hit one plane just as it was going over the horizon was little consolation. For the American cruisers it was even worse. They were not able to join in the long-range shooting at all because their five-inch shells were not the self-destructive type, but impact-only, which required a direct hit.

On the *Wichita's* bridge they listened in admiration to a running account of the various actions transmitted by radio from one of the convoy escorts. The calm voice coming over the monitor from the thick of the fighting described exploding ships and planes and gave torpedo bearings. It was a grandstand seat but a distressing one, as the steady voice continued his commentary. But they were 'doing fine', it said.

When the *Wichita's* crew saw two enemy planes come down and burst into huge sheets of flame as they hit the sea, everyone cheered 'as if we were in New York watching "dem bums" from Brooklyn.' From the cruiser's bridge, Signalman G Edward Young watched through his glasses as a Blohm and Voss plummeted to the sea. It managed to pull out and land on its floats near the convoy's flank. All the ships in the vicinity concentrated fire on the plane. It was incredible that it was not destroyed immediately, but even more so when another Blohm and Voss set down alongside the damaged plane, took off its crew and flew off unscathed.

On the *Lord Austin*, over our hail of fire, we saw another plane land to pick up a pilot who had baled out and was in his dinghy. A destroyer dashed towards them but the plane got away. A surfaced U-boat that seemed to be filming the action picked up another ditched pilot and quickly submerged.

Then, just as suddenly as it had begun, the tumultuous thunder of explosives subsided. The heavy silence was broken only by intermittent firing at several reconnaissance and rescue planes that were still circling after the departure of the torpedo bombers. The convoy steamed on, still in surprisingly orderly formation after an action which seemed to have lasted for hours, but which in reality was over in a few minutes.

Behind was a scene of devastation. The sea was covered with patches of burning fuel oil, with here and there a ship's lifeboat and pieces of shot-down bombers. Far astern a small group of German fliers were adrift in their inflated 'doughnut'; above them, slowly descending, was a red distress flare suspended by its tiny parachute. Pilots were also standing on the wings of downed planes, waiting to be picked up by the daring rescue aircraft.

When a lookout on the *Lord Middleton* reported an object in the water off the port bow, the trawler steamed to investigate, closing up her four-inch gun. She was about 1,500 yards off when another German seaplane landed to pick up a ditched crew. The *Lord Middleton* opened fire. The fall of shot was very close but it was the only shot she made, for after it the recoil system on the old gun broke down. The enemy plane took off with its rescued crew right before their eyes. Good luck to them, it took some nerve. It was several hours before the trawler got her old gun working again.

There were also British and American seamen in the water. Some were fired on by an enemy plane, though this, in turn, fell victim to one of the corvettes. Other aircraft gunned the rescue ships.

Our three stricken vessels had dropped well astern, with the destroyers and corvettes now round them. The *Navarino* and the *William Hooper* were both listing and smoking as the *Rathlin* moved slowly through blazing wreckage, her nets and scrambling lines out to pick up men struggling in the icy water. Among those she dragged to safety were some who were just able to make it over the side on to her crowded little deck before breathing their last. But she saved more than 60 men from the *William Hooper* and some survivors from the *Navarino* were taken aboard by the *Zaafaran*.

Among those rescued was a bemused Filipino who had been sitting on a crate on deck when his ship was torpedoed. All he could say when he was picked up was: 'I go up, I come down. As I come down I see aeroplane go under me.'

It had seemed that the *Azerbaijan* was done for as she disappeared under her funereal pall of smoke, but now there was a shout from the bridge of the destroyer *Ledbury*: 'Good God, the women are putting the fire out!' The women crew members showed great resourcefulness, though some of their male companions were not made of such stern stuff. Four of them, along with a commissar, quickly abandoned ship in a lifeboat and were picked up by the *Zamalek*, while watchers from the *Aldersdale* also saw the tanker lose a boatload of crew when the ship's forward boat was launched before the aft one: the launching gear towed the boat under and the occupants were flung into the sea. The *Zaafaran* crew rescued some Russians who seemed to have been blown overboard, or had jumped. One had badly injured legs, and with the sea covered with oil they had great difficulty pulling him aboard: willing hands constantly slipped in the oil.

More seamen from the *Azerbaijan* had tumbled into a lifeboat and were starting to pull away when a machine gun suddenly began spraying bullets in the water all round the boat. The gunner was a woman. Another woman with a loud-hailer was shouting at them and waving her arm for them to come back. The rowers stopped, there was another burst from the machine gunner, and back they went. They climbed aboard – and stayed to help the women fight the fires. The *Azerbaijan*'s cargo was mainly less inflammable linseed oil, not petrol, and it was this that had spouted skywards. So with his 'volunteers', the tanker's captain was able to save his ship. After a time the rear ships of the convoy saw to their amazement that she was free of her great column of smoke and moving again. Her top speed was 15 knots so she was able to make a good effort and catch us up. The captain had won through but at a high personal cost, for an early fatal casualty had been the ship's radio operator – his wife.

On the *Donbass*, the other Russian tanker, the women crew waved cheerfully to the escorts. There were young women and middle-aged women, one of the latter large and plump, in a long dark skirt covered with a sacking apron down to her boots, her crowning glory a cloth cap. Haunting images like this would live long in the memory.

The *Ledbury* and the *Offa* pulled out to drive off a new threat by the U-boats. The *Offa* had already accounted for one torpedo bomber. While waiting for the Heinkels to come within range after the early alert, the captain of her 'X' gun, Leading Seaman Tommy Ferns, marched his crew round the gun with broomsticks at the slope to the strains of 'Colonel Bogey' coming over the ship's loudspeakers.

Twelve enemy planes had been destroyed for certain – they had sunk. There were probably more, and in addition many were so heavily damaged that they were unlikely to survive the return flight to Norway. Even so, our claims were conservative. The *Wainwright* claimed only one plane – that was definitely seen to sink – with reports of three others having been downed yet to be verified by her captain. She left us to return to the cruiser squadron amid rousing cheers from the merchant ships nearest to her and with a congratulatory signal on her fine shooting from the *Pozarica*, to whom she replied: 'Thank you. We are enjoying the celebrations.' Later she signalled briefly to the *Wichita*: 'We have had the fireworks we were talking about.'

It was astonishing that the enemy's mass of torpedoes had not achieved more hits. This, of course, owed much to good luck, but also to the skill of some merchant masters and the alert escorts. There were many narrow escapes. The *Offa* skilfully avoided three torpedoes and the *Palomares* took the full force of the attack on her starboard side. Her company would never forget incidents like seeing a torpedo running alongside her. She would have been destroyed but for the captain's astute seamanship.

Aboard her sister ship, the *Pozarica*, it was almost impossible to walk along the upper deck for empty shell cases. One incident showed how hard her crew had worked in the heat of the battle. Charles Gooch ran to his station, took the four-inch fixed shells from the cradle and pushed them up the chute to the gun deck. He was muffled up in the clothes he had been wearing on bridge lookout: thick jumper, overcoat, duffle coat and boots, with a long scarf wrapped round his head. When the action ended he was stripped to the waist and in stockinged feet.

Some of the casualties on the escorts had been injured by the heavy crossfire: the four-inch gun trainer on the corvette *Poppy* got a machine-gun bullet in his buttock from the wild firing from the destroyer *Leamington* on her port beam. He showed the neat round hole to his comrades afterwards, seemingly unperturbed about the incident. The *Poppy* had several brushes with torpedoes. During one hectic moment Sub Lieutenant Denis Brooke, at his action station aft by the pom-pom, alerted the gunner to a torpedo emerging from under the ship's port side. The gunner tracked it towards the merchantmen. There was a small explosion: he may have upset its course. Generally torpedoes ran deep when targeting the heavily laden merchant ships and passed harmlessly under the small vessels.

The *Keppel* experienced her closest shave just after the leader of the enemy aircraft had crashed not far off her stern. Men were still gazing at the spot where the Heinkel had nose-dived when they were suddenly aware of a dead straight line in the calm sea streaking straight towards where they were standing, directly above the ship's ammunition store. In a semi-trance they just stood and gaped. All Harold Williams could think of – in a curiously detached kind of way – was how many pieces he would be blown into. Before any panic could spread the ship's stern veered smartly to starboard and the danger was averted. The incident rated just one brief sentence in the log: 'Torpedo passed astern of *Keppel*.'

As our last bullet was fired on the *Lord Austin* the skipper came down from the bridge, his blue eyes blazing with excitement. 'Well,' he said to us in a voice cracked with shouting, 'that was a good bit of action, wasn't it?'

A good bit of action it certainly was and the first real taste for many of us. Inevitably, as on other ships, we now suffered from the reaction. Although some of us had leapt and cheered as blazing enemy planes had gone down into the sea, we now remembered that men had been inside those flaming orange balls. Enemies, fanatical Nazis, were out to destroy us, but they were men, and brave men at that.

We steamed on now in perfect formation, leaving the *William Hooper* and the *Navarino* to be sunk within the hour by the escorts. Three merchantmen were now lost, but we had beaten off the enemy's first great air attack. Would there be another? And what of the U-boats, so far held at bay by the destroyers? We still had four or five days to go and we had mixed feelings about our chances of getting through. Our chief concern was our stocks of ammunition. We had used quite a bit of it. If there were more heavy attacks how long could we last out?

For Cdr. Broome, steaming the *Keppel* through the convoy, it was 'a tonic' to see the ships 'all in station and looking prouder than ever. I think we all felt that the enemy had realised that PQ 17 meant business and that feeling did us good.' In his diary he said he thought PQ 17 could gel anywhere as long as the ammunition lasted out. This feeling was shared by Commodore Dowding. So we steamed on into the Barents Sea, buoyed by the high confidence of our two leaders.

The *Keppel* sent a signal to the *Empire Tide*: 'Can you kill shadows?' The CAM ship apparently did not receive the message, for her Hurricane did not fly off. In any case, the evening sky was soon clear of all but a few white clouds. The 'Shads' seemed to have gone. While the lookouts scanned a cold quiet sea, however, there was intense activity inside the radio cabins.

The telegraphists on the escorts knew something was in the air when most of the signals now received from the Admiralty bore the prefix 'OU' – 'Most Immediate' – which was used only in cases of the utmost urgency. The first signal, addressed to the nearby cruisers, had an ominous ring: 'Most Immediate. Cruiser force withdraw to westward at high speed.'

Admiral Hamilton's cruisers were in any case to have withdrawn shortly as originally agreed; they were not to be risked in the U-boat-infested Barents Sea. But for the Admiralty now to order their withdrawal at high speed seemed to indicate only one thing: that the 'missing' German surface ships had now been located by Allied reconnaissance and there was an immediate threat to the cruisers. Admiral Hamilton had earlier received a message ordering him to remain with the convoy pending further information. This urgent signal seemed to confirm the worst fears.

Just twelve minutes later there came a second signal, this time addressed to Cdr. Broome: 'Immediate. Owing to threat from surface ships convoy is to disperse and proceed to Russian ports.'

The shock of this had scarcely registered before there was a third signal, timed 13 minutes after the other: 'Most Immediate. Convoy is to scatter.'

Cdr. Broome described the situation: 'This one was lethal, it exploded in my hand.' If any lingering doubts had remained this last despairing signal dispelled it: the cruisers were threatened, but so was the convoy itself. It must be the *Tirpitz*. The battleship must be on her way. Only she could have caused such complete and utter panic in the Admiralty. For our merchant ships to disperse was one thing, and bad enough, but to scatter was quite another. When dispersing, the ships in a convoy were required to abandon formation and make their way to port at top speed. As all our ships were bound for Archangel – some projected calls at Murmansk had been cancelled – they would have had to remain in company and so have the chance, however slight, of safety in numbers. In scattering, however, they would steam off north, east and south. Each ship would be entirely on her own.

It was an appalling situation. Admiral Hamilton and Cdr. Broome had to obey orders, much as they disliked them, in the belief that the Admiralty had vital information not known to the commanders at sea. They were not just being alerted and left to make their own decisions on the spot. The officers and men of the naval escorts could just about grasp the reasons for the urgent signals. But what of the merchantmen? All they could see was the Navy abandoning them to their fate. And what of the pledge we escorts had made to protect the merchantmen at all costs, a pledge never before broken in naval history?

All at once the outer escorts closed in with flags hoisted and Aldis lamps flashing. For a short time the other ships were left wondering what on earth was happening.

At 8.32 p.m. the *Keppel* signalled: 'All convoy scatter and proceed to Russian ports. Escorts – negative destroyers – proceed independently to Archangel. Destroyers join *Keppel*.' The instruction came as such a tremendous shock to Commodore Dowding that he twice asked for it to be repeated. When he finally hoisted the two-letter flag signal on the *River Afton* – the No. 8 pennant meaning 'Scatter and proceed at your utmost speed' – his own utter astonishment and dismay were matched by the incredulity of the merchant masters, who could not believe their eyes. The remarks made on the *London* and the *Washington* were unrepeatable. At that moment all the merchant seamen felt like the proverbial sacrificial lamb. It seemed incredible that they should be left to their own devices.

When the radio operator on the old *Washington* came up to the bridge to report that he had intercepted messages that the convoy's protecting fleet and escorts were to withdraw, and that there was a wild rumour that the *Tirpitz* and her consorts were on the prowl to intercept the convoy, Captain Julius Richter refused to believe it. 'I thought these messages were only scuttlebut rumours or some hoax message the Germans were sending out to decoy the escorts away from the convoy,' he said. But what initially began as rumour soon turned out to be fact. The signal was hoisted on the *River Afton*. 'I called my naval gunnery officer and ships' officers to the bridge to tell them of the fateful message and what to expect from here on.' As we were discussing our hopeless situation one of the greatest naval tragedies of the war unfolded as the escorts withdrew one by one.'

On the *Lord Austin*, too, still up starboard, our skipper refused to believe it when a signalman reported the flag hoist signal to scatter. 'Don't be a bloody fool,' he said. 'Get the proper signal on the lamp!' The signalman did so, and that was it. PQ 17 had ceased to exist.

In spite of the unbelievable situation the merchant masters responded as one. Their ships broke formation and spread out over the calm waters. From our position on the starboard flank we saw the vast array of vessels gradually melt away on all sides. The *Keppel's* final signal to the Commodore was: 'Sorry to leave you like this. Looks like being a bloody business. Goodbye and good luck.' She had hoisted the signal 'CHARLIE-MIKE' ('Join Me') for the other five destroyers to follow her in line towards the enemy.

Cdr. Broome believed action was imminent. 'No enemy warships were in sight but in my hand I held the assurance of the First Sea Lord that they soon would be. Having made certain that the Commodore saw the situation as I did, my next instinctive step was to place myself and my destroyers under the order of the cruiser admiral.

'As we steamed through the convoy and down its wake for the last time, our guns, torpedo tubes, smoke floats and all were being manned and checked, for there was no doubt in our minds that we were moving out to fight. My impression was that the fog bank to the westward which the cruisers were approaching was probably where the enemy was hiding.'

Capt. Hobson of the *Aldersdale* tried to contact the *Keppel*'s commodore to ask whether or not he should join up with the escorts. He was unsuccessful. So the tanker struck out on her own, an extremely hazardous business with her load. During the battle with the torpedo bombers her gunners had earned a signal from the commodore: 'Damn good shooting – keep it up!' They would have exacting need of their guns now. Our two submarines had already been instructed by the *Keppel* to act independently.

The cruisers had turned quickly to westward, passing the splintering convoy at a swift 25 knots. Their departure was so abrupt that a Walrus catapulted off half an hour before returned from patrol to find its mother ship gone. Efforts to recall the plane had been unsuccessful. It was action stations on the *Palomares*, who was still in company with a few other ships as the Walrus approached. They had already suffered the attention of a loitering 'Shad' that had returned in time to see the break-up of the convoy. The Walrus tried to contact the *Palomares* by its lamp. As the pilot circled round he suddenly realised that the 'Shad' was closing in and his Walrus was to be its victim.

The *Palomares* opened fire but the Walrus, trying to evade the enemy, flew right into the line of sight. Only a prompt 'Cease fire!' from the bridge averted a calamity. The 'Shad' beat a hasty retreat out of range. Now the Walrus could exchange messages. It did not have enough fuel to follow the cruisers so it landed on the sea alongside the *Palomares*. The crew were hauled aboard and the aircraft taken in tow. It was a strange sight to see the 'ack-ack' ship steaming on with the tiny plane bobbing along behind. The *Palomares* had been on the starboard side of the convoy, so she steamed south-east while the *Pozarica* headed north. As we and all the other close escorts drew away in a silent sea dotted with icebergs, the six destroyers, in line ahead, steamed away from us at full speed.

Aboard the *Keppel*, Cdr. Broome addressed the ship's company. No one wanted to leave the merchant ships, he said, but the Admiralty had received information that the *Tirpitz* had left Trondheim with her escorts. The battleship, with her superior fire power, could stand off and pick off every ship as long as her ammunition lasted. The job of the screening force of cruisers and destroyers was to proceed at full speed to intercept her. As the cruisers raced quickly westward, Admiral Hamilton on the *London* also broadcast to the ship's company, explaining the order to scatter. The *Tirpitz*, the *Hipper* and several destroyers had left Trondheim Fjord, he said, and were possibly converging on the convoy. The *London* made immediate preparations for surface action.

On all the destroyers in the *Keppel's* flotilla the crews had gone to action stations and put on their tin hats, certain they were about to be committed to a bloody death-or-glory action with heavy surface units. In the tense atmosphere aboard the *Fury* the medical officer quietly laid out all his instruments and dressings in the sick bay. After a time, however, when no enemy mastheads appeared on the horizon, there was a growing realisation that they might not be racing to meet a German fleet but simply carrying out a tactical withdrawal. It was a shocking situation: all those defenceless merchant ships left behind to fend for themselves.

Everyone on the bridge of the *Offa* had seen the agony in the captain's face as he sent the message 'God be with you' to one of the 'ack-ack' ships. An animated argument soon broke out on the bridge. First Lieutenant W D O'Brien recalled:

'The captain (Lieutenant Commander Alastair Ewing), the navigating officer (Lieutenant David Unwin), myself and several others all expressed in various degrees the horror we felt at what we had been told to do. "We can't do this. We can't leave the convoy." Yet we were doing so. Someone argued, reasonably, that the *Tirpitz* must be just over the horizon, yet she did not appear. Then we discussed at length the desirability of having a "breakdown", stopping the ship, waiting for the others to disappear over the horizon and then turning round to rejoin the convoy. We very, very nearly did this.

'To this day I blame myself for not pressing this policy more forcefully to my captain, but always we came back to the belief that we could not be doing what we were doing without a purpose, and that soon something more would be told to us and the enemy would appear. Nothing more was told to us, no enemy appeared, and the distance between us and the convoy opened steadily. Our instinct that we should turn back was right. It was a moment to disobey. There must always be a sense of shame that we did not do so.'

The destroyers and cruisers continued a nightmare dash at high speed through fog and a sea scattered with icebergs. The faster ships zig-zagged as a precaution against U-boats, but those like the *Wilton*, a Hunt-class destroyer with limited speed, went flat out on a steady course and still barely managed to keep up. At one stage the *Wilton* received an ironic signal from one of the cruisers: 'Don't rupture yourselves!' A sister destroyer signalled in commiseration: 'I feel like a bloody Italian!' It summed up everyone's feelings.

After some hours of tearing along, the destroyer *Ledbury* asked permission to ease down: the pace was threatening her boilers, and joints were leaking. There was poor visibility and a good deal of floating ice about. On the bridge peering into the murk, the lookouts began to imagine they saw ships and icebergs everywhere. Nerves were on edge. The squadron still kept in tight formation, each ship towing a fog buoy astern to avert collision.

Even so, the lookout astern on the *Keppel* suddenly heard many more voices than usual. He lowered the binoculars he had been using to peer out into the mist just in time to see a blacker wall than fog closing in on the destroyer. It was the port side of a much larger vessel – and it was only a matter of feet away. The great ship drew away with as much speed as she had approached. Then the air was full of the discordant sound of sirens. The *London* had avoided sending the *Keppel* to the bottom by a fraction.

As the cruiser squadron continued its fast run, plaintive signals began to come in from the scattered merchant ships, many miles to the east. 'We are being bombed. We are under attack by U-boats.' The despairing messages made the destroyer men especially sick at heart. Their ships were not big vessels, to be protected like the cruisers at all costs from a damaging torpedo, and they could have put up a real fight against the U-boats. It was now clear that the *Tirpitz* had not steamed to attack the convoy. So what had gone wrong?

Cdr. Broome signalled to the admiral that he was ready and willing to go back, but it was too late. Admiral Hamilton signalled all ships:

'I know you will all be feeling as distressed as we are to leave that fine collection of ships to find their own way to harbour. The enemy, under cover of his shore-based aircraft, has succeeded in concentrating a vastly superior force in this area. We were therefore ordered to withdraw. We are all sorry that the great work of the close escort (the destroyers) could not be completed. I am sure we shall all have a chance of settling this score with the enemy soon.'

Aboard the USS *Wainwright* feelings were very strong. There were no mitigating circumstances: they had flatly deserted the convoy. Even though the destroyer, on her return to Hvalfjord, would be credited with destroying seven aircraft and would proudly paint seven swastikas on her stack, it was a hollow triumph.

On the USS *Wichita*, with feelings running equally high, the crew marshalled the facts known from all the reports and signals received, and made an effort to view the action in a more positive light. A summary was quickly put together and printed in the ship's paper as the cruiser sped westward. The paper was dated 5 July 1942. Within 24 hours of the fateful 'scatter' signal, it was read by everyone on board. It explained:

'Cruiser Squadron One, consisting of USS *Wichita*, USS *Tuscaloosa*, HMS *Norfolk* and HMS *London*, under immediate command of Admiral Hamilton, was ordered to patrol an area adjacent to PQ 17 and to act as a covering force in the event of a surprise attack by enemy surface units. Our instructions were explicit. We were not to go beyond Bear Island unless an enemy threat was imminent and then under no conditions to go beyond 25 degrees E longitude. The convoy had been sighted early by a Nazi patrol plane, and subsequent intelligence from Headquarters suspected that the enemy had, indeed, been moving ships and planes northward. After all, the last few convoys had been far too successful for his taste and it was not likely that he would sit down and let things go on that way. Reconnaissance of German bases had failed for several days because of thick weather, but about three days ago the RAF reported that all of the main Nazi naval units had left their ports and were presumably sliding northward up the Norwegian coastline with heavy air protection.

'Admiral Hamilton, hoping that we might be able to "take a crack" at some of the Nazi pocket battleships, kept covering PQ 17 several degrees beyond the ultimate line specified in our original instructions. The convoy was told to take advantage of the heavy mists by steering a course a great deal farther north than expected. Much to their surprise we were still covering them at a position nearly 30 degrees E longitude.

'When attacks by enemy aircraft began everyone in the squadron wanted to join in the fight and help them out. But our mission was clearly specified and were we to rush in and be anti-aircraft ships we would leave ourselves open for a lucky torpedo or bomb hit – thereby crippling our strength for any full-scale naval engagement.

'It would have been a gallant but strategically foolhardy gesture. After all, the convoy was well supplied with local escorts equipped for defence against air or torpedo attacks. Another materialistic consideration was that the damaging of one cruiser is more serious than the loss of a dozen fully loaded merchant ships. The ships and their cargo can be manufactured in a few months. Highly complex mechanisms, such as modern naval craft, take a good two years and a fortune to build. The recent loss on Russian convoys of the cruisers *Edinburgh* and *Trinidad*, due to their anxiety to "mix it" at the wrong time, definitely decided the High Command not to place other forces in a similar predicament, where without fighter protection they would be victims of enemy bombers.'

After briefly describing the events of 4 July, including the torpedo-bombers' attack, the *Wichita's* paper continued:

'And then the big news broke. Allied Intelligence reports had confirmed our suspicions. In fact, the situation was worse than we expected. All of the main heavy units of the German fleet had crept through the fog to the northern tip of Norway. They were reinforced by the addition of hundreds of shore-based planes moved up specially for this operation. A fresh squadron of U-boats was also under way. Already we had gone far beyond the limits of where we could meet the enemy on even terms and where our farthest point east was to be. Now he had the unlimited help of bombers and torpedo planes operating from nearby bases. We, for our part, had no means of combating this combined attack and the Russians were still too far away to be of assistance. A new full-scale attack was being launched, so the convoy was ordered to disperse and, by various routes, make for Russian ports. As they proceeded, Russian ships and aircraft would give them what protection they could.

'Our main battle fleet was still some way away and despite the fact that there was a carrier with them our combined forces could not combat the preponderance of air, surface and under-sea power which could be thrown at us. The German ships could operate far enough off from shore to carry on a surface battle while at the same time be close enough to have an umbrella of fighter planes hovering over them the whole time. One of the first lessons of military strategy is "always, if you can, meet your enemy on ground of your own choosing and be able to concentrate superior forces at his weakest point". If this is impossible then the next lesson is to retire until trapped and have to slug it out, but we were lucky enough to avoid that disastrous alternative.' And finally, after reiterating Admiral Hamilton's signal: 'I am sure we shall all have a chance of settling this score with the enemy soon.'

The *Wichita*'s paper concluded: 'We, too, are sure. None of us likes the feeling of seeming to run away but it must be remembered that we are in possession of only limited information. No one can accuse us of ever having a faint heart. The *Wainwright* and the *Rowan* showed that. And what they gave them is only a taste of what is coming. Nor can anyone say the British lack guts. After all, they have been fighting this war for nearly three years. For one whole year they fought it alone, without allies, without a trained Army and without equipment, their fleet spread thin around the seven seas of the world. Anyone who has seen the people of London, of Liverpool, Bristol, Portsmouth, Coventry or Southampton can testify as to their worth. Anyone who has seen the commandos in action, was at Dunkirk, or at Malta, would be a good witness. No, we are kinfolk and allies in more ways than one. Our combined spirit and purpose will certainly triumph. Our force, in going beyond its designated turning point in attempting to lure the enemy fleet towards us, did its share. We all would like to have done more. But war takes a lot of patience and broad thinking as well as action and courage. We've only been at this game for seven months. We're fresh and all we need is the chance – and we may be surprised at how soon that chance comes. In the words of a Signalman 2nd Class: "We'll get those sons of bitches yet, by God!" And so we will! The ship is now proceeding SW to Hvalfjord, Iceland.'

Far behind them, scattering in all directions in the Barents Sea, were our 31 merchant ships and tankers, and the escorts. It was every ship for herself now.

Already, after the initial bewilderment and anger, recrimination began. The feeling continued down the years: the feeling that we had been used as a piece of cheese for the German mouse. But in the dying hours of Independence Day there was above all a sense of horror and fear – a fear that no man who survived would be ashamed to confess.

Chapter 5

Black Sunday

Instant flight was the only hope of safety for any ship. Crews faced the threat of German surface raiders appearing over the horizon at any moment.

Some of the escorts, like the corvette *Poppy*, which had been on the convoy's starboard hand, considered pairing off. She picked her way through the dispersing ships and sought out her fellow 'new girl', the *Lotus*, on the port side. Before any mutual tactics could be agreed between them, however, the *Pozarica* asked the corvettes to screen her. The 'ack-ack' ship had only a defensive asdic set and her commander was no doubt thinking of the menacing U-boats in the vicinity. So the *Poppy*, the *Lotus* and *La Malouine*, which flew the French flag as well as the British ensign, but whose crew were all Royal Navy, joined the *Pozarica* in heading north-east for the ice barrier – with many an apprehensive glance towards the glaring south-western horizon. A 'Shad' followed the hurrying group and was there to see them meet up with the *Rathlin*, which was carrying more than 60 survivors. The little rescue ship strained to reach her top speed of 12 knots to keep in company, black smoke belching from her funnel as the stoke-hold gang toiled with their shovels.

The minesweeper *Halcyon* struck north for the ice field, while the other two sweepers, the *Salamander* and the *Britomart* headed south-east along with the *Palomares* and the remaining corvette, the *Dianella*. This left only us four trawlers, the slowest ships in the convoy and the ones with the poorest chance of reaching safety. The *River Afton* and the trawler *Ayrshire* both signalled our skipper asking if we would join them, but since the escorts' orders were to proceed 'independently' our skipper declined. So the *Ayrshire* went off north. Our skipper would have liked to have gone with her, but eventually the captain of the *Lord Middleton*, as the senior officer, took command of the remaining trawlers. So, in line ahead with the *Lord Middleton* and the *Northern Gem*, we steamed north-east at our best speed to find the ice edge.

Some of the merchantmen were still scattered about in the distance, though the majority had vanished from view. Some were heading direct to the northern ice for protection from the U-boats – on one side at least. Others turned to make a dash eastwards. An added difficulty for many of them was keeping to a true course. In convoy their course had been set by the naval vessels, which were equipped with non-magnetic gyro compasses. Many of the merchantmen had only magnetic compasses, which were of little use in these latitudes. The farther north they ran, the more the variation of the earth's magnetic force pulled their compasses off, until it was almost impossible to make a true course.

So 4 July reached its incredible end. As we trawlers punished our boilers in all-out flight, the merchant ships we had been forced to abandon sailed alone to their fate. For all of them there was a brief, unnerving period of quiet as the surprised and jubilant enemy aircraft and U-boats mustered for the kill. Then the long, tragic hours of 5 July – Black Sunday – began.

The first to fall victim to the U-boats was, bitterly enough, an American vessel making her second bid to reach Russia. The USS *Carlton* had been on PQ 16. Four days out from Iceland on this convoy she was damaged by a near miss during a dive-bomber attack and had to be towed back to Hvalfjord by a trawler. Now, in the early hours of Sunday morning, some seven hours after scattering, she was quite alone on a calm sea, pushing along at her best speed of nearly 12 knots under some thinly protective patches of haze. Her master was endeavouring to hold her on a steady course east south-east for the White Sea.

Her five lookouts were given no warning of the U-boat stalking them. At 5.10 a.m. a torpedo struck her on the starboard side amidships, penetrating one of the two deeptanks containing 5,000 barrels of Navy Special. Ignited by the explosion, fire spread swiftly over a wide area. A sheet of flame leapt from the engine room and a column of water, thrown up from starboard, together with oil from the deeptanks, fell on to the midship housing. The two starboard lifeboats were hurtled on to the well deck. Hatch covers were blown off and the cargo – flour – thrown up on deck. Partitions in the crew's living quarters amidships collapsed and the gun turrets on the poop deck buckled.

The engine room, where the explosion killed two men, flooded immediately. With no one left to control the engines, the propeller continued to turn for several minutes until the fire room was flooded. All power was off and the emergency radio transmitter was smashed. The ship's gunners, having no sight of the attacker, quickly abandoned ship along with the others, on the captain's orders. He saw that his ship was sinking rapidly and feared that the 200 tons of TNT she was carrying might explode at any second. Seamen slid down ropes or jumped into the sea, swimming to the four life rafts and the one remaining lifeboat – another had been lost in a storm. All 32 surviving crew and 11 armed guards managed to scramble out or be pulled from the sea.

The *Carlton* settled rapidly on an even keel and sank in 12 minutes. The U-boat surfaced and watched her last dying moments but made no attempt to communicate with the survivors. She disappeared from sight inside half an hour, leaving them alone in the icy expanse of the Barents Sea.

To the north of the *Carlton* and within an hour of her sinking, the British *Empire Byron* was struck by a torpedo amidships. Ship's carpenter Frederick Cooper rushed on deck to find it a shambles. Wreckage was strewn all about and the motor trucks the ship had been carrying were no longer to be seen: they had been blown sky high.

The ship, which had been making a hard 11 knots, was hit in No. 3 hold under the gunners' mess deck. One gunner had just taken his watchmates a mug of cocoa each and had gone back below to the mess deck to replace his mug when the explosion struck under his feet and killed him. It shifted two big central cases containing aircraft, which slid across and pinned six gunners against the ship's starboard side.

When Captain John Wharton quickly gave the order to abandon ship Cooper ran aft to launch the remaining two life rafts. As he did so he heard screams for help in No. 3 hatch. The companion ladder had been blown up, so he lowered a rope and climbed down. Tanks and lorries moving wildly had stove in all the accommodation. The ship's stern was already well submerged under water and bodies were floating around in four feet of water.

Cooper managed to drag four dazed men to the companion, climbed up the rope and heaved each of them up after him. He went back a fifth time and tried to free the gunners pinned against the ship's side, as others had tried to do by desperately stripping the hatch, but to no avail. He took the hands of one man who was trapped by the legs. The terrified man kept shouting, 'For Christ's sake, don't leave me, Chippy. Chop my bastard legs off.' The water crept higher and higher until Cooper could feel the trapped man's life ebbing away in his hands. He could do no more. As he climbed the rope for the last time tears streamed down his face.

He quickly put lifejackets on the four men he had rescued and rolled them into the sea to be picked up later. Then, the last man to leave the ship, he dived over the side. He swam hard for nearly half a mile to reach the ship's jollyboat, which was floating empty.

Ten men went down with the *Empire Byron*, which sank in 20 minutes, stern first and flag flying. Besides those killed and trapped, another man lost had reached the lifeboat station but said he had forgotten his bank book and must go back for it. He was never seen again. Nor was an exhausted fireman. He was woken up by the crew, but simply turned over and went back to sleep. In the confusion, he was forgotten.

Two lifeboats got away safely, though one of the forward life rafts was smashed against the ship's side before the painter could be cast loose. Cooper, in the jollyboat, picked up several of his shipmates from the sea.

The U-boat surfaced. It circled the wreck, approached them out of the mist and handed over the third engineer, whom its crew had picked up out of the sea. The U-boat commander asked the name of the ship, her destination and cargo, and for her captain. He was told the last they had seen of him was on the bridge. In fact, he was in one of the lifeboats, but had stuffed his uniform coat under the seats. Instead the U-boat took an Army captain prisoner: he had been going to Russia to instruct the Russians in the use of the tanks the *Empire Byron* was carrying. Then, while cameras on the U-boat recorded the scene, the commander handed them sausages, black bread and cognac, and gave them a course to steer by. He expressed his regret at having to sink their ship, wished them a safe passage and ordered his men to give a salute – the British salute – before the U-boat drew away and submerged.

A new wave of enemy aircraft was now over the southern horizon. Its first victim was the *Peter Kerr*, which had headed south. Her master, Captain W A Butler, had elected to continue on a rhumb-line course for the White Sea, so, as the most southerly placed of all the merchantmen, she was the first to fall foul of the planes. In the late hours of Sunday morning three Junkers 88s swooped to attack. The *Peter Kerr* fought back, but though the tracer bullets from her small anti-aircraft guns hit the planes they made little impression. After some near misses one plane finally succeeded in dropping three bombs into the ship's hatch, between the bridge and the engine room. The explosions rocked the freighter, setting her ablaze, and with all the fire-fighting lines ruptured, the crew had no chance at all of saving her.

Capt. Butler gave the order to abandon ship and two lifeboats were launched without difficulty on to the glassy-smooth sea. 'Thank God I've got my good leg on,' exclaimed Chief Engineer Herbert Burkhead as he dropped into a lifeboat. He wore a wooden leg and always carried a spare, but one was his favourite.

The attacking planes circled the boats. As one passed over them very low an engine backfired. A fireman thought they were being strafed and leaped over the side. But the pilots were simply taking pictures, and when they had done so flew off with a jubilant wave.

No one among the *Peter Kerr*'s 36 crew and 12 gunners was even slightly injured. They saw two vessels to the north under attack and decided that to return to their blazing ship would be extremely foolhardy. The merchantman was already settling in the water as they pulled away.

More U-boats now joined the kill. Some miles to the north the *Honomu* was steaming flat out at nearly 11 knots when, unseen by her ten lookouts, a torpedo struck her on the starboard side. The explosion completely demolished the fire room, shutting off all power and blasting the radio out of commission. The ship began to settle immediately. With no sign yet of her attacker her guns were useless. Nearly 40 of her company abandoned ship in good order but another 19 men were unaccounted for. Most were believed killed either by the first torpedo or the second, which struck her port side shortly afterwards. The ship sank rapidly, disappearing by the stern in ten minutes.

Soon after she had gone two U-boats surfaced close to the wreckage, while another broke water about a quarter of a mile away. The U-boat that approached the lifeboat and rafts had a victory 'V' over three dice painted on its conning tower. Its commander ordered the *Honomu*'s captain aboard and he was taken prisoner. The survivors were then asked if they had sufficient drinking water and were given some canned meat and bread. They were bound to be picked up in a few days, the Germans said magnanimously. Then the three U-boats made off to the east.

East of the *Honomu* the *Fairfield City* and the *Daniel Morgan* were now both subjected to heavy attacks by the continuing wave of dive bombers and other aircraft. Junkers 88s soon stopped the *Fairfield City*, rocking her with several near misses and two direct hits. Her crew abandoned ship, pulling away from her as she quickly settled in the water.

Three miles away the *Daniel Morgan* retaliated strongly, fighting off her attackers for more than two hours. Her captain had set course for the islands of Novaya Zemlya, far across the Barents Sea. Now she was making a valiant 13 knots, zig-zagging to give a broadside rather than a fore and aft target for the dive bombers, as Heinkel 115s, Junkers 88s and 'Shads' all joined in the running attack. Her guns blazed away continuously, disabling two Junkers 88s. One landed in the water some distance from the ship, while the other flew off with black smoke pouring from it. The dive bombers dropped an astonishing 80 bombs. Thirty were near misses, but three were direct hits. They badly damaged and flooded two of the ship's holds, finally slowing her down. As she lost speed a torpedo struck her cruelly on the starboard side, stopping the engines and wrecking the steering gear. The ship's three-inch gun had jammed through overheating and her ammunition was almost spent. It was the end. In her desperate battle there had been only one casualty, a seaman killed in one of the bomb explosions, but now, as all hands abandoned ship in the lifeboats, two men were drowned when a boat capsized.

The *Daniel Morgan* sank by the stern. Soon afterwards a U-boat surfaced and approached the lifeboats, demanding the ship's name, tonnage and cargo. The captain gave false answers. One of the Germans took photographs of the survivors and they were then ordered to follow the U-boat. This they did, pulling behind it for about an hour and a half in a southerly direction, when the U-boat suddenly made off at full speed.

The survivors carried on, now resigned to a despairingly long, cold haul to land. A few hours later, however, a surprise rescuer, the tanker *Donbass*, came over the horizon. Though utterly exhausted, the *Daniel Morgan*'s gunners volunteered to man the Russians' forward gun. Shortly afterwards they scored a direct hit on a diving Junkers 88, also beating off attacks by two others.

All day long, however, the slaughter of ships went on. Four vessels came in sight of each other as they steamed eastwards: the tanker *Aldersdale*, the *Zaafaran*, the *Ocean Freedom* and the *Salamander*.

The tanker had been shadowed for hours by a lone bomber circling in a bright, clear sky – too bright for comfort

– so the crew were glad to find some cloud cover and close up a little with the *Salamander* and the *Ocean Freedom*. Most of the *Aldersdale*'s company felt just a weariness, a loneliness and a fatalistic 'let it happen soon and get it over with'. It seemed impossible for any merchant ship to escape and Capt. Hobson's decision to head for Novaya Zemlya was regarded as just a gesture in the direction of safety. Nevertheless her gunners were prepared to give as good as they got.

The *Zaafaran*, carrying her survivors from the previous day's battle with the torpedo bombers, had pushed on at speed when she was warned by an escort that the German heavy ships were believed to be only 30 miles away. Captain Owen Morris of the *Zamalek* had invited the *Zaafaran*'s captain, Charles McGowan, to steam in company with him, but there was some rivalry between the two rescue ships, especially between the masters, and Capt. McGowan had refused. The *Zaafaran*'s flat-out speed was a good half a knot more than the *Zamalek*'s so she was able to draw well ahead. Her crew were thankful. They cursed the *Zamalek* for the heavy smoke she made: when there was no wind a black cloud hung above her like a signal, ready to betray their position. Besides, on the radio she was the target of some of Lord Haw-Haw's direst threats. So the *Zaafaran* sped on. As she did so ship's carpenter James Ramsay brought out a bottle of whisky he had been saving to take home. Being a good Scotsman he could not bear to lose it if they had to go over the side, so in the early hours he drank the lot with some of the gunners.

It was late morning when a group of marauding planes descended on the four ships. Three Junkers 88s swooped down to bomb the *Aldersdale*. One was successful. As Gunner Thomas Urwin blazed away with his Oerlikon he saw the grey bombs drop off the port-side beam. They exploded near and under the ship's stern, splitting her engines right across. The aft flying bridge buckled, the pump room flooded, steam poured from the engine skylight and there was a stink of oil and petrol everywhere. One of the junior engineers, answering an anxious call from the bridge asking if anyone had been hurt, replied, 'Hell, what colour's blood?'

With the tanker immobilised and rescue close at hand, Capt. Hobson decided to abandon ship. One of the emergency duties of Third Officer Henry Phillips was to dump the ship's confidential documents. When he went into the chart room he found the navigator, Charlie Cairns, almost in tears. It was chaos. Newly corrected charts, coloured inks, glue and other cartographical debris lay all over the deck. Cairns's comments on the wasted effort were unrepeatable. When Phillips reached the lifeboat station he found that both boats had cast off, leaving six of them on board: the captain, the chief officer, the chief engineer, himself and two others. Each boat had assumed they were in the other one. They made their way aft and launched the jollyboat – after first seeing off some of the captain's rum.

They were all soon picked up by the minesweeper *Salamander*. Before abandoning their own vessel, Gunner Urwin and his colleagues had taken the Oerlikons off the mountings, their barrels red hot. These were now slung over to the minesweeper.

Aboard the *Salamander* Capt. Hobson and Lieutenant Mottram, her commander, talked over the situation and decided to try and tow the tanker. Just as efforts were being made to fix up a tow, the *Salamander* received orders to proceed with all speed. Capt. Hobson was given five minutes to decide whether to return to his ship or remain with the minesweeper. Reluctantly he chose to stay, so they decided to try and sink the tanker by gunfire. The result was as hilarious as it was sad.

The first shell from the *Salamander*'s four-inch took some of her stanchions and wires away; when the order was given to elevate the gun it rose to its maximum and the breech block fell off. It was therefore decided to set the tanker ablaze by firing incendiary bullets into the pump room to explode her aviation spirit. The bullets simply rebounded off her shell plating – fortunately, some thought, for she might have taken them all with her in the resulting explosion. Finally some depth charges were heaved at her engine-room plating. Three or four charges were sent over, but still the *Aldersdale* did not sink, though as they drew away her stern was well down and her fore-foot clear of the water.

The other ships in the group had managed to fight off the aircraft, but not for long. The *Ocean Freedom* and the *Zaafaran* had each pulled away on their own: a single determined plane now dived on the *Zaafaran*, dropping three bombs across her. The middle bomb was either a very near miss on the starboard side amidships or it struck under the waterline: after the shock of the explosion the rescue ship was quickly down by the stern, covered with steam and with her engines stopped. Carpenter Ramsay, his left hand badly gashed in the explosion, made for the boat deck where some frightened passenger survivors had swung the jollyboat out. Tough Capt. McGowan threatened them and ordered them to get out of it. However, the boat was lowered and Ramsay and a deck hand tried to lower the heavier boats. None of the lifeboats had ever been swung out before. The jollyboat was on the ordinary swing-out davits, but the others were on heavy patent wind-out davits and were still resting on the chocks. After winding for some time Ramsay and his helper discovered that the davits had burst through the deck and the boats could not be lowered. Ramsay ran to the boats on the starboard side and found that exactly the same thing had happened there.

By this time the *Zaafaran* was pretty far down in the water. Capt. McGowan shouted for Ramsay to look after himself. The carpenter ran forward and released the raft on the port side. It was immediately crowded, so he crossed to the other side and went over into the water. He swam to a raft which kept overturning: it was built for ten men and there were more than 20 scrambling for places. Ramsay hung on to the side of the raft with the others and as they slowly drifted clear of the ship, the *Zaafaran* suddenly upended and went down stern first. It had all happened in four minutes.

Surprisingly, the sea was quite warm: one of the quirks of the Gulf Stream. Ramsay and his shipmates managed to reach two rafts and scramble aboard. By this time it had become foggy, and with no other ship in sight the outlook was miserable. After drifting for three or more anxious hours they sighted the *Salamander* far off. Then they saw the smoke-belching *Zamalek*. The ship they had cursed they now blessed – once they had got over their initial shock. It was strange to board a ship which, according to one of Lord Haw-Haw's last broadcasts over *Zaafaran*'s radio, was listed among those already sunk.

When they counted heads they found that only one man had been lost, a gunner. There was a brief clash on the *Zamalek* when Capt. McGowan, the senior of the two masters, went up on the bridge with the idea of taking charge. He was put smartly in his place by Captain Morris, who, though not physically a big man, had the courage of a lion. Capt. McGowan went below and brooded for the rest of the voyage. He had had to swallow quite a lot in losing his ship and being rescued by his slower rival. Capt. Morris had already had some arguments over tactics with his own naval gunnery officer, who at times seemed to think he was running the ship. Capt. Morris gave the officer short thrift: after the 'scatter' order the Navy was very low in the estimation of the rescue ship's company.

Meanwhile the *Earlston* was steaming up in the north, towards the ice barrier. She was alone now, though in the early morning her crew had glimpsed the bow of the *Empire Byron* not far off. After scattering, the *Earlston* had turned all steam off the winches to get maximum pressure on her engines. She succeeded in pushing her speed to nearly 14 knots: one of her company said she 'got a wiggle on'.

A few hours after the *Empire Byron* had gone, when the *Earlston*'s crew had just sat down to their Sunday dinner, the alarm bells rang. Five torpedo planes were swooping in on the port bow. The ship's old four-inch opened up at long range and planted its second shell right under the nose of one plane, which swerved and shuddered but dropped a torpedo that streamed straight for the ship. The command 'Hard a port' rang out and the ship began to swing, agonizingly slowly. But they made it, avoiding the torpedo by just 20 feet as it shot on parallel to them along the ship's side. The planes flew off, the damaged one lagging behind the others very low on the water, but now two U-boats were sighted astern. The four-inch crew opened up again but had to stop firing when the U-boats manoeuvred between two lifeboats of survivors from another ship. Then eight Junkers 88s droned in on the starboard beam. One peeled off to attack.

'Here he comes!' came the shout from the monkey island, 'right out of the sun!' For a few seconds all was quiet, then every hand on the ship burst into action. Down came the plane, closer and closer. Would it never pull out? They saw the bomb doors open and the bombs float out, the fins swaying about as they whistled down. One bomb fell to port, the other to starboard. There was a great splash and water burst over the ship, but she was not hit. The Junkers, however, never came out of its dive, smacking down into the sea on the port side. A second bomber flew in – though not so low. It dropped its bombs feet ahead of the ship and sheered smartly away. But still the ship steamed on unharmed. Then a third plane, two more bombs, but still no damage. From then on the *Earlston*'s gunners had no time to count: they loaded and fired as fast as they could as the other planes came in and more bombs straddled the ship.

Then came the unlucky one. Its force lifted the *Earlston* right out of the water. All the pipes in the engine room fractured, the pumps were blown off their bed plates, and the whole engine seemed to have shifted nine inches across the engine room, which flooded fast. There was nothing more they could do. There was no point in remaining aboard. With no power the ship was a sitting duck; the best way of saving her crew's lives was to take to the boats. At 3.10 p.m., three hours and ten minutes after the alarm bells had rung for the final action of the *Earlston*, Captain Stenwick gave the order to abandon ship.

The first thought of Lance Bombardier Richard Crossley on leaving his gun station was to grab some warm clothing. He hurried below and grabbed his Army-issue sheepskin jerkin, together with half a pound of tobacco he had been saving to take home for his father. He then ran back to help get the lifeboats over the side. There were two, plus a dinghy and a raft. The dinghy was holed and started to sink, but all the ship's company got safely away, though the planes deliberately fired on them as they were getting into the boats. Besides the ship's crew and gunners there were five passengers: a Ministry of Supply man bound for Russia, another civil servant and three Russian seamen whose ship had been sunk.

The planes continued to circle the lifeboats and also made another run over the ship, but without dropping any more bombs. Then four U-boats surfaced: two within 200 yards of each other, another half a mile away and the fourth a mile distant. Now the *Earlston*'s crew knew that the best decision had been made: if they had not taken to the boats it was more than likely that there would have been no boats to take to. The three nearest U-boats formed a triangle around the two lifeboats. The commander of one ordered the boat carrying Norwegian-born Capt. Stenwick to come alongside and he was taken aboard. He appealed for help for his crew but it was refused. A final 'Cheerio!' and he was gone. When the crew asked for a course to steer by the U-boat commander replied coldly, 'We are all at war – just find your own way!'

Three torpedoes were now fired at the helpless ship, which lay absolutely still and broken on the calm sea. Two missed and the third struck her amidships, but still did not sink her. The U-boats submerged. The Junkers 88s were still about and one flew very low over the boats, as if to machine gun them, but instead it gave a brief victory roll and flew off. The lifeboats joined up and pulled away together. The enemy planes resumed attacks on the crippled ship, flying down almost to masthead height before releasing their bombs, yet were still unable to hit her. Finally one succeeded in dropping a bomb in the *Earlston*'s No. 1 hold where the naval ammunition was stored. There was an enormous dirty blue flash as the ship went up like a firework, the whole fore-end blowing to bits and the naval pinnace across her deck disintegrating in mid-air. All the survivors saw of the rest of the ship was the stern as it rose out of the water and turned over, disappearing beneath the surface. It was 4.30 p.m.

To the east, just as the *Earlston* was abandoned, the American *Pankraft*, a very old West Coast freighter, was also steaming hard alone at a manful ten knots when seven Junkers 88s swept towards her out of the sun. Three attacked the ship, keeping out of range of her fast firing machine guns, and dropped nine bombs. Six fell wide, but of the other three one dropped directly on to No. 3 hold, amidships between the bridge and the crew's quarters. Fortunately it landed in a large heap of bagged coal stacked on top of the hatch cover, which took the main force of the explosion. But the other two bombs were near misses, which buckled the ship's plates: her oil and steam connections were ruptured, the engine room began taking water and the engines were stopped.

The main transmitter went dead so the captain could not order abandon ship over the loudspeaker system. Radioman J E Blackwell left the radio shack to find that all the lifeboats had been lowered and had pulled away some 25 yards or more, except one, which still had the painter line tied to the ship but had drifted about eight feet away. He went back into the shack for the other operator. Then they climbed down the sea ladder and pulled themselves through the water by the painter line until they were hauled into the waiting lifeboat.

The captain was already in one of the other lifeboats. To the intense anger of the crew he and the chief officer had been among the first to leave. Some men believed that the damage to the ship could be repaired, enabling her to continue. Afterwards they accused the captain and chief officer of being incompetent in handling the ship. The captain had disposed of all his confidential American papers, but in his haste to abandon ship all the British papers were left on board.

In the confusion the second mate had stepped forward and taken the responsibility for seeing all the ship's company safely away. Radioman Blackwell and his colleague believed six or seven planes were coming in low to drop their bombs and machine gun the decks.

Aboard *the Bolton Castle* the crew's tea was laid out ready on the galley tables: cold meats, salads, fruit, cakes and pastries. Later on, during the long days in an open lifeboat, Chief Cook Leonard Osmundsen was to think longingly of all that food. Most of the ship's gunners were busy firing at circling Focke-Wulfs and 'Shads' when out of the blue, in a straight dive, a Stuka appeared. It straddled the ship from port to starboard, in a direct hit. The whole top part of the ship just forward of the bridge was torn apart. The blast hurled a gunner on the bridge into the sea. Those on the *Washington* thought the British ship virtually disintegrated. Amazingly, the ammunition she was carrying did not explode.

Cook Osmundsen dashed out on deck to the nearest lifeboat station, where the seamen were already lowering the boats. Though the ship was listing heavily to starboard they managed to launch two lifeboats and began pulling like blazes away from the rapidly sinking ship. Miraculously there were no casualties. Even the gunner blown overboard was pulled from the water after a few minutes and, though in very bad shape, suffering from cold and exposure, was later brought round in one of the lifeboats.

For 36 hours the *Bolton Castle*'s tireless gunners had kept the enemy aircraft at bay. Now the stricken freighter died in five minutes. Suddenly she lifted herself out of the water and began to slide under, stern first, the red duster still flying as she slipped below the surface.

A plane swooped over the lifeboats with a burst of machine-gun fire but no one was hit. Then other aircraft flew in low. They were taking photographs. As they flew off, one pilot waved his hand as if showing the survivors which way to sail, but Norway and a prison camp were in that direction, so they decided to strike due east. After collecting all the bits and pieces floating around that might come in useful, they discarded a third lifeboat, sharing out its rations between the captain's motorboat and the sailboat. Then, with the power boat towing the other one, they pulled away.

Scarcely had the *Bolton Castle* been hit than it was the turn of the *Paulus Potter*. Her British gunners kept the attacking planes at bay until, for a third time, a stick of bombs dropped close to the ship. All the earlier near misses had sprung her plates and shifted her engines. These last bombs, narrowly missing the four-inch gun platform, blew the ship's rudder off and damaged her propeller. The captain ordered abandon ship, but Gunner David Richards and his comrades, who had a shell in the breech of the four-inch, continued firing at an aircraft flying astern. The plane lost height and dropped its bombs in the sea.

The four gunners were the last of the crew into the lifeboats, along with the captain and second mate. The planes continued to spray the *Paulus Potter* with machine-gun fire but did not attack the four lifeboats. When they had flown off the motorboat took the other three boats in tow, away from the helpless, burning ship.

And then it was the *Washington*'s turn. More bombers appeared overhead and attacked her in force, dive bombing and strafing the decks, which were packed with tanks and truck chassis. The ship's small guns blazed away with no effect. Finally a stick of bombs exploded close on the starboard side, fracturing her side plates. She listed heavily, taking in water, while the deck cargo burst into flames from incendiary shellfire. Another stick of bombs astern disabled the steering gear. Captain Richter ordered abandon ship.

The entire crew got away safely in two lifeboats while the bombers continued to rake the ship with machine-gun fire. Because of the great danger of the fire spreading to the 500 tons of TNT stowed under her deck the boats pulled away from the fiercely burning ship as fast as possible. Soon afterwards four bombers circled low over the boats, but only to take more pictures. The pilots waved as they flew off, leaving the *Washington*'s survivors to take up the oars for the long, daunting pull – some 360 miles – to Novaya Zemlya.

Only hours later the USS *Olopana* steamed up, finding the lifeboats from the three ships. She slowed and stopped. The *Olopana* had been lucky so far, though her master, Captain Stone, was doubtful if his luck would hold out much longer. The *Washington*'s Capt. Richter boarded the *Olopana* by Jacob's ladder. He was asked if any of his crew wished to join the *Olopana* and take a chance with her. When he returned to his lifeboat, however, and put it to the men their answer was firm. 'I hollered back to Capt. Stone on the bridge,' he said. 'We are not coming aboard as my crew feel safer in the lifeboats. Wish you luck. Be on your way.'

So it was with the survivors of the *Bolton Castle* and the *Paulus Potter*, who also chose to remain in their lifeboats. They were more willing to fight the open sea than board a ship they believed to be doomed. During these exchanges a panic started: there were sudden cries that the bombers were returning. Some of the *Olopana*'s crew took to the boats and lay off, while the rest of the crew, her master and all the gunners stayed aboard. It proved to be a false alarm. The tiny specks of 'enemy aircraft' spotted on the horizon turned out to be nothing more than a flock of birds. The *Olopana* men returned to their ship, handed out cigarettes and loaves of bread to the lifeboats and steamed on their way.

Many miles to the south-east a U-boat was claiming the enemy's last victim of the day: the commodore's ship. The *River Afton* was steaming for Novaya Zemlya when, totally without warning, a torpedo struck her in the port quarter engine room. It was 8.15 p.m. W N Marsh should have finished his four-hour watch at 8 p.m. but the crew were having to double up, so his watch carried on. He had just returned to the gun box when the torpedo hit the ship, causing an explosion. He ducked into the box and when he lifted his head again all he could see was a hole where the ship's stern had been. The port lifeboat had vanished and so had the three or four gunners operating the four-inch gun. They were never seen again.

Marsh and his shipmate Gilbert White, both Newfoundlanders, ran to their emergency stations. Marsh helped lower the starboard lifeboat and White released the rafts, cool-headed action to which many men owed their lives. It took a great effort to lower the lifeboat because the warps were covered with debris, and when they got into the boat it capsized with the speed the ship was still making. Nearly 20 men were trapped under the boat and drowned. Marsh dived over the side just in time and swam to one of the rafts. Three other men, one a badly injured fireman, struggled through the icy water to join him.

A second torpedo crashed into the engine room as the boats were being lowered. Adam O'Hagan rushed to lower the jollyboat on the second mate's orders, but this also capsized because the ship was still making way. O'Hagan got away with others on a raft. Among those not so fortunate was the ship's chief mate.

The U-boat manoeuvred and sent a third torpedo crashing into the stricken ship's starboard side. Only then did Commodore Dowding abandon her, one of the last men to leave. He found safety on a raft along with two seamen.

The surfaced U-boat moved alongside Marsh's raft and ordered one of the four men to come aboard and give particulars of the *River Afton*'s cargo. The commander then handed them some wine and bread and took photographs. He told them to steer due east 200 miles to land, to Novaya Zemlya. They asked if he would take the injured fireman aboard. He said he was sorry, but he was 'full up'.

Later Marsh and his comrades were joined by another raft and the refloated jollyboat, which was carrying the ship's master, Captain Charlton, and another officer; the two men had had a struggle to keep the little boat afloat. All around in the rising mist there was wreckage and rafts with men clinging to them, with here and there the floating bodies of the dead.

Fourteen ships had been lost in one desperately black day. It was a huge figure. With the three ships sunk earlier, PQ 17's losses now equalled the entire losses of all the 16 previous convoys to Russia. But the mass destruction was not over yet.

Chapter 6

Flight to Funk Creek

BRODIE.

Sunday afternoon. The *Pozarica*, her corvettes, the *Poppy* and the *Lotus*, and the *Rathlin* were steaming eastwards alongside the ice edge. A Junkers 88 swooped in, shadowed by a Blohm and Voss, but did not attack.

Increasingly harrowing signals were coming in from the stricken merchant ships. Both the *Poppy* and the *Lotus* requested permission to turn back to help survivors, but the *Poppy*'s request was refused. Some of her company felt very bitter about this, urging their commander, Lieutenant N K Boyd RNR, to turn back despite his orders, but he was in his first command and in no position to disregard the orders of a Royal Navy four-ring captain. Feelings were running so high among some of the *Poppy*'s officers that they accused – unjustly it turned out – Captain Lawford of the *Pozarica* of saving his own skin before that of the convoy. When tempers cooled, his situation was clear: with 300 souls on board a converted banana boat it would have been foolhardy to break up the defensive unit formed by the *Pozarica*'s anti-aircraft guns and the corvettes' anti-submarine capacity. Alone, each stood far less chance of survival.

It was not unreasonable, however, for one corvette to go back. The commander of the *Lotus*, Lieutenant H J Hall RNR, was a senior escort officer and so in a stronger position than the others. He turned his corvette back, apparently into the face of the approaching enemy battleships, to rescue those he could. His ship had not been gone long before the *Pozarica* picked up a stark warning signal from the Admiralty: 'Most likely time of enemy surface attack now tonight 5th/6th or early tomorrow morning July 6th.'

From the *Pozarica* Capt. Lawford relayed the news by loud-hailer to the corvette commanders and the master of the *Rathlin*. It was clear they could not attempt a direct descent to the White Sea. They would have to continue skirting the ice barrier and make for the two islands of Novaya Zemlya, perhaps finding refuge in the narrow Matochkin Strait that divides them. If the ships reached the Strait but could not continue south to the White Sea, their companies might have to consider going ashore and making their way south overland.

At 6 p.m. Capt. Lawford gave his ship's company a full briefing. If they met enemy destroyers, he said, they stood a chance of defeating them, but they would have little hope of out-gunning the battleships. If they engaged them, it would be curtains for them all. Nervous laughter hid the company's fears. 'Get as much sleep as you can,' the captain said, 'and make peace with your Maker.'

The four ships steamed on, spread out sideways in a wide formation, hoping from their silhouettes to deceive the enemy into thinking they were a more impressive force than they actually were. Little more than an hour after her captain's speech the *Pozarica* intercepted another signal. The good news was piped over the ship's loudspeakers: the Russian submarine, the *Red Star*, had scored two hits on the *Tirpitz*, which had slowed speed. All the other German units were closing around her. Huge cheers erupted.

But as the hours went by without confirmation, many stood on the after-deck looking for signs of ships appearing astern over the horizon. When two masts did appear there was a general alert followed by an anxious interval, until the lookouts identified the vessel. It was the *Samuel Chase*. When she was close enough she signalled. Could she join them?

So now there were five ships, steaming somewhere north of the 77th parallel, bound for Novaya Zemlya. Alongside the ice edge they had a brush with a U-boat, which had been stalking the *Samuel Chase*. A torpedo approached the merchantman from her seaward side. She managed to avoid it, but it struck the ice wall and exploded, bringing down huge falls of ice. The *Poppy* chased the U-boat under the ice with shells from her four-inch, but they fell short. Eventually the *Rathlin* found the other ships too fast for her, and she dropped astern.

Far from the *Pozarica*, we three trawlers – the *Lord Austin*, the *Lord Middleton* and the *Northern Gem* – had forged our slow way ahead. We heard an occasional dull, rumbling explosion in the distance followed by a rising cloud of black smoke. On the *Northern Gem* the crew had slung out their two lifeboats ready for a quick getaway; with the sea calm and little rolling movement in the ship it was possible to lower them almost level with the ship's rail. They were packed with extra food, clothing, blankets, water, rum, guns, ammunition, tobacco and cigarettes. Each man put on extra clothing and made sure his lifebelt was on him or close at hand. One seaman packed a suitcase.

Old Frampton, the *Northern Gem*'s second engineer, had been recalled to service after being pensioned off. He now found himself on a ship that was hardly a top-notch naval vessel such as those he had served on all his life. He put his pension book and other private papers into an oilskin bag and hung it from his neck under his vest. We and the *Lord Middleton* also loaded our small boats with extra stores and got them ready for instant lowering. On each ship confidential books were put into weighted bags.

As we neared the edge of the ice field we had to skirt carefully round huge sheets of ice. The glare of the sun on them was so dazzling it hurt the eyes. As we passed an enormous iceberg the alarm bells shrilled: three enemy aircraft had been sighted flying towards us. They paid us no attention, however, making for a merchantman far away on the horizon. We had been bombarded by distress calls from the merchant ships and the ship ahead, we reckoned, must be the *Pankraft*, whose signal we had just received. Other Junkers 88s were seen flying in for the kill. As the merchantman lay motionless beam-on to us, a spiral of smoke rising from her, we could see the planes attacking from a very low level: sticks of bombs fell around the ship, one after the other. When the planes had dropped their bomb loads, back they droned. Would they attack us now? One of our signalmen stood alert on deck with a bag containing the thick, heavy, red Fleet codebooks, ready to hurl it over the side if the planes descended. 'No, not yet!' came the caution from the bridge. 'Not yet!'

The planes drew near, flying high above us. But they did not drop any bombs and flew on, apparently taking little notice of our slowly moving vessels. With some of the planes still circling, we could see scattered little blobs on the ocean around the *Pankraft*. They could have been U-boats or seaplanes that had landed with the intention of capturing the ship, so we proceeded warily. But no, they were lifeboats. As we came nearer they turned and headed in our direction.

Our skipper signalled the *Lord Middleton*: if we picked up the survivors she could sink the crippled ship. There was no answer. Then the *Lord Middleton* signalled to us all to alter course, almost to reverse. Our surprised skipper, aware of our duty to go straight to the aid of the merchant seamen, signalled the *Northern Gem*'s commander, asking if he would disregard the order and come with us to the rescue. The *Northern Gem*'s master replied that he was bound to obey the senior officer, so all three trawlers turned and made for a sheltering fog bank. This was too much for our skipper, however, who boldly turned again and steamed alone towards the *Pankraft*, presenting a perfect target as we moved to within two miles of the merchantman. The planes, which had apparently used all their bombs, started machine gunning the merchantman: we could see it all quite clearly. Then the bombers ceased their fire and flew towards us. Unbelievably, they passed overhead without opening fire.

We were joined eventually by the *Lord Middleton* and the *Northern Gem*, but just as we all neared the lifeboats, the craft suddenly turned and pulled furiously away from us. Then, moving fast into sight, we saw the *Lotus*, heading straight for the stricken freighter. Her lamp blinked as she swept by. She signalled that she would take care of the survivors; we were to keep going like hell in an easterly direction, because according to an Admiralty signal, a strong force of enemy vessels, including the *Tirpitz*, was following at 25 knots. It was the first we had heard about this because our wireless reception from the Admiralty was so poor.

Only afterwards did we learn the reason for the lifeboats' curious behaviour in turning away from us. They had been unable to make out our signals and thought we were a U-boat about to torpedo the *Pankraft*. When the *Lotus* arrived and they saw our guns apparently trained on each other, they thought they were going to be caught up in open lifeboats in the middle of a naval gun battle.

The *Lotus* began to pump shells into the motionless *Pankraft*, which was soon burning fiercely. In a very short space of time the *Lotus* had all the survivors safely aboard. She overtook us again at a cool 18 knots – almost double our speed. She signalled: '*Pankraft* went up – bigger and better bangs all the time! Clear area with all despatch – two enemy capital ships and eight destroyers nearer and still approaching. Good luck, Harry Tate's Navy!'

We needed no second bidding to get a move on. Three extra men were put in the stokehold and for the next few hours we heard the sound of shovels clinking with a new urgency as they heaped coal on the fires. Our safety valve was screwed down and we steamed all out. The engines crashed away as if they would fall through the bottom of the ship, smoke poured from the stack in gigantic clouds and the whole vessel reeked with the stench of steam, the Chief threatening to 'blow the bugger up any minute'. She was doing a fantastic 11 to 12 knots, more than she had ever done before. But the engines could not stand such violent treatment for too long.

As we pushed on into the early hours of the next day, 6 July, the buffeting ice and intermittent fog occasionally separated us from the other trawlers. Our mutual plan had now been made, however: we were to aim for the remote Matochkin Strait, anchor there under the cliffs, put out our fires and lie low till the enemy's assaults had subsided. If necessary we would leave the ships and try to make it on foot overland until we reached a settlement. It was not an attractive prospect, but better than the possibility of freezing to death in an open boat.

At intervals more enemy planes flew near, sometimes diving to take a look at us before flying on. This contemptuous indifference to our presence was rather a slight to our dignity as warships. Even so our main fear was that German HQ would get so tired of getting reports of three trawlers that a force would be sent to finish us off.

As the *Lord Middleton* steamed on, temporarily alone, there was a shout from one of her lookouts: 'Enemy aircraft!' The plane, he reported, was signalling the ship by lamp. The captain and a signalman were called. Sure enough the flashing signals continued. 'What the hell does he want?' the captain said. The signalman studied the high flying aircraft. 'Sorry, sir,' he said, 'I can't make it out. He must be speaking German.' 'In that case,' the captain said, 'he is not signalling to us but to someone over the horizon – surface craft. Bosun, turn out the lifeboats, get the codebooks ready for dumping and tell the crew to be ready to abandon ship at short notice.'

It was some time before the truth of the anxious situation dawned on them: the mysterious 'signals' were being caused by the sun striking the perspex dome of the enemy scout plane. Red faces all round.

Later on four bombers circled the *Lord Austin*, when we, too, were alone, but they did not attack, obviously looking for bigger game. But relief dropped to zero when a message from the Admiralty reported the position of three enemy destroyers between us and Novaya Zemlya. Could we escape them and get through? We were still steaming flat out, with the ship shaking so much it felt as if the boilers would explode. Sparks and clouds of heavy smoke belched from the funnel, covering us like a smoke screen.

At last, at 7.50 p.m. on 6 July, we sighted land. Three hours later we reached the rocky coast of Novaya Zemlya's north island. By this time our Chief was insisting that if he did not 'blow his tubes' the boilers would burst, so the ship was stopped for this to be done. Waiting was an eerie and nerve-wracking experience for us all. The ship lay practically motionless, cloaked in a silence you could almost feel, broken only occasionally by the helmsman making a wheel adjustment or by the sound of hammering from the bowels of the ship as the engine-room staff carried out the repairs. We felt this disturbing noise must be carrying through the water to the listening equipment of some underwater prowler. To cap it all we discovered that we had stopped in approximately the same position as the three enemy destroyers reported earlier.

Our skipper held a pow-wow with the *Lord Middleton* and the *Northern Gem* over the loud-hailers. Then thankfully we were under way again, taking the lead from the other two trawlers as we steamed south along the rugged, uninviting coast, searching for the Matochkin Strait, as unknown to us as the land we were now looking at, a God-forsaken island we had not even noticed on the map before. We found an opening which seemed likely to be the place we wanted, but our inadequate charts, dated 1904, showed only one landmark – a light on a wooden tower on the cliffs – whereas here there were two 'towers'. There was no sign of life – and no knowing what we might find. Just then, over the *Northern Gem*'s loud-hailer, news came of a signal warning that an enemy force was operating only ten miles away – almost in sight of us. All three of us quickly put on steam.

Another more up-to-date chart had now been found and our skipper signalled the *Lord Middleton*, as senior ship, to lead us in, past the headland of rock that had to be Matochkin. However, the *Lord Middleton* replied – twice – that we should lead. To make sure this happened, she abruptly steamed off down the coast. We later discovered the reason for her odd behaviour: she had thrown all her codebooks overboard and so would not be able to answer a challenge from another ship.

So the *Lord Austin* went in with all guns manned. From behind the rock a light suddenly flickered out: 'What ship?' It was the *Poppy*, guarding the entrance to the Strait. Suddenly, we were safe.

We realised for the first time what a wonderful morning it was. At 2 a.m. on 7 July, the sun was so strong that it burned our faces, but this trick of Arctic time no longer registered. For the past hectic days many of us had given up trying to keep track of the clock; the actual hours were merely figures for the log. Up forward on the *Lord Austin* a seaman was taking soundings in the twisting entrance to the Strait with a lead-line and the help, or hindrance, of half a dozen supporters. His soft Scots tones floated back to us:

'It's nay bother, nay bother at all.' The whole ship's company was up on deck. Signals flickered like summer lightning between us and the *Poppy*, going something like this: 'What kind of a time have you had?' 'Pretty bloody.' 'How about you?' 'Much the same. This looks better, though.' 'Yes, it's quite snug here.'

Then we were round the bend and the sparkling morning took on a new glory, for the most cheering sight met our eyes. Lying peacefully at anchor in a small natural harbour were no fewer than a dozen other ships from the convoy: the *Palomares*, the *Pozarica*, all three minesweepers – the *Halcyon*, the *Salamander* and the *Britomart* – together with *La Malouine* and the *Zamalek*. But there were only five merchant ships: the *Ocean Freedom*, the *Samuel Chase*, the *Hoosier*, *El Capitan* and the *Benjamin Harrison*. Were these all that were left?

As we passed by the 'ack-ack' ships there was a shout from one of them. 'My word, you won't arf cop it – you're adrift to hell. What have you been doing. Fishing?'

Minutes later our anchor rattled out of the hawsepipe. Apart from those on watch, everyone moved towards their bunks. The desire for sleep was overpowering.

The *Palomares* had been first to reach Matochkin. She had made most of the early part of the journey on her own, still towing the Walrus. There was quite a scare when the lookout in her crow's nest saw a ship coming up astern: a warrant officer gunner who was sent up the mast to check reported that it was definitely a warship. Everyone thought the enemy had finally caught up with them and there was a tense interval before the approaching ship began to signal. Thankfully, it was the *Salamander*, with her four-inch gun jammed, asking: could she stay in company? So finally there were three or four of them all heading for the Strait.

As the *Palomares* steamed close to Matochkin her navigator found a mistake on his chart: the height of a mountain shown was too great by an extra nought. It was another example of the inadequacy of the charts for this region of the Arctic. No one had anticipated being in this area and it explained why they could not get a range on their radar. The 'ack-ack' ship had sailed cautiously into the Strait and, turning the corner out of sight of the open sea, anchored where she could cover the opening at short range, bringing up armour-piercing shells ready for use should the enemy close in. And then the other ships had arrived.

The stoic inhabitants of a small Russian settlement on the shore of the south island showed little surprise at the 'invasion'. The settlement was just a collection of austere wooden buildings, the occupants roughly clad traders and hunters with their womenfolk, children and hunting dogs. A trading ship flying the Soviet flag was moored alongside a small jetty. As some of the British ships arrived they were 'inspected' by a Russian naval officer, a bizarre figure in a long black overcoat, who cruised the Strait in a little motor-powered fishing boat with a machine gun mounted in the bows. He spoke no English but was affable enough over the odd whisky and was pleased by such courtesies as the *Britomart* hoisting the Russian flag. His one-man crew, a Russian sailor, was similarly amenable as he and the British sailors exchanged cigarettes.

After the *Palomares* had come the first merchantmen, *El Capitan* and the *Benjamin Harrison*, followed by the *Salamander* with the *Ocean Freedom*, then the *Hoosier*, the *Zamalek* and the *Pozarica* group. The radar operators on the *Palomares* had picked up the *Pozarica*'s radar long before they saw her.

Like the naval craft, the merchant skippers had also made for Novaya Zemlya with various emergency plans. The *Hoosier*, heading north, had got stuck in ice fields several times, though thankfully running into sheltering snowstorms and fog. She had met up in the ice floes with other ships, but then lost them. Her captain had aimed to anchor in the Strait and send a radio message for rescue. The master of *El Capitan* had also hoped to find an inlet to lie up in for about a week before attempting to cross to the entrance to the White Sea. The Panamanian freighter had also got through by seeking every fog bank for shelter and frequently altering her course to avoid danger areas as the distress signals came in from ships being attacked.

We found a new strength and optimism in our re-formed numbers and there was another triumph when, shortly after the arrival of our three trawlers, the *Lotus* steamed in carrying more than 80 survivors: her decks teemed with heads. There were great cheers as she came slowly into the Strait, the rescued men waving. Hours after rescuing the *Pankraft*'s crew and shelling the ship, the gallant little corvette had come upon wreckage, floating corpses and the half-frozen survivors of the *River Afton* on their rafts: the grim ordeal of these men had lasted for five hours.

The survivors were spread among the bigger ships, where they were made welcome. They occupied any space they could find. They had lost everything and a dry billet and food seemed little enough to offer them after having had to abandon them out in the icy sea. Aboard the *Pozarica* there was instant fellowship as the survivors volunteered for the various action stations. One survivor was a full-blooded American Indian from the *Pankraft*, called 'Cherokee' by his mates, who opted to help as a machine-gun loader and became in some ways more efficient than his opposite number. The *Salamander* also distributed some of the survivors she was carrying among the bigger ships.

Except for the missing trawler *Ayrshire* and the corvette *Dianella*, all the escorts were now present, a total of 11 of us to shepherd the five remaining merchant vessels and the rescue ship. All thoughts of abandoning ship and making a long march overland were quietly dropped. So was the idea of waiting in the Strait for a few days until the enemy had withdrawn. Bottled up as we were, with no room to manoeuvre against raiding aircraft, and with the possibility of U-boats gathering off the entrance to pounce whenever we left, there seemed to be no alternative but to leave the Strait as soon as possible. On the *Palomares* they had seen an enemy plane searching for us. It was glimpsed for a few seconds between the two hills at the mouth of the Strait, but fortunately it did not see the ships.

Our depleted stocks of ammunition were another factor in the decision to make a quick dash to the White Sea. Most of our ships were in a similar position to the *Halcyon*, who, at the time the convoy broke up, had used up nearly half of her four-inch shells. She had reached Matochkin with very little fuel left, and she was by no means the only one.

At 11 a.m., not many hours after our own arrival, the captains held a conference aboard the *Palomares* to plan a course of action to get the small group of ships to the White Sea and Archangel. Someone suggested scuttling the ships and living ashore, but the idea was passed over as if unheard. The *Palomares* managed to get a message through to the Senior Naval Officer North Russia, and in reply was given a course to follow to reach Archangel. The messages were passed via the radio station ashore to avoid using ships' radios, which might be detected by the Germans.

It was decided that we would sail at 6 p.m. On the *Lord Austin* new orders were shouted: 'Stand by to heave in. We're going to coal.' For men who had scarcely had time to close their eyes it took a superhuman effort to get to their feet again, but somehow it was done and our tired company cursed and shoved each other up the ladder. We went alongside the coal-burning *Ocean Freedom*. Soon the bags were coming over the side and we were exchanging yarns with her crew and throwing them cigarettes and tobacco, for the merchant seamen had completely run out of stock.

It was either in Capt. Walker's dayroom on the *Ocean Freedom* or in the wardroom of the *Lord Austin* that an explicit new name was coined for Matochkin Strait. It was Funk Creek.

In our exhausted state we had only managed to haul ten tons of coal over from the *Ocean Freedom* before sailing time; we might just make Archangel on our supply. The Walrus, which the *Palomares* had towed for hundreds of miles, was hoisted to the deck of the *Ocean Freedom*, which was appointed lead ship of our re-formed convoy of 17 ships. The plan was to steam south hugging the coast of Novaya Zemlya, so we had open water and the U-boats only on our starboard side, then on south towards the Russian coast, turning back west to approach the entrance to the White Sea. Promptly, we weaved out of Funk Creek into a shrouding mist. The *Lord Austin* brought up the rear. She was the last vessel to leave our temporary bolthole.

In the meantime, far from the sheltering crags of Matochkin, the slaughter had gone on. When our ships had been converging on the Strait the previous day, 6 July, the enemy aircraft had found another easy kill. The *Pan Atlantic* from Mobile, USA, had taken a south-easterly course that led her below Matochkin on a push to the White Sea. She hoped to meet up with Russian air support on the way. As she steamed along, however, the patrolling bombers found their prey and flew in to attack. The *Pan Atlantic* received at least one direct hit and was quickly ablaze, sinking within minutes. Several men were lost, among them the chief engineer. As the ship was abandoned, young Third Engineer Richard Tallon, finding one of his shipmates without a lifejacket, took off his own and handed it to him, with the quip that back home he had swum the Mobile River, so why not the Barents Sea? The gallant lad was never seen again.

In the early hours of the following day, at the precise moment we trawlers were entering Matochkin, the killing began all over again. The planes' grim work was now taken over by the U-boats, which had raced for Novaya Zemlya to head off other merchantmen fleeing there.

At 2 a.m. on 7 July the British *Hartlebury* was steaming alone towards Novaya Zemlya's south island. As yet she was unscathed, with her many lookouts alert, but the end came very suddenly when two torpedoes rocked the ship. Gunner Arthur Carter was off watch and asleep when the torpedoes struck. When he opened his eyes the first thing he saw were flames coming through a bulkhead. He was dressed only in Army trousers, shirt and pullover, with socks and sea-boot stockings on his feet. As he leaped up to dash on to deck the first thing on his mind was his lifebelt. He had to have it. He found it, grabbed it and ran, but he had to rush back three times when it caught between the handrail on the bulkhead and was torn from his grasp. When he finally reached the deck, the *Hartlebury* was listing at an angle of 45 degrees. As everyone automatically took up their allotted stations for abandoning ship, Carter saw that his closest shipmate, a gunner who had been on watch, was very dazed though he did not appear to have been hit.

The debris-strewn deck was covered with what appeared to be a mixture of flour and water, so slippery that men could not keep their feet. Some seamen launching a lifeboat were halfway through the job when the bow went straight down and the boat just hung. Amid confused shouting another boat was quickly lowered and landed perfectly on the water – but there was no plug in the bottom and by the time a man had scrambled down the rope the boat was flooded.

The ship was still moving. Carter saw the life raft on the forward rigging being cut free and as it came sliding down the side of the ship he somehow scrambled on to it – just how he could never remember. As they paddled away from the ship a third torpedo struck her in the engine room, and with a tremendous explosion the two ends of the *Hartlebury* stood straight up in the sea, then quickly disappeared.

There were 13 men on Carter's raft, one of them the first mate. Carter was relieved to see that his friend, the dazed gunner, had managed to get to another raft, but he heard afterwards that his friend and a seaman both died on the raft. They were buried at sea.

The U-boat surfaced a short time after the *Hartlebury* sank. There was quite a crowd on the conning tower and two men were pointing machine guns at the rafts. It gave the British seamen a bad scare: they remembered recent newspaper headlines that said that all ships' survivors were being shot, especially gunners. Carter was convinced that from this moment his auburn hair began to turn white.

The U-boat, a wolf's head on its conning tower, closed in on his raft of 13 men. Three officers in turn addressed them in English. 'What ship are you? Where were you bound? What do you want to go to Russia for? You are not Bolsheviks, are you?'

One officer told them the direction in which land lay. He asked if they had a compass (they had) and apologised for not taking any prisoners as he was already full. The survivors were then thrown two bottles of Schnapps and seven loaves, motion pictures were taken of them and the U-boat moved off. The first mate saved the lives of the 13 men, many of whom were thinly dressed. There were two sheets of canvas in the raft's locker. He folded one in half lengthways and put it round them all, then stretched the other completely over them so they were in a canvas 'igloo'. He then kept everyone awake, talking, singing and moving their limbs as best they could as the raft drifted on.

At this time, well to the south, the *Alcoa Ranger* from Philadelphia was making a good 13 knots on an easterly course that would have brought her below the southern tip of Novaya Zemlya. Although attacked earlier by planes she had escaped damage, and now, as she steamed along in clear weather, there seemed nothing to threaten her on a quiet, calm sea. Then two enemy scout planes suddenly appeared. When one closed in and circled the ship but did not attack, the *Alcoa Ranger*'s master, convinced they were cornered, gave the surprising order to display international flags meaning 'Unconditional surrender', called for the Stars and Stripes to be struck and the ship abandoned. The second mate promptly took command, however, and asked for volunteers to sail the ship on. The master changed his mind, ordered the flag to be hoisted again and the guns manned, and took charge once more.

Then, without warning, a shadowing U-boat struck. At 8.30 a.m. a torpedo exploded on the vessel's starboard side, opening a large hole that made her list heavily. The ship was immediately reversed to kill speed and her engines secured; distress signals were sent and the ship's papers dropped overboard in an iron box. All hands then abandoned ship. To the intense anger of the crew, the master gave no leadership at all in handling the lifeboats, but in spite of this everyone managed to get away safely. The U-boat, an unusually large one, surfaced and began to shell the freighter. The survivors counted more than 60 shells exploding on contact with the ship: it seemed that the U-boat's gunners had been given the go-ahead for a leisurely round of target practice. The *Alcoa Ranger* went down by the bows three hours later, at 11.30 a.m., just as our captains at Matochkin were holding their conference.

The U-boat came alongside the master's lifeboat. Its commander asked in broken English the name of the ship, her destination and cargo. Many pictures were taken of the survivors. They were told the direction of land and asked whether they had sufficient provisions. Then the U-boat quickly moved on south.

A few hours of quiet followed, but the U-boats operating off the island coast were by no means through. The Liberty ship with the proud name of the *John Witherspoon* was already steaming on a fatal course that would bring her near the stricken *Alcoa Ranger*. She had scattered north and east to seek some refuge along the shore of Novaya Zemlya; north and east, that is, largely by guesswork, for there were times at the wheel when Ferocious O'Flaherty saw the magnetic compass fluctuate by as much as 70 or 80 degrees. The crew had only to glance astern to see from the wake that the ship was meandering dangerously all over the ocean.

O'Flaherty asked the first mate: 'Do you think it will do any good if I keep looking aft to try and compensate for this?' 'Ah, what's the use?' was the mate's dry reply. 'We'll never reach Russia anyway.'

After a time he noticed that O'Flaherty was holding a course on something straight ahead. He asked what it was. 'A cloud,' said O'Flaherty. 'Whoever heard of steering by a cloud?' the mate said. 'Well,' said O'Flaherty, 'take a look aft. The ship's wake is a lot straighter than it has been.'

The mate decided he had important papers to attend to. With time to plot the arc of the sun they could have made a fair course, but everyone felt sure that time was short and none of the officers had the heart for it. German scout planes had been on the horizon for a very long time and they had never realised before how much a gliding seagull could look like an approaching enemy aircraft. All hands reacted in the same way to the harmless seagulls: they cursed the birds roundly. Although the *John Witherspoon* finally escaped from the hunting planes, however, when the aircraft disappeared and the ship was sailing alone beneath an empty sky everyone sensed danger was even more imminent. Everyone felt a U-boat attack must come. With their nerves ragged from the constant harassment of the past three days many even looked forward to the tranquillity of bobbing around in a lifeboat.

When the attack did come, on the afternoon of 7 July, there was no prior hint of it. At 4.15 p.m. a torpedo struck No. 3 hold on the starboard side and sent the Liberty ship far over on her port, scattering equipment and men. She flopped back to starboard with a heavy list, and lying with her starboard main deck awash started to turn in short circles like a wounded bird. The torpedo might have blown her completely in two had it not been for the cargo of truck tyres in No. 3 hatch. They absorbed a great deal of the shock, with many tyres floating out of the hole made by the explosion.

Everyone had been so on edge that they were in action before the officer of the watch got his hand to the alarm bell. The after gun crew fired only one shot at an object, with heated disagreements over whether it was a U-boat. It was all they had time for before the steep list of the ship made their gun and the forward gun useless. The two lifeboats on the starboard boat deck were hanging from their davits, one in pieces and the other of doubtful use. Since everyone was certain that the U-boat would send another torpedo into the ship from the port side where the two remaining boats hung, they acted quickly. All the company converged on the two lifeboats except the captain, who remained on a wing of the bridge. A raft was also launched from its cradle in the shrouds.

O'Flaherty and another seaman, who were below when the torpedo struck, were both without jackets when they hit the cold air on the boat deck. It would take a few minutes to swing out the boats and that was all O'Flaherty needed to run back to his room on the deck below. The law of salvage was in order and you could grab the nearest jacket, but someone had already observed that law and the most valuable object in O'Flaherty's room was gone. He went back up to the boat deck so quickly that reason had not caught up with him: he could find a garment in the same way that he had lost his own. He went back down again, in and out of rooms – nothing. By now he was flying. He went back up to the boat deck again to check how many seconds he reckoned he had left.

The experience of breaking a routine to abandon ship often made men act without reason. Even so, the crew looked askance at him: he had been running up and down the ladder with no obvious purpose. For a third time he turned and bounded down the ladder, to the port side this time, and grabbed a jacket lying on a bunk. No seaman ever went up a ladder so fast after that. Only his toes touched metal as he flashed back to the boat deck and tumbled into the last boat as the men on the boat falls prepared to lower it.

The captain had come down from the bridge but remained on deck, motioning to them to move off. Just then an engineer and an oiler wandered out of the midship house, apparently stunned. In the confusion the lifeboat was released from the ship's side and the two men on the falls had to drop into the water. The oiler, suddenly coming to life, ran to a raft and released it. He and the engineer grabbed the captain and forced him over the side on to it.

One of the two men on the boat falls who had dropped into the water was knocked unconscious by the shock of plunging into the cold sea. The men in the lifeboat grabbed their oars and went after him, while the other boat, drifting down wind, intercepted his partner. The first man was lost, however. The lifeboat, buffeted by the waves, was unable to save him. He showed no sign of life as the seas pushed him further away until they lost sight of him in the streaming grey waves.

The ship was still turning in short circles. When, as expected, a second torpedo was fired at her the men in the nearest lifeboat could feel its hiss through the bottom of the boat as it headed for the ship. With a thud, it hit No. 3 hatch again, this time on the port side. The *John Witherspoon* did not even have the dignity of going down in one piece. She ripped herself completely open around the hull like a tin can until the bow and stern almost met, then plunged like a stone.

The U-boat surfaced, a wolf's head on its conning tower. A gun was trained on the survivors while a camera took pictures. The commander asked in good English, 'Is anybody hurt?' 'No,' said the radio operator. 'Do you need any food or water?' 'No.' 'How many tons of cargo did you have aboard?' 'I don't know.' Undeterred, the German commander produced a sheet of paper and told them exactly how many tons their ship had carried. 'Where is your captain?' he asked. 'We don't know.'

In fact, the captain had shifted from the raft and was lying in the bottom of the second boat, to avoid capture. None of the other ship's officers wore uniformed clothing. The U-boat commander studied the survivors while his craft drifted about 50 feet away from them. Then with a point he said, 'Land is over that way,' gave a wave and started down the hatch. They waved back and watched the U-boat slowly submerge.

With the drama of the sinking over and their ship gone, the men in the boats – one a sailboat, the other a motorboat – began to register the cold and the loneliness of the sea around them. As they pulled away, the final drama of that day was drawing to a close some miles to the north, almost in the path of our re-formed convoy now steaming out from Matochkin Strait.

The *Olopana*, having been rejected as a rescue ship by survivors of the *Washington*, the *Bolton Castle* and the *Paulus Potter*, had continued on for hundreds of miles until she was almost within striking distance of the coast of Novaya Zemlya's south island. Her journey had not been uneventful. Early on, when the crew panicked and made to abandon ship, Capt. Stone calmly discussed the situation with the British gunners. Their firm answer was that it was their duty to stand fast at the guns until the ship was put out of action. This quietened the panic and restored morale. The gunners arranged with the captain that if the ship was attacked from the air they would stay aboard while her two lifeboats pulled away: they would light a smoke float on deck to pretend that the ship had been hit. It seemed much their best course after finding that their machine-gun bullets and tracers simply bounced off attacking planes.

The smoke-float ruse worked well the first time it was tried, and on the afternoon of 7 July, after fighting off an attack by a Heinkel bomber, they let off another float on the forecastle head. The plane must have thought they were hit for it never returned, but the *Olopana*'s radio officer heard the pilot transmitting to a U-boat. After that the end was not long in coming. At 10.55 p.m. a torpedo struck the ship on the starboard side, killing all the *kanakas* in the boiler room. Some seamen and a gunner were also lost.

Gunner Edward Hennessey was asleep in the radio room when the torpedo hit. He had come off watch and the radio room was the nearest position to his gun station. He rushed on deck to find utter chaos. The explosion had flung the starboard lifeboat on to the deck, smashing it to bits. He looked over the rail where the torpedo had entered but could see nothing but clouds of steam. He then looked down to the engine room but could not see in there either for the billowing steam. In a panic someone let the forward falls of the port lifeboat go and it was swept away. A raft was also lost, but all the survivors managed to get away on the remaining three rafts.

The U-boat surfaced – that wolf's head emblem again – and shelled the reeling ship for 15 minutes. When it had finished the *Olopana* was well on fire and sinking by the stern, clouds of yellow smoke rising from the smashed and holed drums of chemicals stacked in her foredeck. The U-boat came alongside the rafts and again the questions were asked. 'Are you Bolsheviks? No? Then why are you helping Russia?' The commander asked if they had enough food, pointed out the direction of land and boasted, 'The ships of your convoy are all at the bottom of the sea.'

It was a sickening parting shot for the survivors to stomach that lonely midnight on the Barents Sea. The *Olopana* was the 22nd ship to die – but she was still not the last.

Chapter 7

Bloody Marvellous!

BRODIE.

O ur re-formed convoy was quickly spotted by a lurking U-boat as we steamed into the mist outside Funk Creek. As the *Lord Austin* was the last ship out of the narrow Strait we had a good sight of the enemy craft not many miles off. When one of the corvettes opened fire it submerged quite slowly. There were reports of more U-boats in the area. These were now our main danger, for word had reached us that the enemy's large ships had returned to anchor in Norway.

The mist turned to fog, our oldest enemy becoming once again our firmest friend: if this kept up all the way we might manage the rest of our journey unmolested. Before midnight the fog cleared for a while, then came down thicker than ever, making near collisions frequent: we just missed hitting the *Zamalek* by a coat of paint. The *Benjamin Harrison* lost touch completely and her skipper, after trying for 12 hours to find the convoy, turned back for the Strait, not caring to journey through alone.

By next morning, 8 July, the fog had improved – to our benefit. There was just enough visibility to keep contact with each other, but enough of a blanket to make us invisible from the air. We sent up a prayer to the 'god of fogs' to keep it just like that. Now that the immediate danger had passed each man again found himself with an intense craving for sleep. The odd three hours here and there just seemed to aggravate the complaint; about three days' sleep would have been nearer the mark. On the wheel, staring into the bright, hypnotic square of light in which the block markings of the compass card turned and swam before your eyes, it required every ounce of willpower not to drop off.

In the afternoon, however, the fog became thick and heavy, and there was a new chill in the air. Sirens hooted and we slowed just in time to avoid ramming the ship ahead. From it came the cry, 'Look out! Bad ice coming!' In a few minutes we were in the midst of pack ice, which grew thicker as we moved forwards. Soon every vessel was twisting and dodging to turn round and get out before it was too late and we were gripped fast. A chorus of sirens blared out.

On the *Lord Austin* we had a real scare when a huge merchantman loomed out of the fog right across our bows. There was no room to manoeuvre so we quickly stopped the engines. Then there was a warning shout from the lookout: we were drifting stern first on to the grandfather of all ice blocks. The *Lord Austin* was rising and falling in the swell. If she touched that mammoth chunk it would slice off her propeller and rudder. We were saved by the alertness of Signalman Gordon Hooper. He seized his lamp and flashed urgent SOSs to the other ship, which, quickly understanding the danger, promptly moved off and allowed us to restart our engines – just in the nick of time.

The *Lord Middleton* had a similarly alarming experience. Completely surrounded by ice, she kept going at about six knots when suddenly the alarm bells went off and everyone rushed on deck as a 10,000-ton merchantman loomed up in the greyness. Neither ship could stop nor go astern as the ice would have smashed their propellers, nor could they turn to port or starboard because of the ice packed all round them. The trawler's two smallboats were quickly over the side and the crew all ready to leave ship when the merchant skipper acted. He increased speed, hoping that the freighter would pass the collision point before the trawler reached it. It was a very close decision. As the merchantman passed dead ahead of the *Lord Middleton* there was scarcely a couple of yards between them. If she had hit the little trawler she would have turned her over and gone on without a scratch.

The struggling ships tried to maintain contact by fog horns and radio transmission. This was probably how we gave away our position to the listening enemy. As the *Lord Austin* retraced her passage we kept running into new ice fields. We took turns as lookout right up in the bows. In our sleepless state the ice seemed to take on odd shapes in the murky greyness. Sometimes a lookout would swear he had seen a U-boat ahead; once an 'E-boat' was reported to be heading straight for us. It was now bitterly cold so it was vital to keep contact with the main body of ships: to become detached from the convoy here would be grim. A signal was intercepted warning of an enemy warship in the area. On top of this we were worried about our coal supplies; all this going back and dodging around was eating into our scanty stock. Would we ever reach Russia?

All the other 15 ships were busy fighting their own battles with the ice. Among the merchant vessels, *El Capitan* and the *Samuel Chase* got through, but the *Hoosier* got completely lost. When eventually she sighted land Capt. Holmgrun went in close to shore and signalled, but there was no reply. Then the crew saw men walking along the lonely shore: a part of Novaya Zemlya. The captain landed and had a conversation in sign language. Then he was able to return to his ship and set a course to catch up with the others.

Our friends on the *Ocean Freedom* suffered most in the chaotic conditions. Earlier on she had been in company with the *Northern Gem*, with the trawler keeping to her port bow. One of the *Northern Gem*'s crew laconically observed, 'There's no bloody freedom in this ocean.' When they first came out of the fog the two vessels were still together but there were no other ships in sight; it was a lonely position to be in and the crews were sure they were being watched. When the two skippers saw a new bank of fog on the port bow they both made for it as fast as they could. Then they met the ice. As the *Ocean Freedom* steamed at a much reduced speed, skirting the ice as best as she could in the fog, the crew's nerves were more strained than in any of the previous actions they had been in. In no time the ship seemed to be entirely hemmed in. Floundering around like a man in a maze trying to find a way out, she came across the *Northern Gem* again, now stuck fast in the ice. With her greater size and weight the merchant ship pushed through the ice, releasing the trawler and herself.

Now in more or less clear water, Capt. Walker decided to crack on as fast as he could, taking the lead from the *Northern Gem* in case they encountered more ice. Very soon they did. Still in heavy fog, the *Ocean Freedom* ran full tilt into thick pack ice. Fortunately the trawler was not astern or she would have run into her back; instead the *Northern Gem* ran up alongside, rising on top of the ice almost to her foremast. She went astern and stopped. Coxswain S A Kerslake went anxiously to inspect the forepeak. It was snuff dry: no sign of water or damage. The old girl had brought them through again; they certainly had built her well in Bremerhaven.

On the *Ocean Freedom*, however, it was a different picture. After taking the full impact of the ice, her stem was gone from the waterline down. The frames and plates along each side were buckled and twisted, and the forepeak flooded immediately. The chief officer and carpenter anxiously inspected the damage and the No. 1 hailed the bridge: 'The forepeak is open to the sea. Abaft the collision bulkhead she's tight – try going ahead.' Capt. Walker eased the ship forward, gradually building up speed. Then another shout: 'She's still holding. Give her the works!' And so, as the fog began to clear, the two ships piled on steam in an effort to catch up with us. The *Ocean Freedom*'s speed was retarded by her mangled bow but was still enough for her to keep one step ahead of the *Northern Gem*.

In fog up ahead the *Palomares* had her hectic moments. She was steaming along with the *Pozarica* immediately astern when she hit a barrier of ice head on, giving the men in the forward mess decks a nasty shock. There was such a thunderous noise below decks that there was a general scramble aft before it became clear that the enemy had not, in fact, scored a direct hit. But the *Palomares* was well and truly stuck in the ice. Only after a great strain on the engines did she eventually free herself.

There were many bitter comments about the Russians having given them a route that led straight into the ice. The *Pozarica* took quick evasive action, only narrowly escaping ramming her sister ship. As she continued slowly on, Charles Gooch was on the upper deck off duty. He was looking over the side and peering into the fog when suddenly the bows of *El Capitan* loomed up so close he could have touched her with his hand. Here again, however, the *Pozarica* was lucky and did not collide. Then in a sudden break in the fog, almost under the 'ack-ack' ship's bows, a lifeboat with a red sail up was spotted. The men in it shouted as they were seen by the careering ships. The lifeboat held 19 men from the *John Witherspoon*, many of them frostbitten and all in a very weak state. They were now picked up by *El Capitan*.

All the ships were now retreating westwards from the pack ice that was sweeping round the southern tip of Novaya Zemlya. We would have to steam back for many miles before being able to turn south again for a last push down to the entrance to the White Sea. Our convoy pressed on, skirting the ice on the port side and praying for it to clear.

The early hours of 9 July brought a clear sea. The fog was much less dense but just thick enough to give us adequate cover. On the *Lord Austin* we passed over a huge patch of oil, the sombre marker of a recently sunk merchantman. Then the fog lifted completely and, like all the scattered ships, we were looking out for our companions. Surprisingly, a strong nucleus of the convoy had kept within fair distance of one another and very shortly we found ourselves in company with both 'ack-ack' ships and all three corvettes, along with the *Lord Middleton*, the *Britomart*, the *Hoosier*, *El Capitan* and the *Zamalek*.

Soon a few black specks were spotted out to port. *La Malouine* raced over. She found two lifeboats with survivors from the *Pan Atlantic*; others had already been picked up earlier by the *Pozarica*.

That day we finally left the ice and swung south, the corvettes kept busy dropping depth charges against shadowing U-boats. We began to pass occasional logs floating in the sea, a comforting indication that we were now approaching Russia, even if we still had quite a distance to go. Any moment we hoped to see a squadron of Red Air Force planes come into view. When two planes were sighted during the afternoon, however, they were not Soviet. They hovered just above the horizon like giant dragonflies; we had seen planes like them somewhere before. One was a Blohm and Voss, the other a Heinkel 115. They flew round the convoy in opposite directions, an ominous patrol busily reporting back to base and to the U-boats. Almost at the same time a U-boat surfaced some miles off, scrutinised the convoy and then quickly dived. The game was about to begin all over again.

It did so in the late evening. The lead ships of our sorry remnant of PQ 17 were about 80 miles off the Russian coast. Aboard the *Palomares* the radar gave the first warning of approaching aircraft: they were about 70 miles away. Long blasts on the 'ack-ack' ship's sirens were followed by a hoist of flags. As the other vessels were alerted, the radio operators on every naval ship broke silence, making frantic efforts to contact the signal stations at Archangel and Murmansk with an appeal for fighter protection. On the *Palomares* they called up in code, by radio and in plain language, in English and Russian, on several wavelengths. There was no answer to all the urgent messages. Was there something wrong with the wavelengths? Or were they being jammed by the Germans? The plain fact was that our operators could not get through and we needed air support quickly.

On the *Lord Austin*, haggard-eyed, we searched the horizon. We did not have long to wait. Soon five tiny specks were seen flying very high. Round went our guns, but the planes were much too high for them. Boomp! Boomp! Boomp! went the high-angle four-inches of the 'ack-acks'. How we wished we had such a gun. Puffs of black smoke appeared in the raiders' path, but the five planes did not swerve off from their course. They flew straight on. Then, when they were quite near, they broke formation to swoop down from different points.

One plane put its nose down for a dive: three spouts of water rose into the air off our port bow. There was no sound, only a massive shudder through the ship's hull. Another five specks were coming in from a different quarter; then more, and still more, always in fives. They picked their targets and dived, though never very low. Three bombs floated down from each plane, looking like large silver Indian clubs, slowly at first, then faster and faster as they came nearer. When they were almost half way down you could tell which ship was their target. We would wait, holding our breath, until three great waterspouts mushroomed up, completely hiding the marked ship. Then the curtain of water would drop and you could see the vessel still sailing steadily on course, her decks lined with men soaked to the skin by the mighty splash.

The *Pozarica* heeled over from the force of three bombs, turned a complete circle to port and stopped dead. She signalled: 'Three very near misses but we think we are OK.' The *Palomares* steamed over at a furious pace to check on her sister ship. She came up to cross our bows fast, a voice on her bridge crackling harshly through the loud-hailer: 'Ahoy, *Lord Austin* – take care! We are coming through you all!' There was a heart-stopping moment as she loomed high above us. We slowed and turned hard to starboard as the 'ack-ack' surged past with no more than 20 feet between us. She swept by, still firing. A plane dropped a stick of bombs at her. They missed. Instead the whistling explosives came for us, the slower ship. Two bombs hit the sea on either side of us ahead, the third came wobbling down straight for our deck.

Our junior 'sparks', Telegraphist Johnny Rose, captured the tension of those fleeting seconds before it descended. He wrote in his diary: 'We saw the bomb get bigger and bigger, and I remember thinking that if I continued to look up into the air, my mouth would be dragged open and the bomb would fall right into it. It was surprising how smartly I snapped my jaws together. George was standing by my side, looking up – his boiling hot mug of cocoa tilting over, its contents dribbling and splashing down his chest and stomach and legs, soaking into his clothes unnoticed (he showed me the scalds afterwards but said he hadn't felt them). Jock had a lump of corned 'dog' in his great fist, which he was squeezing until it oozed between his fingers. The oaths he was muttering were sweet to hear. Jim Morris, the only one who seemed unperturbed, had seen the bomb but had turned away to make a lightning sketch of others falling alongside the *Lotus*.

'The coxswain behind me was straining his ears to hear the orders from the bridge. Already he had the wheel hard to port, and the old tub was answering painfully slowly. Johnny was there on the Lewis, one eye on his Junkers target, the other on the whistling missile. Sweat ran down his face but he was still firing, as were the two men on the twin point-five platform, sending streams of bullets towards the planes. The skipper was yelling again and again, "Keep her hard to port!" and watching the bows shudder slowly round. The four-inch gun crew on their platform could do nothing. They simply stood there waiting for the inevitable, not knowing whether to crouch or stay as they were. Ron, on the bridge, clutched at the loose halyard ends, saying the word "Jesus" over and over again to himself. My knees felt like jelly, my stomach had shrunk into a tight ball of painful gristle. My head thudded and ached and I couldn't look upwards any longer.'

The scream of the bomb was ear-splitting. Then, after what seemed an eternity, it was down and smacking into the sea just off our bow, sending up a giant waterspout that doused the ship and all of us in its icy wave. Amazingly, it had not exploded. If it had done so our bows would have been smashed in. And if our skipper had not turned to port split seconds earlier, the bomb, whether it exploded or not, could have hit the magazine and taken us all to the bottom.

The *Pozarica* was soon under way again and the *Palomares*, firing fiercely as ever, returned through the ships to take up her former position.

Shrapnel fell like snowflakes in the heavy barrage as every vessel began a new fight for life. The attack had begun at 9 p.m. After only 15 minutes the *Hoosier* was abruptly out of the battle. A V-shaped formation of bombers went for her, flying so high that her small guns were useless. Then the planes peeled off to dive and loose their bombs. Finally a stick of three fell just short of the ship's No. 3 lifeboat, passing under the freighter and exploding, lifting her completely out of the water. Her steam-turbine main engine jarred back on its foundation, jammed and would not run. All the steam gauges and small steam lines were broken, and the fuel-oil pump was knocked off its base. The chief engineer told Capt. Holmgrun that the ship was unable to run.

Reluctantly the master gave orders to abandon. Bombs were still dropping as the crew went over the side into the lifeboats. There was no panic, however, though three men who had finally cracked up under the strain had to be helped over by the others.

As the *Hoosier* swung out of line and drifted astern with steam pouring from her we saw the *Poppy* race to her aid. She helped the survivors aboard as they rowed over in their boats crammed with luggage and provisions. When the steam cloud had cleared the *Poppy*'s commander tried to persuade the *Hoosier*'s master to return to his ship and see if the engine would run, but Capt. Holmgrun said this was impossible. So, to avoid leaving such a costly prize to drift, possibly to the enemy-held coast of Finland, Sub Lieutenant Denis Brooke was ordered to sink her with the *Poppy*'s four-inch. He was told where the *Hoosier*'s tons of ammunition were stored, but though they put more than 30 shells into the freighter, peppering the hull and setting off a fire inside her, they got no spectacular results. The *Hoosier* was left settling slowly in the water.

More high-level bombers now came over near the *Poppy*. Brooke thought one was low enough to have a crack at. 'I suppose the bombardment of *Hoosier* had perhaps gone to my head a bit,' he said, 'for I omitted to ask the captain's permission to open fire. I didn't get the gun trainer or layer to use sights but merely got them to raise the old four-inch, with such un-nautical expressions as "Up a bit. Right a bit. Fire!"

By this time the mouth of the barrel was near the wing of the bridge and the captain and company were as shattered by the blast as some of the canvas screens.

'It was nothing to the blast which poured down on me afterwards from the captain wanting to know what the bloody hell I was up to. With some satisfaction I saw the shell explode in front of the bomber, which sharply altered course away. I pointed this out to the captain, who was not impressed and merely called it a waste of valuable ammunition on aircraft that had obviously dropped their bombs. Suitably abashed, I watched the next wave of bombers course slowly over, with the *Poppy* holding a steady course at full speed. Fascinated, I saw a single stick of three bombs fall from one aircraft and produce towering geysers of water on our port bow, near enough to wet the foredeck. I didn't dare look the captain in the face.'

When the *Poppy* finally caught up with us the convoy was still under continuous attack. The *Hoosier*'s gunnery officer and his men asked what they could do to help the corvette's crew. They were allocated to ammunition hoists and gun loading. Many of the seamen, however, though they had not wetted their feet crossing on to the *Poppy*, behaved like survivors for the rest of the voyage, putting quite a strain on Anglo-American relations. Admittedly they had brought with them some welcome supplies of tinned food, but members of the *Poppy*'s company even had to stop some of them, before they finally left the ship, throwing what was left overboard rather than leave it behind for the naval men. Seeds of misunderstanding were already germinating.

The *Hoosier* died at five minutes past 1 a.m. on 10 July, three hours after she had been abandoned. There were two terrific explosions. The *Poppy*'s commander came down from the bridge to tell Capt. Holmgrun. 'Your ship has exploded twice and is now sinking.' 'God bless her,' replied the master. 'May she rest in peace.' All his crew admired the old man for the way in which he had stood up under the strain while younger men were breaking.

All this time the bombing had continued, hour after hour, with short intervals as some planes withdrew and others arrived to take their place. Men on the guns just had time between attacks to replace new belts and pans of ammunition, light up a cigarette, take a few puffs, and then it was tin hats on, cigarettes out, and back to their guns to meet the next group of bombers. The planes attacked in long, dodging 85-degree dives. The majority of them were Junkers 88s, though there were also some Heinkel 115s. During one lull a U-boat contact was reported. Away went the *Lotus* to drop venomous 'ash-cans' over the spot. Then fresh quintets of planes approached. Whether by accident or design they made the corvette their target. We saw stick after stick of bombs fall around her as she writhed and dodged. She seemed certain to be hit, they fell so closely. But no. As the last trio of waterspouts subsided, she was still in one piece and still under way. She was a stout little ship, that corvette.

A boatload of exhausted survivors from the *John Witherspoon* picked up by *La Malouine* saw how the corvette dodged the bombers. O'Flaherty said: 'An officer lay on his back just forward of the wheelhouse and dead centre of the ship, focusing his binoculars on the underside of each plane as it dipped down to release its bombs. If a bomb disappeared from his view he said nothing. If it remained in view it meant that it was heading for us, and he would order the helmsman to turn either way without taking his eyes away from his line of vision. This method avoided the error of zigging when you should be zagging. It was very tiresome on the eyes, calling for frequent changes of watchers. It was also a strain on the animal instinct to evade, until you drew an imaginary line from the centre of the ship to the belly of the plane and realised that the blighters were right. All the same, it was a weird experience to be sailing along on a straight course while bombs dropped around us, being averted by a combination of drift, speed and the coolness of the men on the corvette.'

From the *Lord Austin* we saw the *Lord Middleton*'s narrow escape. She was lying astern of us when three bombers came in close, one right over her. Nine bombs fell each side and astern, the nearest only feet away. All we could see was one huge spout of water, yet she sailed through magnificently.

One of the greatest surprises was how the *Zamalek* managed to keep going, for she could scarcely be seen for the great eruptions of water around her. She was singled out for attack. Only a miracle and expert handling by Capt. Morris saved her from going down with heavy loss of life. She was crowded with more than 200 survivors and all the officers and crew were sharing their cabins and mess space. The chief engineer alone had eight 'guests' in his cabin – and food was running very short. Kept very secret from the survivors was the fact that she carried 60 tons of depth charges for use by Russian-based aircraft, with several hundred gallons of petrol for the launch stored on deck. As the bombs rained down, the fuel pipes in her engine room fractured and a generator was put out of action.

Chief Engineer A S Dawson was alone at his post in the engine room, the others at stations on deck, when suddenly all the lights in the ship went out. He calmly told the bridge of his plight and several engineers among the survivors, including the *Zaafaran*'s Chief Engineer Miller, went below to help him right the main switch and fuse.

From the *Lord Austin* we saw a smoking plane turn away and try to make altitude. It failed. As its pilot and gunner parachuted down to the sea near the *Zamalek*, she was alerted. 'Well,' she started to reply, 'if the Bosch behave … ' Then she was straddled again by near misses. When she emerged from the splashes she was still flashing: 'I was about to say before being so rudely interrupted that if the Bosch behave I will go back for them, but now following this little packet from the Fatherland, if they haven't frozen to death in this water they can either start swimming or bloody well tread water.'

As the bombing continued some planes dropped parachute mines ahead of the convoy. A sweeper went ahead to clear a passage through them. The escorts' radio operators made more efforts to contact the Russian signal stations, but again without result.

During one of the earlier brief spells between the waves of attackers someone on the *Palomares* saw blood running down the mast on to the deck. He remembered that the lookout was still up in the crow's nest: he had not had time to get down before the first bombers were upon them. As all eyes gazed upwards the man was seen hanging perilously over the edge of the nest with an ominous hole visible at the bottom of it. He had been hit by a low-angled shot from one of the other escorts. A rope was specially rigged to bring him down. He had lost a lot of blood and a large part of his backside, which was sewn up by the ship's doctor. Remarkably, after being treated in hospital in Archangel, the sailor was ultimately left with just a pronounced limp.

The *Pozarica*'s guns were loaded and fired over and over again until everyone became insensitive to the noise. The decks became cluttered with empty shell cases, the gun barrels grew hot and the paint peeled off in large flakes. In between attacks the guns were trained into the wind to let the icy air flow through and cool them down. At one of the twin Lewis guns, where the rejected cartridge cases were now waist high, Mayne and 'Cherokee' had just reloaded for Taffy Cooke when Mayne caught sight of a Heinkel 115 flying in just above the waves. It obviously intended to loose its two torpedoes at the 'ack-ack' ship.

Mayne signalled to Cooke, who opened fire. The gunner gave the aircraft the two magazines full, 90 rounds in all. The three men saw the Heinkel drop to the sea and sink fast from the weight of its torpedoes. Cooke undoubtedly saved the ship since the other guns were too busy with the aircraft overhead. His action was carried out in desperate conditions, with blast from the four-inch gun muzzles just above their heads. When Leading Seaman Berry reported Cooke's feat to the bridge he got the typical naval reply: 'Very good.'

Because the planes were flying so high, we on the *Lord Austin* could not fire our four-inch very often. Our gunner grumbled and swore as the gun was trained first from one side and then the other. When a Junkers 88 swooped low enough for us to get in a burst with the point-five we saw that its wings were tipped with yellow: the mark of one of Goering's special squadrons. Crack pilots they may have been, but fortunately they lacked the daredevil courage of the torpedo bombers of Independence Day. They pulled out of their dives at about 500 feet to release their load. Having dropped its load, a plane would continue to make feint attacks to draw the convoy's fire from the real attackers.

As the bombs came down the fish went up, dropping back on to the sea dead or stunned by the explosions until the water was covered with them. It was good fresh fish. Even in mid-action our hungry stomachs protested at the sight of all that food going begging.

Now *El Capitan* with her deckload of aircraft was running the gauntlet. At the same time another plane dived for us. Again it seemed we were done for, but either the pilot decided against wasting his cargo on such small fry or the bombs jammed in their racks, for he peeled off and we turned our attention once more to *El Capitan*. Up went the waterspouts, but she always reappeared. Suddenly the planes were making off, but to our dismay we saw the merchantman was losing way. We were immediately signalled by the *Palomares*. 'Out scramble nets!' ordered our skipper. 'Stand by to pick up survivors.'

Early in the bombing three bombs had fallen astern of *El Capitan*. Her afterpeak, also the gun crew's quarters, had begun taking water, but the situation was not critical. She had survived many more attacks, only to be crippled now in the last gasp of more than seven hours' continuous bombing. It was 5.30 a.m. on 10 July. Three bombs landed within 20 feet of the ship on the starboard side, blowing in the sea valves and bursting fuel and water pipes to the main engines. The starboard side of the engine room was completely wrecked and two holds began taking water.

The boats were lowered from the helpless merchantman. Men tumbled into them and started rowing towards us. Our skipper bellowed over the loud-hailer, 'Bring some guns if you can!', at which they paused to dismantle the lighter machine guns. We helped them aboard without ceremony, grabbing outstretched hands and dragging them quickly over the side on to the deck. We let all but one of their boats drift away. Our decks were now very crowded. Then the order: 'Stand by, the four-inch crew.'

El Capitan's old captain, a Norwegian, warned us not to hit her in No. 2 hold: it was full of TNT and we would all be blasted to kingdom come. He stood on our bridge with tears in his eyes as the shells crashed into his ship. At only a cable distant it was impossible to miss. Our own feelings were pretty mixed when they told us her fridges were still stuffed with turkeys and other delights for Independence Day, for by this time our rations were very meagre. With six hits below the waterline and three holds flooding, it would not be long before the huge vessel disappeared below the surface. We had no means of knowing it then – but she was the 24th ship to die. Her machine guns were fixed to the sides of our bridge and our skipper took charge of her gunners' revolvers. He did not like the idea of having any armed men on his ship.

During the rescue operation and shelling the bombers had left us alone, but now they returned for another shot at the settling *El Capitan* – and at us. The *Lord Austin* was shaking alarmingly from more near misses. With our condenser badly damaged and plates buckled it would not have taken very much more to put us under, but they eventually drew away and left us suddenly staring at an empty sky.

We had a senior asdic rating who, early in the voyage, had been found by the skipper sleeping behind the funnel. Having been torpedoed, he had sworn never to sleep below decks again. But he was a good hand and the skipper fixed him up a cabin in a passage off the deck. Now, as we all relaxed, he approached the skipper. 'Sir,' he said warmly, 'I thank you. You were bloody marvellous!'

By this time the convoy was almost out of sight on the horizon and we made speed to catch up. Fortunately they slowed and waited for us, and for the gallant *Zamalek*. The *Pozarica*'s captain took his ship in as close as possible to the *Zamalek* and everyone aboard raised a cheer to the rescue ship. Answering cheers rang back from her crowded decks: a strange, moving incident in that desolate sea.

Soon after we rejoined the convoy the aircraft warning was sounded: a little speck had been seen far ahead. Everyone thought it must be another German plane coming in to assess the results of the long raid, but then it dropped flares, a green and a red, and the convoy sent up answering flares. As the aircraft came nearer we saw it was an antiquated flying boat with a pusher screw. It was friendly! It was Russian! Everyone waved and cheered and capered wildly about. Apart from the Walrus from the cruisers it was the first friendly aircraft we had seen since leaving Iceland. The flying boat flew low over us, the pilot returning our greetings, then it turned and flew off. Surely it would not be long now before the convoy had some fighter support.

Some miles away from us, however, the *Samuel Chase* was in serious difficulty. Just after passing Cape Kanin, the *Halcyon* came upon her. She was drifting helplessly. Her master signalled: 'Two direct hits, three near misses, main steam line broken. Shall we abandon ship?' The *Halcyon*'s captain determined to try to save the situation. He replied: 'Do not abandon ship. We will take you in tow.' A very fine piece of seamanship followed. The minesweeper had reciprocating engines, which enabled her to pull a considerable weight. Very efficiently, a strong tow was shot over to the *Samuel Chase*, the *Halcyon* gradually increased engine revolutions and both screws began to thrust. The merchantman began to move.

The two vessels made a steady five knots south to the White Sea, ready to cut clear if they should be attacked. After some hours the Americans, fired no doubt by the example of the little 1,000-ton sweeper, managed to get their engines going again and finish the journey under their own steam. In recognition of the *Halcyon*'s assistance, the master of the *Samuel Chase* asked that the minesweeper be allowed to escort him to harbour, which she did.

On the *Lord Austin* we had turned to looking after our guests from *El Capitan*. There was a mix of nationalities: Americans from both north and south, Argentines, Poles, English and Chinese. Besides her crew there were also the survivors from the *John Witherspoon*, whom she had been carrying. Some of these were suffering badly from frostbitten hands and feet, with the threat of gangrene setting in. They were all given a double tot of rum and then we began to tackle the problem of feeding and finding sleeping room for 89 extra bodies. The Chinese were very helpful, offering to give a hand in the mess and the galley, and refusing to sleep anywhere but under the whaleback on deck.

The survivors as a whole were quite cool, cheerful and fatalistic, though inevitably, once all danger had receded, there were grouses about the crowded conditions on a ship with accommodation for 50 officers and men, which now had to carry 140. We had to improvise nine sittings for meals – the galley never stopped – and there was a desperate shortage of cutlery. The white Americans did not like eating or even mixing with the coloured seamen and in the confined space quarrels sprang up between them. Men flopped down to sleep everywhere, on the floors of the mess deck, the wardroom, and along the corridors all over the ship. Those who could not find space below had to sleep on the open deck. Some survivors had no compunction about taking a crew member's bunk while he was on watch and refusing to get out of it afterwards.

They were used to a considerable standard of luxury on their merchant ships and found it hard to cope with the spartan conditions of a trawler. Not least the sanitary arrangements. There were just two lavatories or 'heads' for our crew, nerve-racking places to perform in at the best of times. Now the situation was chaotic: the sight of bare bottoms sticking out over the sides of the ship became a familiar one.

The only survivors happily unaffected were the stokers. Joining their brethren below, they followed the long-standing tradition of manning the shovels that were put into the furnace.

Far behind us as we raced for the White Sea, the damaged *Ocean Freedom*, with the *Northern Gem*, was straining every nut and bolt to catch up. Eventually, from about eight miles astern, she sighted our depleted group. She made an even greater effort to reach us, but about three miles from Cape Kanin she was attacked by several aircraft. There were only about eight or nine planes, but to Capt. Walker and his company it seemed like the entire Luftwaffe as they gave the *Ocean Freedom* their undivided attention. Time and again she was straddled by bombs, shivering and shuddering under the storming attack. Her gyro compass and bridge instruments were shattered, the magnetic compass blown out of its gimbals, and the plates along both sides of the ship further buckled by the bomb explosions. Huge columns of water boiled up each side of the ship and enveloped her. As the water cascaded down it was like coming up to the surface from a great depth, only to be enveloped again and again. The bridge was awash and the gunners totally submerged. Washed out of their gun pits, they scrambled back again, numbed and soaked to the skin but with their trigger-fingers still working. Still the planes failed to plant a bomb directly on her, hampered in their efforts by those resolute trigger-fingers.

On the *Northern Gem*, too, the trawler was fighting with everything she had, adding to the din. Then suddenly the planes were gone, leaving the *Ocean Freedom* practically out of ammunition and her decks covered with empty shell cases. Incredibly, she was still intact and gamely steaming. Her only bad casualty was a gunner who had been hurled from his platform on to a hatch, injuring his spine.

Far ahead of the *Ocean Freedom* our group had at last sighted the coast on our port hand. The last hours of 10 July had seen the odd phenomenon of sunset and sunrise at the same time. It was now a dazzling morning, 11 July. More survivors in open boats were spotted and picked up, again some badly frostbitten. The sea was glassy and there was a striking mirage. The ships ahead looked like tall, elongated, slender trees, their smoke taking the place of branches. Those beam-on to us looked like great square islands, and the hills ahead seemed to be chasing each other madly across the landscape. At first we thought the strain had been too much for us, that we were seeing things, but after a time we became accustomed to it, though the lookouts kept reporting our own ships as submarine periscopes.

We nosed into one of the little harbours at the entrance to the White Sea for a brief spell, then steamed on together into the White Sea itself, where we were met by Russian armed trawlers and wood-burning destroyers painted in fantastic camouflage. Further into the White Sea two British minesweepers passed us, their magnetic sweeps out, combing for enemy-laid mines. It was a comforting sight to see these few vessels. We discovered that the sea, in spite of its name, was a dirty brown colour, with logs floating everywhere.

During the afternoon two Junkers 88s swept out of the clouds to drop a stick of bombs each. One of the sticks fell about 100 feet off the *Pozarica*'s starboard quarter, giving the crew quite a shock. But it was the enemy's last fling.

Some of the stragglers among the ships now came up over the horizon and joined us, including the indomitable *Ocean Freedom*. We pressed on down the White Sea without further incident.

That night as the sun, an enormous, quivering red ball, dropped to the horizon, the whole sea between skyline and ship became a blood-red corridor that looked as if it was on fire. Around the molten glow a deepening dusk lasted for ten minutes before the sun reappeared over the horizon. It was the nearest thing to darkness we had seen for about ten days.

The morning of Sunday 12 July was cloudy with drizzle. As the *Lord Austin*'s bows cleaved the water, throwing up a muddy-brown wave, the rain stopped, the clouds cleared and the sun shone strongly. We dropped anchor off the mouth of the North Dvina river that led to Archangel. 'Oh, what a wonderful night we've had tonight,' played over the *Pozarica*'s loudspeakers. The *Palomares* checked the number of survivors on board each vessel: one alone had more than 300 and the total approached the thousand mark. One thousand men without their ships: what a desperately broken and miserable fleet we were.

The pilot boat arrived and we had our first sight of the Russians. A smart naval officer boarded the *Lord Austin* and had a rather involved conversation with our skipper, who refused to go further until the men suffering from frostbite were transferred to a ship where proper medical attention was available. This done, our pilot came aboard and we set off up the river, which twisted and turned like a snake. Tired though we were, every man was on deck to take his first look at the Soviet Union. There were logs everywhere, in the river and piled high on the banks. Women working among them laughed and waved as we passed, as did other women from the doors and windows of their wooden dwellings. Passing boats dipped their flags and the crews waved. In spite of the poverty of our numbers we were getting a royal welcome.

There were sandy beaches and behind them splashes of green: plantations of young trees. Further back still from the river stretched great pine forests. Immense barges, larger than any we had ever seen, swept past us. Full-sized wooden houses were built on them, and they had spacious decks; some were even topped by windmills. All dipped their red flags, showing the hammer and sickle.

The *Pozarica* ran on to a sandbank and stuck fast. Hands jumped up and down on the forecastle but they could not shift her, so she had to wait there several hours for high tide. It seemed a mortifying end to her journey as we all steamed past her to our respective wharfs a few miles from Archangel.

The *Lord Austin* came alongside a wooden quay at the village of Maimaksa, where to our great relief our survivors were transferred to a larger ship to continue to Archangel. As soon as we tied up, children swarmed on to the jetty offering to barter badges and emblems for cigarettes, chocolate or soap. They were joined by old women begging for bread.

After a few hours we moved on to moor at a huge wooden quay – it was said the Russians had built it in two weeks – at a village on the opposite side of the river to Archangel. Here we met up with others from our convoy and swapped experiences. As the bits and pieces were put together the full extent of the catastrophe began to take shape. At 10 a.m. next day, 13 July, the survivors were 'counted off' on the jetty – a long business – and a 'missing list' compiled.

Then several of the escorts prepared to steam back at once to the Barents Sea to begin a rescue search. There was good news of the *Dianella*, which had won through on her own, unscathed. After scattering, the corvette had cracked on at full speed for Archangel. On reaching the White Sea she was challenged by three Russian torpedo boats and quickly ran up a couple of Union Jacks to assure them of her identity. Then she hurried on. She was the first ship among us to reach Archangel – and the first out again to begin rescue work.

Better news still brought our total of merchant ships safe to four, together with the reappearance of the plucky *Rathlin*. It turned out that she had arrived at Archangel before us, almost down to her last scrap of coal, and had a rousing tale to tell. After slipping back from the *Pozarica* group, up north in the ice, Captain Augustus Banning had pushed his ship on alone, thrusting right up alongside the polar ice field. Off Cape Zhelaniya, the most northerly tip of Novaya Zemlya, she reached a point 78 degrees 45 minutes N, 700 nautical miles from the Pole and a record high at that time for any British ship of the last century. Turning south and steaming along the coast of Novaya Zemlya, she had then met up with the American USS *Bellingham*.

The *Bellingham* had had a remarkably lucky escape from an enemy plane. The aircraft circled the ship several times and finally started in from her stern for the kill. At that moment a fog bank loomed and Captain Mortenson ran his ship hard into it. The confused plane released its bombs on an iceberg off the *Bellingham*'s starboard side, blowing it apart, but the ship was safe.

And so on 8 July, while we in the re-formed convoy were steaming from Funk Creek, the *Rathlin* and the *Bellingham* had forged ahead and were moving through broken ice near the approaches to the White Sea. The rescue ship, with her companion about 500 yards astern, was going flat out at a punishing 12 knots when suddenly the morning calm was broken by the heavy drone of an aircraft. It was a Focke-Wulf Condor – a long-distance convoy raider – out on morning patrol from Petsamo base in Finland. Flying out of the morning mist it swooped in a long shallow dive over the two ships, releasing three heavy-calibre bombs. Fortunately all were near misses. Then it turned to make another run in, this time at almost masthead height.

Everyone knew that if the plane got them now it was God help them, for the *Rathlin* was carrying a staggering 240 men, many of them survivors so shaken up by their recent immersion in an ice-packed sea that they refused to go below and spent their time huddled round the funnel casing on deck. The ship did not have enough lifeboats or rafts to accommodate half their number. As the Condor passed over, its rear gunner opened up with cannon fire at the *Bellingham*, whose funnel and superstructure were riddled like a soup strainer. The *Rathlin*'s stern-gun crew replied with their new, rapid-firing Bofors, and to their amazement got the plane with their first few rounds. The Condor veered off to port. At first a dull red glow was seen in the forward cockpit, then seconds later the whole of its fuselage burst into bright orange flame. It bucked and crashed into a dead flat sea about a quarter of a mile away, the wreckage still burning fiercely.

The Rathlin's rescue launch was soon away, but as they approached the downed plane it slowly sank. All that was left were scattered papers and burning bits and pieces spread over a wide area. Of the aircraft's probable crew of seven, just two bodies floated face downwards, the early morning sun glinting on their half-opened parachutes. The launch turned back and the *Rathlin* quickly resumed her course: the Condor had been sending out radio messages before the attack and more planes might be on the way. But no other aircraft appeared. The two ships safely entered the White Sea, where they were met by an ancient Russian destroyer.

They arrived at the mouth of the North Dvina two days before us. There they found a third ship waiting for the pilot: the Russian tanker, the *Donbass*. She had won through on her own despite a torpedo tearing a hole in her bows: the sea poured in and out as if in a fantastic Fingal's Cave. Her survival owed much to the efforts of the *Daniel Morgan*'s gunners. A high-ranking commissar was sent to thank them personally for all they had done.

Lord Haw-Haw's radio message was now one of complete triumph: 'Mr Churchill, you have not told the British people the truth about your latest convoy to Russia. I will tell you the truth. The whole of that convoy has gone to the bottom, not one of your merchant ships has reached Russia.'

A communiqué put out by the German High Command was only slightly more temperate. This claimed that one US cruiser and 28 merchant ships had been sunk, ten other vessels damaged and a number of American seamen rescued and taken prisoner.

What the Germans sank for a cruiser we never did find out, but the picture on the naval side at Archangel was one that did nothing to improve the feelings now boiling up among many American survivors. Twelve of the 13 escort ships had arrived safely: the only vessel not accounted for was the trawler *Ayrshire*. Against this we had with us only four out of 33 merchantmen – the *Ocean Freedom*, the *Samuel Chase*, the *Bellingham* and the *Donbass*, together with two rescue ships.

What of the rest? Soon word arrived that some ships had successfully reached Novaya Zemlya, and on 16 July, four days after our arrival, Commodore Dowding set off in the *Poppy*, accompanied by the *Lotus* and *La Malouine*, to salvage what he could of his ravaged convoy. Meantime on the *Lord Austin* we began to coal up, a lengthy job, in preparation for patrol duties.

Chapter 8

Snatched from
the Sea

BRODIE.

Although desperately short of medical facilities, the Russians gave our host of survivors what hospital treatment and comfort they could. There were many bad cases of exposure and frostbite, and more to come, resulting in amputations, but for the majority of survivors their main need was sleep and treatment to regain full use of their limbs. After this, they were billeted out in public buildings all over the town.

Ferocious O'Flaherty, of the *John Witherspoon*, said: 'We were delivered to hospital, a plain one-storey building with a statue of Lenin in front, where the nurses put us to bed and began pill medication. We all had partly frozen feet. For 11 days and nights I could not sleep soundly. If I moved my feet suddenly, even the touch of the blankets would awaken me. The rest of our boat's crew were in a similar condition. Each night a nurse would make the rounds with pills, saying "Schleep, schleep."

'The beds had no springs and the mattresses felt like straw, but we were grateful to the staff, for they were doing the best that could be managed with what was on hand. We did not expect the doctors to have time for us as they were too busy with more serious cases of frozen limbs: one young merchant seaman lost both feet, one hand and part of the other.

'After 11 days and nights of this a friend and myself were able to hobble outside. We were the only two who recovered this fast; others of our boat's crew were still hobbling weeks later and one man had to be carried about. This after 72 hours in an open lifeboat.'

The reception some of the survivors got was not without humour, such as that experienced by Third Officer Phillips of the *Aldersdale,* one of those marshalled into a large hall which formed part of a hospital. He recalled:

'From the collection room we were ushered about six at a time into a reception room. Ranged across one end of the room was a row of trestle tables and seated behind these, like wizened oranges, were half a dozen elderly Russian matrons, who obviously spoke no English. Through sign language we understood that we were to strip off to an undefined limit. In front of each woman was a notebook, and as we removed each garment, giving the name in English, it was written down phonetically in Russian. Eventually we were stripped down to underpants and vests. Short, tall, paunchy or thin, we were faced by six near hysterically laughing nurses – and the dilemma of how far to go. After much discussion we stripped down to the buff and made our way through an adjoining door to an enormous shower room.

'The showers were set high up and were controlled by a small boy. After setting the temperature, some muscular nurses came in and proceeded to scrub us with an ersatz loofah on the end of a short stick, the more masculine-looking of us being singled out for some special female comments – earthy Russian type. From here we were issued with white pyjamas, which were our uniform for a long time. We walked, talked, danced and even slept in the damn things.

'The hospital was fairly comfortable and the food plain and monotonous. Porridge was the staple: we even had it with meat and gravy. The staff, being female, were hotly pursued by the more virile survivors, with varying degrees of success. Little English was spoken, though the resident medical officer was a handsome woman who spoke English with a Home Counties accent – and she had never been out of Russia in her life. She was a tower of strength to us.'

Gunner Urwin of the *Aldersdale*, one of those lucky ones who simply needed three days rest, went out on to the green outside the hospital and saw some of the staff cutting from the lawn what looked like dandelion leaves. 'We asked in our sign language and pidgin English what they were for and the answer was "Soupo korosh" – meaning soup was good when laced with rabbit meat (but there was no rabbit). Dinner was boiled wheat with two meat-cube sized pieces of yak, which seemed to have died of old age.'

Hospital life for Third Officer Phillips' group came to an end. 'We were given back our clothes in a typically Russian method. The ceremony was a shambles and took place in the same room where we had stripped off before our giggling audience. The doors of the room opened and before us on the floor lay a mound of miscellaneous clothing – our clothes. The ensuing chaos was hilarious and pathetic, but after scrabbling and bartering, we ended up decently, if ridiculously dressed. At least the pyjamas returned to their original purpose. I had managed to preserve my blue Burberry and guarded it with my life. It had served as dressing gown, overcoat and raincoat.

'We transferred from our pleasant hospital to the Intourist Hotel: top floor, six to a room, one bulb at the foot of the next floor up as lighting, sparse beds and close neighbours in the form of voracious bed bugs. It was not until we turned in and extinguished the solitary distant bulb that they visited us for supper. Not just a family but the whole generation from Peter the Great on. Next day we attempted to smoke them out with paraffin wads and merely succeeded in almost setting fire to the hotel. Eventually a naval debugging squad sprayed the room but I never slept there again, bunking in a room on the floor below which was occupied by RAF personnel.'

It says much for the majority of the survivors that they were able to hold on to a good sense of humour, especially those from the open boats, for they were far worse off than us. They were men without ships, with only the clothes they stood up in, and though our own food situation rapidly became critical, they were on poorer rations even than us.

Our own first impression of the Archangel area was that quayside swarming with children, who offered an amazing variety of souvenir badges. They were a lively, talkative crowd of youngsters, dressed in a patchwork of clothing, who were to dog us throughout our stay. They had badges to commemorate everything and everyone: the Russian Army, Navy and Air Force, all branches of the civil defence, for shooting, athletics, agriculture, doctors, nurses, commissars, inspectors, drivers and people working in civil aviation. All the badges seemed well made, with enamelled designs, and the price, in cigarettes or chocolate, varied according to the class of the emblem. A common 'Red Star' could be had for two or three cigarettes, but a comprehensive air-raid model, showing aircraft, searchlight, 'ack-ack' gun, gas mask and all, might cost ten cigarettes. A brisk trade was done at first, for we were well stocked with the necessary currency, but later on it was to become a problem whether to smoke our slender ration and eat the 'nutty', or to barter for more souvenirs.

And there were the old women, pinched and poverty stricken, begging for food. On the first morning after we docked we threw our stale bread over the side of the *Lord Austin* as usual, only to see the women produce long fishing nets, fish out the bread pieces, dry them in the sun and eat them. After this we were warned not to throw any food into the river.

This brought about a difficult situation when the Russians, knowing that we were short of food, generously offered us some yak meat, all they could spare from their own scanty resources. Two carcasses were carried aboard – rather blue-looking and with a distinct odour about them – and hung up in the meat safe. After our first meal from them we decided unanimously that it would be better to stay hungry.

Next day the carcasses had signs of life in them, so the problem of how to dispose of them arose. It would have been discourteous and ungrateful to return them to the Russians and they could not be ditched over the side. We decided to burn them in the stokehold. Two men were detailed for the job – one insisted on wearing his gas mask. They lugged the carcasses along the deck and lowered them into the stokehold using the ash chute. But they had reckoned without our chief engineer. Refusing to have them anywhere near his domain, he hoisted the yak up the chute again. It took the duty officer much coaxing and persuasion before the chief relented and let the carcasses be cremated in his fires.

The quay hummed with activity as our pitifully few merchant ships were unloaded. Middle-aged women, hardy and strong, did the bulk of the work while green-capped commissars with revolvers in their belts paced the closely guarded quayside. It was said that these commissars had discovered a Russian stowaway in a ship about to sail back for Britain and had shot him on the spot – as they did an unfortunate stevedore who pocketed a tin of peaches.

We moved up river and began coaling from the *Ocean Freedom*. It was a long, arduous job bagging the coal in the merchantman's hold and slinging it over to our decks. There was a heatwave now – surprising, considering that we were so close to the Arctic Circle – and there were mosquitoes: thousands of them. They were not malarial, but all the same they raised a nasty lump. At night it was too hot to keep the hatches closed and the mosquitoes came down and bombed us in our bunks. We would almost have preferred Junkers 88s. You had the choice of either sticking your head under the blankets and being suffocated, or keeping it out and being bitten; there were no nets to be had. For some protection during his watch the quartermaster carried a paraffin-soaked rag on the end of a stick, which he waved around his head.

The ships from our convoy, and some merchantmen from the previous convoy, were scattered about the Archangel area at wharfs and jetties along the Dvina, and in small creeks running from it. Most berths were well supplied with sentries and guards, and had high wooden towers in which women with machine guns were stationed. At the bigger wharfs it was impossible to get out of the jetty area without passing a guardhouse and having to identify yourself to the very suspicious and often deliberately obstructive guards. At the smaller quays, however, there might be only a few sentries strolling about the jetty area and you could leave ship and wander into the countryside and round the villages without check, returning in the same way.

And so, while coaling from the *Ocean Freedom*, we made our way into a village nearby. We found the villagers, almost all women, very hospitable. They waved from the windows of their large communal dwellings, invited us in and produced tea from a samovar or a bottle of vodka. Some thought we might need more than vodka and were willing to oblige.

The effects of the vodka could be disastrous on those not accustomed to its potency. Some men heeded the warnings to treat it with respect; others did not, to their cost. Bottles of it were bartered by the ubiquitous badge-toting children; some was genuine, some just a hooch concocted of wood-alcohol. Two Americans died after drinking the stuff – it paid to be careful.

The children followed us everywhere: 'Give me smokum, Comerad.' Then, when you refused, pointing to the half-smoked cigarette in your mouth: 'Little smokum, Comerad. Give me little smokum.' And there were the knowing ones, tiny tots some of them, who had 'beeg sister – beeg sister very nice.'

Archangel itself, reached by ferry across the river from us, was a sprawling timber town, the few tall cement buildings in the centre standing like islands among a mass of wooden houses and buildings. There was a general air of shabbiness and dilapidation about the town. Even the new cement buildings showed signs of decay, with large cavities in the sides where the improperly bonded cement had fallen on to the streets.

None of us had ever seen such a concentration of wood. The streets themselves were laid with timber to resist the hard winters, with raised wooden pavements that needed repair. There was also a peculiar stench. The sewers were open and primitive, and this, combined with the smell of pine, formed a sickly odour that hung over the ancient town. Outside the town the flat 'countryside' was covered with a deep layer of sawdust into which your feet sank, and way beyond this stretched vast forests that seemed to go on for ever. It was easy to see why the port was one of the largest timber centres in the world.

Most naval and merchant personnel found the townspeople friendly, hospitable and full of humour, though with a natural suspicion of Allied officers, as they had of their commissars. They only really loosened up with the rank and file. The authorities did not spy on us but there were many regulations to observe. We made allowances for many of the things we found odd. It would have been unfair to judge the Soviet Union by the conditions of life prevailing in a remote port in the summer of 1942, when the Russian armies had their backs to the wall. The battle for Stalingrad was still at its height; the Germans were advancing through the Caucasus, menacing the oil fields. If Baku was taken the Soviet Union would be doomed. Where else could they obtain their oil supplies? Certainly not by the Arctic route. The amount of oil we had brought would hardly keep the war going for half an hour. If convoys were arriving every week that would be another matter, but the arrangement had, of necessity, slipped to one a month. After the disaster of PQ 17 it seemed doubtful whether any further convoys could be risked until there was a reasonable period of darkness to provide cover.

Some Russians could not believe that PQ 17 had started out with as many ships as we claimed. Small wonder. Looking at the sad remains of our merchant armada we found it hard to believe ourselves. Yet the bedraggled, exhausted, frostbitten survivors still coming in provided bitter testimony.

The courtesies the citizens showed us took many men by surprise. They had been very prejudiced against the Russians, imagining them to be little better than the Nazis. Not least the merchant seamen, for whom the flags flying in their honour was a totally unknown experience. The Russians impressed upon them that they were the guests of the Soviet Government because of their attempt to help Russia with supplies.

The courtesies were extended in many little ways. Both naval and merchant men were, for instance, given the 'freedom' of Archangel's single-deck trams. On these trams there was no nonsense about carrying a certain number of passengers: everyone who could get a finger-hold was carried. The smell inside them was unspeakable. Normally only the wounded and pregnant women were allowed to ride out front with the woman driver, but, as visitors, we were allowed to do the same thing – and were not asked to pay – though most of us did.

In the *kinemas* we were speedily taken to the front rows: an alarming experience for some. Signalman Douglas Blarney of the *Palomares* remembered: 'Looking for local experience we entered a *kinema*. It was late as we bought our tickets and went through to the gallery. A heavy Russian period drama was in progress. As we got inside and groped for the nearest seat to the back we suddenly found hands grabbing for us and we were pushed and lifted towards the front of the gallery. For one horrible moment we feared their object was to throw us down into the stalls, but they only meant us to have the position of honour in the front row!'

There were stark reminders everywhere of the plight of the Soviet Union at war. Outside one shop we saw a long line of women, queueing not for food or cigarettes but to buy copies of a poster showing a Russian woman and her child shrinking from a German bayonet. Where else would you find people queueing to buy a war poster? Was it compulsion or patriotism? We never knew the answer.

As for food, there were poignant scenes as women stood in long patient queues outside the communal kitchens, at least one set up inside a beautiful old church. The women carried contraptions like three-tiered cake stands on which they collected their strict ration: one tier for soup, another for black bread, and the third for a morsel of yak or similar meat. Their daily ration was hardly enough for one English meal, even in wartime, and on one day of the week they had to give up their rations for the Red Army. Poor devils, no wonder they looked hungry. Yet in spite of their privations, they remained mostly friendly and cheerful. Platoons of men and women soldiers sang magnificently as they marched, their voices rising high above the never-ending wood piles near the quays.

For most of us visits to Archangel were infrequent, because of its distance from the various quays, the difficulties of travel, and later on because of our dwindling cash and supply of goods to barter. The children who pursued us from ship to shore seemed to have a never-ending supply of rouble notes, probably because in such grim conditions few necessities could be bought. They offered the notes in exchange for cigarettes, chocolate and soap. The barter price of a two-ounce bar of chocolate settled at 30 roubles – nearly 30 old shillings in these pre-decimalisation times – though a bar in a red wrapper could fetch 40. Similarly, cigarettes would produce 40 roubles a packet, but in a red packet would be worth 50. We smiled ironically at these 'red' Russians engaged in 'capitalist' buying and selling, but as we had no means of changing our sterling, it gave us currency.

When we could afford it we could buy food at the International Club in Archangel, which was also used by the more privileged classes of Russians: high-level citizens graded by their importance to the state. The club was well run and, like an oasis in a desert of want, provided fairly good meals to supplement our own spartan rations. The waitresses seemed to regard their job as the best fun in the world, taking a gleeful delight in saying 'feenish' to the dishes that were 'off'. The girls who came into the club were attractive and nicely turned out in summer dresses, in sharp contrast to the other women who were poor and shabby. We were shocked at first though, when some of these pretty girls smiled and showed three or four gruesome metal teeth. Dentures for men and women were made of metal, presumably a wartime measure.

Dances, concerts and sing-songs were put on in the club by the Russian and Allied forces, but only when we could leave our ships and had enough roubles to spend. For the most part it was a tedious existence.

During our first days in port, the final dramas of PQ 17 were being enacted on the bleak Barents Sea. Reports came through of a lifeboat from the *Alcoa Ranger* making land at remote Cape Kanin, followed by news of other men from ships sunk on Black Sunday: like the survivors of the *Peter Kerr*. For two days in dead-calm weather her two lifeboats had been able to make some headway with the oars, then a wind came up that enabled them to make good time sailing. They covered 360 miles in seven and a half days. Second Mate William Connolly had saved his sextant and chronometer and so was able to navigate his boat of 24 men from a chart that had been put ready in the boat. He recalled:

'On leaving the ship the rudder in our boat was broken and we had to steer the whole time with a sweep oar. I was fortunate to be one of the three chosen for this job and by virtue of the extra exercise it afforded we three were the only ones who did not suffer some degree of 'immersion foot' after getting ashore.

'Landfall was made a short distance east of Murmansk and when we were about a mile offshore a Russian torpedo boat came alongside with its machine guns trained on us. After satisfying themselves of our identity they took us in tow and into a nearby submarine base. From there we went on to a hospital where we were all given clean, comfortable bunks. Fortunately no one was in need of medical care but all relished getting a good sleep.

'After a day or two in the hospital we were brought to a nearby barracks for further rest. Most of the soldiers here were Lapp women and they paid no attention whatsoever to us. There was some air action near the barracks but apparently it was not the specific target. After about a week here we were taken to Murmansk where about the only evidence of a city once having been there were the chimneys that remained – all else seemed burned out. Here we were put on an old wood-burning train for Archangel.'

After travelling three days north from Archangel, the *Dianella* picked up the two boatloads of survivors from the *Empire Byron* off Novaya Zemlya. By this time most of the seamen's minds were wandering: they were seeing imaginary clear water and ships. Among them were two young apprentices, aged 15 and 16, both of whom lost toes and one a foot from frostbite. In the jollyboat after the sinking Carpenter Frederick Cooper had rescued the ship's young third radio operator, Dick Phillips. This lad had bravely gone back for the radio receiver after first handing the others the transmitting set; with the lifeboats then gone he had jumped into the sea. It was his first voyage and exposure killed him. He died in Cooper's arms and was buried at sea; he was awarded a posthumous George Medal. Also among the survivors was a badly injured gunner and a fireman who had had his finger nearly torn off while leaving the sinking ship. This man never complained at any time, though he must have suffered agonies from the salt water getting to his bandaged wound. His finger was later amputated in Russia.

Walter Shepherd was in one of the lifeboats. He remembered: 'The second mate organised singing and guessing games but after the second day nobody wanted to know. The third engineer started drinking salt water and became very bad-tempered. He was warned that if he did not stop he would be tied down, but it had no effect. Our ration every six hours consisted of two ounces of water, two Horlicks malted-milk tablets and two small biscuits. Since that time I can't bear to see a tap dripping. We rigged the sails but there was very little breeze. We also shipped the oars, but this was more to keep the blood circulating than anything else. In the end we were too cold and exhausted to do that even. We took turns rubbing each other's feet with whale oil.

' "Planes" were sighted at intervals but they all turned out to be seagulls. As time wore on the snarl set in. Tempers frayed and arguments arose that were quickly quelled by the captain. Suddenly someone shouted, "A ship. Look!" "Another iceberg more likely," said someone else. But it was the *Dianella*. She signalled us: "I will circle round you twice. If I get a ping I'm away. If not, come alongside as quickly as possible and lose no time: you may be a decoy." They put scramble nets over the side and we watched with anxious eyes as they circled us, wondering if a U-boat was lying waiting. But in less than 15 minutes we were all aboard, the two lifeboats bobbing about in our wake. I and several others collapsed on deck and we were helped below. We were given a plate of hot soup and 20 cigarettes. The sailors gave up their bunks for us for 24 hours, and then we slept anywhere we could find. The sailors had not much food but they shared it. We were aboard for six days looking for an American ship which was in difficulty in the ice, but did not find her.'

One of the most dramatic rescues was made high up in the Barents Sea by the *Salamander* and the *Halcyon*, along with a third minesweeper, the *Hazard*. A Russian Catalina out on patrol had spotted three rafts and radioed back their position with an estimate of the direction in which they would drift. The three minesweepers were sent out from Archangel to find the rafts. They were given nine days for the search as they were needed for minesweeping work. This gave them three days to reach the area, three days to look for the rafts, and three days to return.

When they reached the search area the weather was perfect, but the first 24 hours slipped fruitlessly by and everyone began to feel disheartened. 'What sort of a fool's errand is this?' the *Halcyon*'s crew wondered. Every man was strained and tired after the activities of the past two weeks: no one had had more than four hours sleep for what seemed years. However, they were fortunate in having absolute quiet for their search on the sunlit sea: no U-boat echoed on the asdics, no bomber marred the blue sky. As they got back into a regular routine the men's spirits rose and they began to take an interest.

By the afternoon of the third day of the box search the atmosphere was tense. The night hours passed quietly, the sun just on the horizon shedding a path of crinkling liquid gold on the rippling sea. It was an eerie scene but the crew had a sudden inexplicable feeling that perhaps they might find the lost seamen after all. This despite the fact that the survivors had been afloat for 13 days and the minesweepers were only going on calculations made a week before by the Russian pilot. Though they were tackling the impossible, excitement mounted and hopes grew as the search time grew shorter.

At 7.30 a.m., however, the black Arctic fog descended. This seemed the end. Their time was up at noon and they were helpless in the fog. All they could do now was feel their way and hope. At 8.15 a.m. on the *Halcyon* the usual anti-freeze routine on the guns was carried out, with a few test rounds fired by each. All those not on watch below came and stood shivering on the upper deck, cursing the fog or silently praying for it to rise. Sometimes it lifted just enough to let them see the *Salamander*, but not the *Hazard*, which lay 200 yards farther off. At 11 a.m. the coxswain served the rum. Everyone went below for their tot, then returned. There was no argument or lively banter as usual, just a strained silence.

The *Halcyon*'s captain ordered the Very pistols to be fired, the signal for the last lap. For this last half-hour everyone lined the rails, watching, waiting, praying. Then at 11.45, with just 15 minutes to go, a miracle happened. The fog lifted. First they saw the *Salamander* and then the ghostly shape of the *Hazard*. They heard a faint cheer – or was it their overstretched imaginations? No, it was not, for right between each ship was a raft crammed with men waving weakly. They began to shout,

'God Save the King! We knew you would save us.' They had heard the gunfire and paddled wearily towards it.

The minesweepers dropped their scramble nets. On the *Salamander* a seaman's first attempt to throw a line to one of the rafts missed. 'Limey,' said a cracked and dry voice, 'I have been on this raft for 13 days and would do better than that!' After taking 13 men from one raft – there were more than 30 survivors in all from the *Honomu* – the *Salamander* moved off to drop depth charges in case a U-boat was near.

Aboard the *Halcyon* the survivors were too weak, and their feet too swollen, to stand, but otherwise they were in surprisingly good shape. From the first day they had taken turns on the paddles – four hours on and four off – and during the off-period had washed their deadening feet with saltwater. Only a coloured seaman who would not do this later lost part of a foot with frostbite. The U-boat that sank the *Honomu* had surfaced again on the third and sixth days of their ordeal, giving them more water. Every man among them now repeated the same vow: 'If I get back to the United States I'll never go to sea again.'

Other Black Sunday survivors got through to the Russian mainland, among them a boat from the *Bolton Castle*. They had started out with enough water for about an egg-cup full twice a day, and for food, two Horlicks tablets twice daily, a two-inch square ship's biscuit once a day and a teaspoonful of condensed milk. They had a dozen small tins of corned beef but decided to conserve these until later.

The sea got rougher and they had to bale out continuously. Six Arab firemen suffered badly from frostbite. Because of their religion they could not urinate in front of the rest of the company; as the situation worsened one pulled a knife on a young apprentice. After that they were searched and their knives taken away. When they wanted to urinate the rest of the boat's company had to turn their backs. As one man aboard remarked: 'Anything for a quiet life!'

On the fifth day the corned beef was opened, the condensed milk finished and the water reduced to one egg-cup full a day. They sighted another lifeboat and pulled wearily over to it. It was an American boat, empty, but inside it they found a carton of American cigarettes; they had been sharing what few smokes they had. The situation now looked pretty bleak and hopes dwindled. Suddenly, on the seventh day, they saw what they thought was a ship coming up astern. Excitedly they threw flares into the sea, sending up thick clouds of red smoke, but when the ship was only three miles off she suddenly disappeared. They could hardly believe their ill fortune. That night brought heavy seas and bitter cold. On the morning of the eighth day they could still not see anything – but they could distinctly hear the thud of a ship's engine. It was the motor of a Russian submarine beneath them – the 'ship' they had seen the previous day – and soon, in answer to its radioed messages, a Russian trawler arrived.

Chief Cook Osmundsen remembered: 'We were given a good reception by the Russian crew: a slice of sausage and a glass of vodka that knocked several of us out cold.' After 18 hours steaming they were into the Kola inlet leading to Murmansk. 'What a sight! The harbour was crowded with sunken ships, with funnels and masts sticking out of the water everywhere'. There, too, they saw the two Polish submarines from the convoy. 'Nothing could be done for us so we were taken by lorry to hospital in Polyarno. The doctors and nurses there were wonderful to us. I remember being given a mug of hot coffee with plenty of milk and, having finished it, asking for another. The nurse actually ran to get it. Nothing was too much trouble for them.'

The men made good recoveries and it was decided that they should go to a rest camp in the forest country because of enemy bombing. 'A long journey by lorry to get there and we were billeted in a long, narrow shed with shelves like the racks on railway carriages but made of wood, and we were issued with a blanket and straw mattress. We had to sleep on these shelves side by side. Sometimes two mattresses were put together for three men, as there were not enough to go round. The food was awful, the main meal a sort of stew with everything one could think of in it except meat: fish heads, beetroot and so on.

'After a week there it was decided to take us to Archangel, a five-day railway journey around the White Sea coast. On arrival at Archangel we were put up in a schoolhouse. The accommodation was very good indeed and so was the food, except for the black bread. Again, everyone was kind.'

The two lifeboats from the *Earlston*, sunk to the south of the *Bolton Castle*, lost each other in thick fog but met up again. At midday on 6 July both were rowing steadily and having a rousing sing-song as they pulled on the oars in the heavy boats. Then one boat slipped away, leaving the other to forge on through the choppy sea. Among the 33 men in this boat, who hoped to reach Murmansk, was Stoker A J Robinson. 'I must take off my hat to the chief steward,' he said. 'He had put three bottles of brandy and some cigarettes in the boat, so we had a little tot every morning, a godsend.' It was a big blow, however, when they found that the boat's 20-gallon tank of drinking water had burst: they had to use the little that was left very sparingly.

Second Officer David Evans was in command of the boat. He showed exceptional resourcefulness in keeping the boat on course, and when he had to give in to exhaustion, Cadet Andrew Watt, just 19, took over for a spell.

Watt also kept a pencilled 'log' on a single sheet of notepaper. Spirits were still high on the fourth day when he noted: 'July 9, noon. North-easterly breeze; running free due south. Great excitement, sighted two objects astern on horizon, rising fast. What are they? Everyone speculating.'

They thought it was a rescue ship, but to their disappointment it was only a motorboat from the *Bolton Castle*, pulling another boat behind it. They, too, were hoping to make Murmansk. The parties checked courses and exchanged a few words before each continued on their separate way. When the wind became stronger, the *Earlston*'s boat made such good headway by sail that it overtook the other boats, giving them a cheer as it passed by. Then the sea became very rough and the boat was tossed about like a cork.

On the fifth day three men were suffering badly with swollen legs; next day three more. Stoker Robinson rubbed the feet of every man in whale and vegetable oil three times a day. 'I praise the three able seamen who steered the boat for seven days. We could not have gone on much longer without casualties, as some men had begun to drink sea water.' On the seventh day – Sunday again, 12 July – Cadet Watt noted in his log: '5 a.m. Land sighted fine on port bow. Thank God! we all say.' And at noon: 'Volunteers for oars to help make bay.'

Stoker Robinson noted: 'We were all very weak. We came to a little beach and were approached by soldiers. We had landed on the Rybachi Peninsula, right in the Russian front line against the Finns. Among us was a man who could speak Russian, a Government passenger on the *Earlston*, and so he could explain who we were. I thought I was in fair shape and was second out of the boat, but found I just could not stand up. Others fell down around me. The soldiers carried the rest of the men out of the boat and sat them down. They gave us a sip of water – I could have drunk a gallon. We were then put in lorries and taken to a dugout where we had a hot drink, some bread and jam, and a shave. We had to get out quickly as they were expecting a big push at any moment.'

They were taken by lorry to a front-line hospital. The log entry read: 'On arrival, casualties attended to and put to bed, others bathed and given meal (excellent fish and macaroni, coffee, bread and butter). Oh boy, wasn't it good!'

Next day they were taken by lorry and ship to hospital at Polyarno, where they stayed for three days. This was followed by a period in a rest camp before joining a train for Archangel.

The *Earlston*'s other lifeboat was by no means as fortunate. After having to force its way through large areas of pack ice it met a dangerously heavy sea, in which large, floating baulks of redwood were a hazard. Lance Bombardier Richard Crossley was in this boat. He remembered: 'The wind and seas eventually dropped late on the third day or early on the fourth, and we began to row. Several of the crew suffered from exposure. Old Paddy Murphy swore he could see "some lovely big red buses" when we were in the crests of the waves. A pity they did not come up. I would have enjoyed getting one to King's Cross. Later this old chap died after operations to his feet, which became gangrenous. Some others of the crew also lost parts of their feet.

'We just rowed and rowed, never seeing another human being for ten days. I learned a lot about gulls and fulmars and puffins, and we got tangled up in a school of whales. I can vouch that at least one whale had a helluva bad case of halitosis; it surfaced about six feet from us and exhaled over the boat.

'On the tenth day we sighted a plane. It flew over us once. We also sighted a mountainous coast. A small motorboat was seen, but we were too far away to make contact. The first mate was noisily certain that he had made landfall in Russia, and when another fishing boat came out he sent our English-speaking Russian forward to speak to the boatman. After the first hail the Russian turned sadly round, spread out his hands and said, "He is not Russian." The bosun, a Dane, growled: "He is Norwegian!"

'The fisherman guided us through an intricate passage to a small cove near the North Cape. I carried a little Scots seaman up the cliff to the fisherman's house. His wife was very kind to us, bathing the feet of the worst frostbitten and giving us soup. Those of us who could stand and walk went outside to lie down and sleep in the sun. Gunner Officer Lieutenant Hough, Gunner Kidd and myself decided to make a break for Sweden (a stupid idea we learned afterwards), but while we were asleep the first mate, being nervous of German reaction to an escape, sent the bosun to a nearby lighthouse to report our landing. I was awakened by a German boot under my backside and a voice saying, "Raus, raus?"

'We were taken from there to Nordkyn, and eventually to Wilhelmshaven. I was interrogated by an extremely good looking elderly German speaking perfect English. He wanted to know all about our guns and the rest, but I repeated that I would only give my rank, name and number. When he asked where I came from I said "Hull" and he replied, "Don't you mean Kingston-upon-Hull?" which, of course, is the full name of my native city, though hardly anyone uses it. He then said, "Tell me, does Queen Victoria still watch the people going to the lavatories in the square?" This was a reference to the fact that underground conveniences were built on the spot formerly occupied by her statue. They replaced the dear old Queen on top of them. He evidently knew Hull!

'He sent me for three weeks' solitary for my non-co-operation, telling me that they knew all they wanted to know already, just wanted my confirmation. When the Germans left our camp at the end of the war this man was found hiding in a barn nearby by one of my pals, who was undecided whether to kill him or not. He didn't.'

The unluckiest ones of all were the crew of the *Carlton*. Not only was this American merchantman the first ship to die on Black Sunday, but every surviving member of her company fell into enemy hands, so substantiating part of the claim of the boastful German communiqué we heard at Archangel. Six hours after the *Carlton* was sunk, at 5.22 a.m. on 5 July, as the lifeboat and rafts were trying to pull away from the scene, an enemy seaplane landed on the water and picked up two survivors. Shortly afterwards a flying boat descended and took aboard nine gunners and a seaman. In the evening another flying boat picked up 12 more men and handed out rocket flares. Early next morning a seaplane picked up another two men. All were flown to Norway.

The 17 remaining survivors transferred to the one lifeboat and cut the rafts adrift. The second mate, who had clung on to a sextant and charts, set a course for the nearest Russian territory. On the fourth day after the sinking a British plane dropped them a rubber life-suit and some canned food. On the eighth day a U-boat surfaced and came alongside. The young commander, who said he had lived on the US west coast for some time, apologised for not taking them aboard as he was 'still outbound on patrol.' He offered medical aid, which was refused as it was not needed, and gave them a compass, charts, position, time, course and distance to the Norwegian coast. He also handed them water, biscuits, cigarettes and blankets – most of the goods were made in the USA – and told them that 42 U-boats were hunting for the scattered ships.

On the 13th day the first assistant engineer died of exposure and reluctantly the lifeboat was set on course for Norway. Six days later, in a very distressed condition, the men made landfall near the North Cape. Their war was over.

What of the ships and lifeboats that had managed to struggle through to Novaya Zemlya? How many were there? Commodore Dowding's little rescue fleet was soon to find out.

Here the *Empire Tide*, one of only two British merchantmen to survive, figured largely. Her story follows.

Full Ahead
on a Prayer

BRODIE.

When the signal had come for PQ 17 to scatter the *Empire Tide* was steaming along in her position in the middle of the convoy. After their initial shocked disbelief at the incredible order, her captain and chief officer had a hurried consultation and decided to remain right on course, letting the other ships draw away from the *Empire Tide*. Captain Frank Harvey rang 'Full Ahead!'

Treatment for their gunner, who had been wounded in the torpedo-bomber battle earlier, was now a problem. Chief Officer George Leech remembered: 'I had a look at his leg and was appalled by the wound. The bullet must have been spinning, making an entry hole an inch round and an exit hole which was a gaping wound about nine inches across. I spoke urgently to the captain, as it was more than we could handle. We called up an American destroyer by Aldis lamp and asked if she would take the injured man. But they had their orders, and the reply was, "Sorry, we are unable to help you." And off she went with the others. All we could do was to apply dressings and make the man as comfortable as possible.

'We kept going on our course of 020 degrees True at about 13 knots and shortly before midnight came to the edge of the ice pack, which was solid as far as the eye could see on our port bow. We altered course slightly to clear the ice sticking out ahead of us, then resumed our former course when the ice edge curved away again to the north-east. We next ran into fog. The captain and I discussed which was the better course of action – to slow down in the fog or, regardless of risk, keep going at full speed to get as far away as possible from the searching enemy. Our decision was to keep going and pray!'

So the *Empire Tide* made a swift but hazardous passage through the fog. Large ice floes and icebergs loomed dangerously around her, 'but we were pretty desperate by this time. It was not long before SOS messages began to come in as one ship after another was attacked and sunk. One message in particular I cannot forget. It was from the *Earlston* and said: "Am being attacked by seven dive bombers and three U-boats. Have repulsed them so far." I think this deserves to rank with Nelson's "Engage the enemy more closely." '

The Empire Tide's Hurricane fighter, now more than ever, was their greatest asset, a deterrent to the enemy planes. 'The firing point for the catapult was in the carpenter's shop forward. It was the chief officer's job to actually fire the catapult rockets when the aircraft was launched, and before this was done a special "link" connector had to be fitted into the circuit. This was always kept padlocked to the bulkhead beside the firing switch. I had to keep the key constantly with me, and could not hand it to anyone except the two RAF officers we carried. It was returned to me as soon as the periodical checks of the circuit were made.

'From the start of the convoy this key haunted my dreams. I lived in fear that action stations would be sounded and that after rushing to the firing position I would find I had lost the key. The first two days after scattering brought continuous alarms. Time after time when the weather cleared we sighted single aircraft approaching, and immediately action stations was sounded the RAF pilot and myself would make all speed for the Hurricane and firing point respectively.

'From the bridge to the fore well-deck there were three ladders and we learned very quickly how to slide down the handrails without one's feet touching a step, making the fore-deck from the bridge in about ten seconds. The pilot would start the Hurricane, I would unlock the "link" and plug it in (thanking God I had not mislaid the key) and stand by to bang off if we got the green flag from the bridge. On each occasion, however, the enemy was obviously discouraged and kept his distance on sighting the Hurricane on the catapult.'

Stowed away between decks was the *Empire Tide*'s 'secret weapon'. Someone's bright idea at Hvalfjord had been that she should carry a mock Hurricane fighter, so that if the real plane was fired off the dummy could replace it on the catapult and deter other bombers. As it happened this dummy aircraft, made of wood and canvas and painted in regulation colours, was never needed and ultimately disintegrated.

The *Empire Tide* was one of the few ships to have a gyro compass that could take over when her magnetic compasses lost almost all their directional force. She continued hard on course until reaching 78 degrees N, when the captain decided to turn and make for the coast of Novaya Zemlya. The crew sighted the coast early next morning, 6 July, and at this point the *Empire Tide* took a very different course of action from most of the other ships that managed to reach the island. Her captain decided to keep well clear of Matochkin Strait.

Chief Officer Leech noted: 'We thought that if a concentration of surviving ships were anchored there it would be too good a target for the enemy. Luckily we had the Admiralty chart, "Anchorages on the Coast of Novaya Zemlya", and some way south of Matochkin it showed a small anchorage in a bay, the entrance to which was partially obstructed by a reef marked "Extending 1935". We decided to take a chance and anchor there for a few hours so that all hands could have a break from action stations. We approached the bay cautiously, at a very slow speed, taking cross-bearings by gyro, when suddenly the ship shuddered and came to a standstill. We were on the reef. At that very moment the lookout aft sighted an aircraft some distance south of us flying towards the land. It disappeared behind the hills as we sounded action stations again.

'Careful checking of our position showed that according to the chart we should have been in 17 fathoms of water, but the fact remained that, looking over the bow, the reef with all its colours and waving weeds could easily be seen.'

They had to pump all available water and oil overboard, shift cargo and order all hands aft as the main engine was run full astern. Even so it was an agonizing seven hours before the ship finally came off the reef at high tide, a result of the persistent efforts of Chief Engineer Hughes. The fact that the forepeak was filled with concrete saved the ship's bows from being ripped open. Once off the reef they could see daylight through the bottom of the forepeak. They tried unsuccessfully to plug it, but they were in no immediate danger with the bulkhead strong and well shored up for ice.

Thankfully the mystery aircraft did not return during these pretty hopeless hours. Capt. Harvey, having had enough of improperly charted anchorages, now decided to steam on boldly down the coast and risk an all-out dash to the White Sea.

By next morning, 7 July, they had forged on without further incident well down the coast of Novaya Zemlya's south island. Then they sighted a ship ahead. She appeared to be another merchant survivor from the convoy and by 8 a.m. they were slowly gaining on her.

Chief Officer Leech remembered: 'The captain and myself had been continuously on the bridge for the past nine days, taking only occasional sit-downs in the chartroom, and now with the weather fine, the sea smooth and all seemingly peaceful, Capt. Harvey suggested I should go down to his cabin for a quick wash and breakfast, then relieve him to do the same.

'But I had only been down five minutes when I got an urgent message to return to the bridge. The captain asked me to take a good look at the other ship now about six miles ahead. She had turned broadside on to us and he thought she looked a bit odd. I took the telescope and saw at once that she was down by the head, apparently sinking (we discovered afterwards that she was the *Alcoa Ranger*). I then spotted close to the ship three U-boats on the surface – and the white bow wave from one of them as it made full speed towards us. We immediately went hard-a-port and showed our stern. We thought that if they came close enough we could make use of our 12-pounder aft. As we steamed back north at full speed the problem now was where to go.'

They again studied the Admiralty chart and decided to try and enter Moller Bay, well south of Matochkin. 'We gathered from the chart that there was a small Russian settlement there called Mali Karmakulski Stansovische, and it looked as if there was just sufficient room in the bay for the ship to swing to anchor, though the entrance to it was extremely difficult, quite narrow with a right-angled turn to be made. But Capt. Harvey said he would sooner put the ship ashore trying to escape rather than be sunk by the enemy, and I agreed. So a few hours later we reached the approach to the bay, and with the bosun up forward with the leadline, made the turn successfully and anchored right up in the middle.'

A launch came out from the settlement carrying some officials, but there was no difficulty in the *Empire Tide* identifying herself, for among her passengers was a Russian naval officer who spoke perfect English. There were about 50 people in the settlement, families who made a living by hunting and collecting duck eggs, which they sent to the mainland. They were a hospitable crowd and agreed to radio Archangel to report the ship's arrival and ask for medical help for the wounded gunner. Unless enemy aircraft found them now, the *Empire Tide*'s company of 66 were safe for a while.

Further south down the coast two lifeboats of men from the *Olopana* had stumbled ashore, the survivors in one luckily finding a tiny Russian trading post. The other contingent, beaching more to the north, found an open timber lighthouse in which they sheltered. They had not been there long when to their surprise they awoke from an exhausted sleep to see a ship stranded offshore. She was the *Winston Salem*. The American vessel had withstood several enemy attacks only to run hard aground on a sandbank while pulling in close to the island coast in foggy weather. Soon some of her crew came ashore with tins of food and boat stores. The men from the *Olopana* were taken aboard and given a chicken dinner and some warm clothing.

The *Winston Salem* could not be kedged off the sandbank and her crew, fearing air attack, decided for safety to set up permanent camp on the beach. They were unloading more stores on to the beach when a plane came over and caused panic. The ship's gunners had dismantled her light guns, but the plane was only a Russian Catalina. Flying low, it dropped a note to say it had picked up other survivors from the *Olopana* and would return. After some time it did so, flying more *Olopana* men up to the *Empire Tide* in Moller Bay.

The *Winston Salem* remained stuck fast, though her misfortune proved a godsend to others: first to some men from the torpedoed *Hartlebury*. The 13 men on Gunner Arthur Carter's raft, shielding themselves from the cold with a canvas screen, had paddled for two and a half days on a desolate sea before sighting a lifeboat ahead.

'It was the captain's lifeboat from our own ship. In it there had originally been 13 men, but eight had died before we reached her and been put over the side. A ninth man had just died but no one had the strength to haul him over the side until we got into the boat. He was a big, blond Swede. In dying he had slid between the seats and we had the devil of a job to free him. I'm afraid there was no ceremony, just over the side. I remember the great big hole he made in the sea. We all got into the boat with the remaining four men, abandoned the raft and set sail.

'The first mate from our raft was the only officer in the boat and despite an injured arm he was good. Half the crew were put to rowing, the other half rubbing the feet of the rowers. It was awkward but we did our best, and what was important, we were all kept moving. After half a day in the boat we sighted Novaya Zemlya and eventually reached the shore.

'First thing we did on landing was to make a fire to dry ourselves out, then the mate split us into two groups, one to search for wood or anything burnable to keep the fire going, the other to look for anything eatable. Two birds were caught and a few birds' eggs found. The birds were obviously not afraid of us. They just sat there and let us take them. Their feathers seemed to come off as a kind of skin, but they were birds all right. We made a stew, filling a biscuit tin with snow and putting bits of the birds in when it melted. We also made a tent from the lifeboat sails.

'While our scavenging parties were out we left three men by the fire. One was a young seaman with frostbite in both feet.

We had nothing and could do nothing except try to comfort him. However, while he was alone for a short time this lad put his feet in the fire – to warm them, he said – and when we returned to camp they looked terrible, like two big balloons of raw meat. Later he had both legs amputated in Archangel.

'Our parties worked away from the fire in ever widening circles, and the wider we got the higher we got, which is how we came to see a column of smoke rising a long way off. It had to be a ship, so we decided to row along the coast to her. This meant crossing a large bay and rounding a headland, and in the event the tide was too strong for us, but the ship saw our difficulty and sent a lifeboat to help. And so we found the *Winston Salem* aground – and they certainly made us welcome.

'As we got up the rope ladders and over the side, one of the crew was calling, "Coffee this side, tea over there!" In a big saloon were two long tables heaped with eatables, a coffee urn on one table and tea on the other. The ship seemed crammed already with survivors. Her crew scrounged us some clothes; how they had anything left surprised me, as the ship was so packed we had to go ashore again.

'But camping preparations had been under way for some time and all sorts of stores had been put ashore including tents and plenty of blankets, while cases of eggs had been buried in the snow. Three cooks stood on the beach, each with a tin barrel made into a makeshift stove. They were cooking flapjacks, which smelt great, and there was a large tin of molasses. It was a case of help yourself. You just joined the queue, anyone, and went round until you had had enough. After living with the Americans for five days we were sighted by a Russian Catalina, which dropped a message to say that help was coming.'

Still more men came in from the sea to the *Winston Salem*. In the early stages of their long haul across the Barents Sea the two lifeboats of survivors from the USS *Washington*, rowing through heavy ice floes, icebergs and fog, suddenly came upon a motionless ship smoking and burning fiercely. They pulled close and read the name on the stern: the *Pankraft*. Knowing that the fire would eventually reach the abandoned ship's cargo of explosives, they rowed quickly away and stayed on course for Novaya Zemlya. Their limbs were cramped, numb and sore by now, but nothing could be done about this except to take regular exercise by rowing.

Capt. Richter remembered: 'We were not only plagued with cold weather and ice but came upon a school of whales who insisted on being playful and swam dangerously close to the boats, following along with us for hours. Luck was with us that they did not venture to dive under and capsize the boats. When the weather occasionally changed we took full advantage of favourable winds and hoisted sail, giving the crew a rest from rowing and some much needed sleep under what little cover the lifeboats afforded.

'We kept close count of the lapsing days by our watches. On the tenth day the weather cleared and we were joyfully rewarded for our efforts when ahead on the horizon there loomed the white snow-capped mountains of Novaya Zemlya. It gave us all renewed hope and courage. As land was still a good day's rowing away, the crews of both boats now set to with renewed vigour and we found a favourable landing cove along the beach. By dead reckoning, I estimated we had landed just south of Matochkin Strait. The coast was uninhabited, desolate and barren.

'The crew were soon busy building huge bonfires from logs and driftwood, and we lay down to sleep and rest near the fires. Some men suffering from frostbite gained a little relief after vigorous exercise. Sea birds, ducks and geese were plentiful and with good revolver marksmanship the crew managed to bag some much needed food. While we were camped on the beach enemy reconnaissance planes circled the area to investigate, apparently attracted by our bonfires and smoke, but they did not bother us in any way.

'After three days of recuperation on the beach we broke camp and took to the lifeboats again. Keeping close to the shore we headed south, hoping to find a Russian fishing village, but we ran into dense fog and with a stiff inshore breeze it took our utmost efforts to keep the lifeboats from being blown ashore against the rocks.

'Next day the wind subsided and as the weather cleared we saw two other lifeboats ahead. They were from the Dutch *Paulus Potter*. The captain and some of the crew were suffering from severe frostbite, unable to walk and badly needing medical aid. The boats joined up with us and we carried on rowing southward together. Some time the following day, through the light fog and haze, we sighted a ship close in to the beach and pulling to her we found she was the *Winston Salem*, hard aground. Soon we were aboard and being treated to our first hot coffee since abandoning the USS *Washington*.'

The *Winston Salem*'s captain was now waiting for a favourable high tide and the promised help from two Russian tugs to pull his vessel free. He had learned of the *Empire Tide*'s safe anchorage to the north and was expecting two Russian trawlers to pass by the *Winston Salem*; they were persuaded to take the *Washington* and the *Paulus Potter* men and others up to the British ship.

So it was that one of the trawlers steamed into Moller Bay carrying well over 100 American, British and Dutch survivors, including some from the *Alcoa Ranger*, and towing five lifeboats. What with other men flown in by the Catalina, the CAM ship was now crowded to capacity and hard put to stretching out her fast diminishing food stocks to provide rations for more than 200 men. She had only been stored up with three months' supplies for her crew and had been obliged to dig well into these while waiting a month at Hvalfjord for the convoy to sail.

To eke out the rations some American survivors went ashore and caught ducks. There were thousands of the birds; unsuspecting victims were caught quite easily while nesting by a long noose on the end of a pole. The ducks, which had a distinctly fishy flavour, were scarcely a delicacy, but they made a change from beans and Spam. Other Americans went off in a small sailing boat to the *Winston Salem*, returning two days later with 1,000 tins of Spam and 14 bags of brown pinto beans. Oddly enough, most men seemed to thrive on the weird diet, putting on weight.

The ship kept constant gun watch, with some survivors also taking a turn to ease the crew's hours. Twice enemy planes flew over the little bay. Although they did not attack, most of the American survivors decided it was too dangerous to stay on board ship and went off and camped ashore. The very ill were cared for in the settlement's small hut hospital; help for them arrived eventually in the form of a Russian Catalina. Everything moveable, including guns, had been taken out of the plane to make more room for the casualties, and some of the worst cases were loaded on and flown off under the care of a woman doctor.

Besides the low food stocks shortage of water now became a worry, and with the ship's tanks running perilously low, Bosun Bill Medhurst, with the aid of the ship's carpenter, decided to try tapping a stream that ran down into the sea. 'I built a dam of sorts, inserting a five-gallon oil can to which we had fixed a fire hose. We then ran the hose down to a steel lifeboat, which had been well scrubbed out, filled the boat with the crystal-clear water and rowed it back to the ship to be pumped up by a fire pump. We had two days of this, two very uncomfortable days. It was no fun rowing a boat with icy water lapping one's behind!'

One afternoon while they were topping up the ship's freshwater tanks during the long, frustrating wait at Moller Bay, *La Malouine* suddenly appeared at the narrow entrance. She asked how the hell the *Empire Tide* had got into the bay and said she would be back in the morning to escort her to join a convoy to Archangel.

Bosun Medhurst recalled: 'Never was the sight of a warship more welcome! Away went the feeling of being abandoned and there was jubilation throughout the ship. Back came the men who had been living ashore to be housed in one of our 'tween decks. We collected all the lifeboats, hoisted them up to the rail level, leaving them hanging secured that way, hoisted anchor and away we went.

'Imagine our surprise when we got outside to find five other ships waiting. The naval vessels had rounded them up from farther along the coast. Some were a peculiar sight for they had splashed whitewash and white paint all over themselves from truck to water's edge. This camouflage may have helped them when they were anchored against the ice but at sea they stuck out like a sore thumb and they were asked to get the paint off quickly, though they could not really do much before we sailed.'

The strange white ships were the American vessels, the *Silver Sword*, the *Troubadour* and the *Ironclad*, led by the trawler *Ayrshire*. Their adventure began up in the northern ice, where they had all steamed after scattering. The *Ayrshire*, commanded by Lieutenant Leo J A Gradwell RNVR, first headed north-west to Hope Island, but when she met ice she struck out north for the barrier edge.

First Lieutenant Richard Elsden remembered: 'After scatter we spliced the main-brace, got the cook to make heaps of corned beef sandwiches, got up all the four-inch ammunition and stacked it around the gun. We then fixed depth charges and oil drums together with wire, setting the charges to go off at 50 to 60 feet below the surface, the idea being that if we could get under the *Tirpitz*'s bows we would drop the things and they would go off like mines under her. All this helped to keep up morale.'

Soon, like bees round a honey pot, the three merchantmen joined the little trawler, each anxious for naval support. The *Ayrshire* took them under her wing. Second Mate John Behnken of the *Silver Sword* said: 'On scattering we headed due north at our full speed of nine knots and after about 12 hours' steaming reached the ice field, where we joined the *Troubadour*, the *Ironclad* and the trawler. The *Ayrshire*'s commander suggested that our four vessels should form a sort of square to give us the maximum defence against attack. It was then decided to steam right up into the ice as far as we could go.'

Captain George Salveson's *Troubadour*, with her strong ice-breaking bows, led the ships slowly into the ice field at 3 knots until they had pushed 20 miles into it and were firmly entrenched with no open water visible on any side. First Lieut. Elsden walked over the ice to the merchant ships to see how they were fixed for stores and ammunition. On one ship it struck him that the grey decks and cargo must stand out alarmingly from the air so he asked if they had much white paint, found they had, and suggested they should splash it all over the decks and cargo as fast as possible.

On returning to the *Ayrshire* he told Lieut. Gradwell of his idea and Gradwell agreed that all ships should apply the same camouflage – on decks, cargo and starboard side only – as the *Ayrshire*'s officers guessed that the Germans, with their work-to-rule methods, would not go north of them and sight their port sides.

Second Mate Behnken recalled: 'On the *Silver Sword* we painted the masts, most of the superstructure and the hull, then spread white bed linen over the whole of our deck cargo and the hatches. In the flat calm we had no need to secure the linen and there was an abundance of it, as there was of white paint, though we were short of everything else, including food. But the morale of our crew was always good, which may have been partly due to the fact that they were kept so busy.'

It was also decided that the merchant crews should sponge the grease from inside the gun barrels of the tanks carried on deck, and ready them for firing, breaking open the crates of tank ammunition. Some tanks were raised on the outboard sides to give the guns more elevation.

And so for the next two days, as SOS messages came in from the other ships being attacked all over the Barents Sea, the four vessels remained safely hidden in the ice. First Lieut. Elsden frequently walked over to check that all was well on the merchantmen. Once they heard the reverberations in the ice as a ship was bombed just off the ice barrier to the south – probably the *Pankraft*. The *Ayrshire*'s officers discussed whether they should steam out and help, but they decided this would only give away the position of their three charges, so they stayed.

When the situation seemed to have quietened down, the four ships broke out of the ice and steamed east alongside the ice-barrier edge. Searching aircraft flew over them, but thanks to a comforting fog the ships were not spotted and eventually reached the north island of Novaya Zemlya. They went into a bay about 50 miles north of Matochkin, where, as they lay up for 24 hours, the *Ayrshire* took in fresh water from the *Silver Sword*. They then steamed on to find Matochkin. The *Ironclad* ran aground on the coast but the *Ayrshire* managed to tow her off and at last, on 11 July, they all reached the Strait.

Not knowing what their reception might be, the *Ayrshire* sent a heavily armed party in a whaleboat to contact the settlement. They included a man who spoke Polish. In spite of his efforts, along with sign language, the Russians at first refused to radio another message to Archangel, though later they agreed to do so. Some measure of the heartfelt gratitude the three merchant ships felt towards the *Ayrshire* was when the *Troubadour*, towering high above the trawler, showered her fo'c'sle with packets of cigarettes and chocolate – and presented her officers with a brand new coffee percolator.

In the Strait, the *Ayrshire* and her brood found the *Benjamin Harrison* and the damaged *Azerbaijan*. All together they formed quite a refugee fleet. The *Ayrshire*, steaming a long way up the narrow Strait, found another tiny settlement, where she anchored. A Russian armed trawler appeared and the two ships tied up together, looking very much like twins. The Russian crew proved very friendly.

One small bedraggled party of survivors was especially glad of the late arrivals at Matochkin. These were more men from the *Paulus Potter*, who had struggled along the coast until coming to a small Russian weather station. The Russians fed them salmon and black bread and took them up the Strait to join the *Silver Sword*.

Commodore Dowding's rescuing corvettes arrived at Matochkin on 20 July. A Russian icebreaker, the *Murman*, had now joined the ships there and Dowding decided to lead the return convoy in her, as she would be able to force a passage if they encountered strong ice. All ships headed south at once. It was just as well they did, for the next day a U-boat arrived at the Strait and, thwarted because everyone had flown, shelled the settlement.

After picking up the *Empire Tide*, the convoy went on to the *Winston Salem*, but had to leave her: she was still firmly aground, with two Russian tugs standing by. Then it moved southwards towards the Russian coast.

The *Pozarica* and other escorts sailed out from Archangel to meet the remnant convoy as it approached the White Sea, but except for some U-boat alarms, what could have been the most dangerous journey of all was entirely uneventful. There was, however, one disconcerting incident involving the *Murman*. When the U-boat alarm was given, the icebreaker, much to the astonishment and anger of Commodore Dowding, instantly put on speed and high-tailed it away from the slowly moving convoy. It returned only when the danger had passed.

We saw them come into Archangel late on 24 July. It was an incongruous sight, with the *Ayrshire* leading her three merchantmen, all still painted a dazzling white. The battered *Winston Salem* lumbered in four days later. She had finally been rescued from the sandbank thanks to the efforts of the US Naval Attaché in Archangel, Commander Sam Frankel, who flew out to her in a Catalina. The *Winston Salem*'s captain suffered a nervous breakdown.

Now came the reckoning. A total of 22 merchantmen had been lost: 15 American, six British and one Dutch – plus a rescue ship and a British fleet tanker. A total of 24 ships, with enough equipment and supplies for a vast army, lay at the bottom of the Barents Sea. So far as was yet known, some 300 men had died, were missing or had been taken prisoner. Two captains at least had been captured and two others had died.

It was a miracle that the loss of life had not been far greater, but there were many wounded, broken men, and more yet would die as a result of their ordeal. Many would lose limbs or parts of limbs; some, paralysed from the waist down, had to be carried everywhere.

All this, and yet the dreaded *Tirpitz*, the menace from which we had so desperately fled, had never at any time proved more than a threat on a signal pad.

Chapter 10

The Hungry Wait

BRODIE.

The massacre of PQ 17 meant the Admiralty first postponed and then cancelled the sailing date of the next convoy, PQ 18, which had originally been expected to leave Iceland towards the end of July. It was decided that PQ 18 could not run the same risks we had. It would have to wait until an aircraft-carrier escort could be spared or winter darkness returned – or both.

In Archangel we knew nothing of these discussions going on behind the scenes more than 2,000 miles away. We anticipated being at Archangel for no more than two weeks: our supplies were geared to this plan. Instead, as the days and weeks dragged by, what had been an interesting experience, meeting the Russians, turned to extreme boredom and frustration as we waited impatiently for the return home. We knew PQ 18 must sail first: it was the practice for each return convoy to cross the outward-bound one.

Some escorts kept busy with turns of sea duty, but the trawlers generally remained idle. A projected Barents Sea patrol for the *Lord Austin* did not materialise. The corvettes did it instead because there was an acute shortage of coal in Russia and it was thought best that we should hold on to our small supplies for the eventual homeward run. So, after a much needed refit, continual topping up of coal and painting ship became the daily duty.

Life was not helped by the suspicious Russian guards on the jetties, who caused many upsets among the Allied seamen. When the *Empire Tide* got to her unloading berth the spare lifeboats she carried had to be put in the water and tied to the quay. After unloading she shifted half a mile to a new berth. Bosun Medhurst took four men along the quay to collect the boats, but were confronted by two guards with tommy guns. Every time the seamen attempted to man the boats the guns were pushed in their way, so they finally had to leave them.

The guards seemed to object to any contact between our ships. A whaleboat from the *Palomares* went up river to collect some tinned corn from a merchantman to supplement the wardroom stores. When it returned the crew were not allowed out of the boat until an interpreter was called and explained their 'indiscreet behaviour'. These petty incidents, all too numerous, were made more difficult by the language barrier.

A Russian woman sentry wanted to bayonet the No. 1 of a corvette who tried to get ashore. A gunnery officer from the *Palomares* was arrested and held prisoner for a night because he went near some guns carrying a small suitcase – it contained a pair of shoes he had been trying to get mended. Signalman Blarney from the same ship was refused exit from the jetty simply because he was carrying a book. It happened to be the life of Cecil Rhodes, bound in red. The zealous sentry treated it with great suspicion. Once Blarney had given the book to a colleague to take back to the ship all was well and he was allowed to pass.

Ashore, authority ruled everywhere. Great deference was paid to the green-capped commissars: old men, women and children, all that seemed left of the civilian population, stepped off the wooden pavements when these officials walked by. But there was no giving way when green caps and Allied blue caps edged past each other on the planks.

In the hot weather it was impossible to quench your thirst when ashore. Beer was unobtainable, the water not fit for drinking without first boiling it, vodka was definitely not a thirst-quencher – and the Russian tea simply made you more thirsty. Men returned to their ships long before they needed to just to be in time for the evening cup of char. Surgeon Lieutenant McCallum raised cheers on the *Zamalek* when he managed to distil some beer and spirits from the barley and yeast they could spare.

The combination of a lack of mail, a growing shortage of food, the very hot weather, mosquitoes and coaling was beginning to tell. Morale fell to a new low. On every ship the unchanging diet added to the general gloom. Crews were tired of corned beef in various forms: cooked, used in soup or sandwiches, or served just as it was. Watery stews with their invitation to 'find the meat', and the everlasting starchy rice, gave men diarrhoea. And no man thought he would ever be able to look a rice pudding in the face again. The men longed for some potatoes and green vegetables to vary the meagre rations, but all they were offered in place of greens were tiny pills to prevent an outbreak of scurvy.

Three minesweepers that had been in Russian waters for six months should also have gone back to Britain with us – and they were perilously low on stores. The *Pozarica* helped them out, as she did other ships, so her own company found themselves eventually living on 'hard tack': corned beef and biscuits. They notched up the date, 5 August.

Walter Edgley remembered: 'Biscuits, too, were gradually reduced in quantity until four biscuits a day was each man's ration. There was no bread, and tea was an interesting meal with everyone nibbling at their biscuit or biscuits.'

The *Poppy*, doing constant patrols and rescue work, had no bread or meat and her crew also had to live on hard tack. The Russians gave them dried fish but it was so hard they could not eat it. So on patrol they exploded depth charges to kill fresh fish: much to their mortification on one occasion they raised only three fish with one charge.

We found the Russian bread salty, sour and inedible, so on the *Lord Austin* our cook was forced to bake every day, despite his strong protestations that he had never been taught how. The daily bread ration, so long as it lasted, was two rounds per man, and woe betide the messman who did not cut those rounds into equal thicknesses. On the *Salamander*, in response to desperate appeals, the assistant cook said he could bake. He forgot to add the yeast, however, so mess was served with a loaf of bread like a brick.

Stoker Thomas McClements recalled: 'A Scouse seaman came to the rescue. He had done a bit in a bakehouse as a lad. His effort turned out a treat. There were two DSMs sent to the ship for her part played in the convoy, one for the officers, one for the crew. We voted unanimously for this chap to receive the crew's medal – we should have been lost without his knowledge.'

Coxswain Kerslake of the *Northern Gem* had to make the ferry trip to Archangel almost every day to try to forage for food. 'We were down to tea with no milk or sugar, hard biscuits and "pusser's peas". We had flour but no yeast, so we could not bake bread. I never had any success with either British or Russians in Archangel, so we eventually pulled a whaleboat up and down the Dvina, calling on any merchant ship we saw, begging what we could here and there, and luckily from an American ship we managed to get some yeast. What a joy to taste fresh bread again!'

One afternoon, with great ceremony, two Russians brought a sack of green vegetables on board the *Northern Gem*. Her crew looked forward excitedly to fresh cooked greens with the next day's dinner. 'Alas, after half an hour the Russians were back, this time with a guard, and said they had put the sack on the wrong ship, and that it should have gone to one of the minesweepers which had been working from Archangel for so long. We thought it rather funny, but our mouths were watering all the same.'

There was more comedy later on – but with a better outcome. News came through of the Canadians landing at Dieppe. The delighted Russians thought this was the 'second front' they had all been waiting for, so a deputation arrived at the *Palomares* with a gift of yak meat. Two other Russians boarded the *Pozarica* with a sack of cabbages. Next day, when the news came through that the Dieppe forces were being evacuated, the Russians reappeared for their yak and cabbages, explaining they had been delivered by mistake and should have gone to Russian ships farther along the quay. They were out of luck: the meat and greens had been eaten!

Of course, our privations were small compared to those the Russians themselves were enduring. An example was when we on the *Lord Austin* had the small job of running some stores from one place to another along the river. Among the stores were some barrels of flour. The working party of Russians looked emaciated: perhaps they were political prisoners. The barrels were of poor quality and when they had been hoisted aboard a mound of flour was left on the jetty. As soon as the armed guard had driven away in their lorry and we had cast off, the poor devils in the working party threw themselves on the mound and stuffed the flour into their mouths as fast as they could. What they could not eat they pushed into the pockets of their tunics. We wondered what the guards would have done if they had seen them. Would they have been shot? This had happened to others caught pocketing food on the quays.

Four destroyers arrived from home. The *Martin*, the *Marne*, the *Lord Middleton* and the *Blankney* had made a dangerous dash across the Barents Sea jam-packed with ammunition and stacked with four-inch shells, even on the upper deck. This ammunition, along with gun barrels to replace those on which the rifling had gone, was badly needed by the 'ack-ack' ships for the return journey. The destroyers also brought medical supplies and some stores, though these did little to alleviate our food shortages. After initial excitement at the destroyers' arrival, which we hoped was a sign of our early return, it was soon evident that this was not the case. The tedium of life on the Dvina resumed.

One day, to great cheers from the banks, the huge Russian submarine, the *Red Star*, glided up river. This vessel was said to have put two torpedoes into the *Tirpitz*, a claim later rejected by the Admiralty. Two Russian destroyers, their multi-coloured camouflage laid on in Cubist designs, anchored near to the *Lord Austin*'s berth. They bristled with 'ack-ack' guns, which looked as if they had just been wheeled aboard and left on deck. All the same, the ships had a very businesslike air, like the Russian trawlers, whose 'ack-ack' armament put us to shame.

Admiral Stefanov, the Russian Commander in Chief of the White Sea Fleet, went by in his ultra-modern launch. Festooned with flags, its burnished brass gleamed against its shining white background. The funnel was its crowning glory: wide and oval-shaped, it leaned back at an incredible angle. Stefanov inspected the *Pozarica*'s company. An old man, but very firm, he made a powerful speech with much hand waving. They would be returning home and coming east again with more supplies for the glorious Red Army, he told them through his interpreter. 'See to it that you have an aircraft carrier with your convoy to protect it,' he said.

The British admiral accompanying Stefanov told the company they were not forgotten, a statement received with some doubt. When Churchill visited Moscow just before the Dieppe landings, we hoped there might be an improvement in our beggarly situation, but nothing happened. The state of the war remained critical for our hosts. We were relieved to hear that on the Murmansk front things remained static, but elsewhere the Russians were hard pressed. One strong rumour, which caused near panic for a time, was that Russia had capitulated, and that we should get out with all haste before the Germans arrived.

By this time we had begun an orgy of sport to keep ourselves active. Before we had played nothing; now we played everything. We found ourselves down for soccer after dinner, and after tea, rugger, cricket or a weird form of hockey, using a wooden square puck, all played on the wooden-planked quay. In the evening there was shooting and boat pulling, and sessions of swimming in the log-laden Dvina, with the added excitement of trying to miss the submerged logs as you dived in. Besides this, there was a Russian Army assault course near the ships and the Russians had no objection to some of the sailors joining them on it. The Russian recruits were a ragged bunch, their ages ranging from 16 to 60, but they all held themselves well and sang roundly on the march, though with strangely emotionless faces.

At first there was a certain enthusiasm for the various sports, but as the days went by it became too much of a good thing, and because of our poor diet we found we were none too fit. For the men of the *Lord Austin* the situation changed when we moved to another berth. Sports were held here, but in a much milder and more enjoyable form. More importantly, when we decided to row our contesting teams over to a nearby island to play their fixtures, we had the extreme good luck to obtain some potatoes, our first for many weeks. They cost us nearly all our spare woollen clothing in barter, but we could have assured the knitters they had never been put to better use.

Others made their own luck. Sub Lieutenant Brooke of the *Poppy* remembered: 'Our No. 1 mounted an expedition to get some potatoes and one night several officers from the corvettes, clad in dark jerseys and gym shoes, rowed downstream with muffled oars to a field alongside the river, which we had previously reconnoitred. We knew it contained potatoes, and that it was guarded by armed sentries who patrolled the dykes which kept the river out. Choosing our time carefully, we crawled over the dyke and down in among the potato plants. Then, keeping flat on our stomachs, we wriggled down the rows, burrowing in with our hands to get the potatoes without disturbing the plants. We stayed as long as we dared, then scurried back to the boat with our spoils in a sack. It was not a great quantity of vegetables but Queen Elizabeth couldn't have enjoyed Raleigh's potatoes more.'

One mess on the *Pozarica*, after many weeks, also managed to get a brief taste of the now highly prized and almost non-existent vegetable. By absolutely scraping the barrel they gathered together enough cigarettes and chocolate from their small ration to barter for enough potatoes to give them a couple of expensive but glorious meals.

Meanwhile many of the survivors billeted in Archangel were living on black bread, grass soup and barley, and, where fortunate, the inevitable corned beef. They were given Russian tobacco too, when available, though they found it was like birdseed and it would not roll. But at least it burned – using newspaper and toilet rolls for cigarette papers – and was better then the dried tea leaves that some men were reduced to smoking. The American survivors, in particular, found it hard to adjust themselves to the spartan food and conditions; only the Chinese seamen fully retained their poise and manners.

The survivors who were not hospitalised had little to do with their time except to sit in the International Club or find themselves girlfriends. Many found regular sleeping partners, as did some naval officers who 'went native' and lived with girls ashore. For the naval men this side of life varied from a number of steady romantic partnerships with Russian girls to such pathetic episodes as that involving a Russian woman who came down to one of the jetties every night. Aged about 60, her face lined and worn, she stood in a little alcove in the logs, where she received her customers. All she asked in payment was a few squares of chocolate or two or three cigarettes.

The American survivors, understandably restless and impatient, and with the disaster of PQ 17 festering ever more strongly among them, sent representatives to the US Naval Attaché in Archangel, Commander Frankel, demanding better living conditions and a decision on when they would be going back to the States. There was little he could do, but he did hold meetings to tell them about the progress of the war. At one of these meetings they learned that the enemy had known the name and details of every ship in the convoy. Furthermore, it was claimed that in one instance the crew of an enemy seaplane had landed and boarded an abandoned ship. Long afterwards a U-boat commander also claimed to have boarded the *Paulus Potter*, which drifted for a week through the ice floes like a phantom ship, and found her secret codebooks and a complete list of the ships in the convoy.

Since our arrival Archangel had been remarkably free from the attentions of the Luftwaffe, but as short periods of darkness in the night hours returned, the enemy resumed his bombing attacks. We had often wondered what the result might be of a full-scale incendiary attack on this city of wood, where it seemed just by shaking hands with its people you risked getting a splinter in your palm. Even the high air-raid towers from which women kept watch were built of timber, and the fire-fighting apparatus we had seen looked as if it had strayed from the set of an old comic film.

Although the first raid lasted for five hours and huge fires were started, the town was not burnt out. It was sheer man and woman power that saved it, and the closeness of the river. Everyone not actually bedridden turned out to lend a hand. No one sheltered from the raids – for there were no shelters. Hundreds of troops were brought in by ferry and tram from the surrounding villages, and the women worked alongside the men as Russian women always do. Next day Archangel looked very much like its usual self.

A second big raid again produced great fires, and we had to keep our hoses going to protect the decks and the adjoining quay. Yet the result was much the same. Some fires burned for two days afterwards, but the actual amount of damage was surprisingly well contained. The methods of ensuring this were ruthless: to stop fires spreading all intervening obstacles were systematically demolished. On one occasion this brought an unwelcome surprise for some of the Allied survivors who willingly pitched in with the Russian firefighters.

Third Officer Phillips of the *Aldersdale* recalled: 'One particular hut was on a piece of waste ground between two blazing rows of houses. Harries, our chief sparks, and myself recruited some Russians and armed ourselves with a telegraph pole. Harries, being the heftiest, took the leading end of the battering ram, and I the rear, with some Russian volunteers between us. We charged the offending hut, with a view to immediate demolition. Unfortunately the side which presented itself to our assault was the opening one, and as the butt struck the door it flew open and Harries swept inside followed by two of the Russians. A blasphemous yell, silence, and then the emergence of three dripping figures. It had been the communal loo for the surrounding houses. It took hours of nakedness on the banks of the Dvina to get rid of the debris and smell.'

Big news came at last with the arrival of the USS *Tuscaloosa* at Murmansk. The fast cruiser had steamed from the Gyde with three destroyers, all carrying stores. The *Tuscaloosa* also brought a medical unit, which aimed to establish a base hospital to look after convoy survivors because the Russians had a severe shortage of medical supplies. This unit was called 'Operation Dudley' – and it was a flop.

The Russians, for reasons of suspicion, jealousy and pride, refused to allow the unit to land on the ridiculous grounds that the men did not have a visa. The unit was finally put aboard the *Zamalek*, but the medical men wanted to return home with naval ships, so all except one sick-berth petty officer quit the rescue ship, taking their stores with them. This was a blow for Surgeon Lieut. McCallum, who could have done with the men and their help on the return journey later.

However, the *Tuscaloosa*'s mission was also one of repatriation, and she brought blessed release for many survivors, who were taken to Murmansk to join her. Twelve fortunate American merchant crews were taken aboard after the survivors drew lots. Among the crews taken from Archangel by a destroyer were those from the *Washington*, which left three men behind in hospital, and from the *John Witherspoon*.

Ferocious O'Flaherty said: 'I never knew that an American destroyer could look so beautiful until we saw her swing round a jetty towards us. This was the first we had seen of the US Navy since they had left us in the Barents Sea. They tied up just long enough to drop a board across the dock while we scurried over it. We were told that another destroyer had gone before us with the litter cases.

'Before long we were swinging round into the harbour of Murmansk. Here we saw more naval ships. All but one were at anchor, with the *Tuscaloosa* dominating the scene as the largest. They did look good to us. We had been on the run from the Germans for so long that it was encouraging to see the ships feeling safe enough to lie at anchor.

'Going aboard the *Tuscaloosa* was like entering a luxury hotel after the plain fare at Archangel. Plenty of sailors were on hand to help carry the weak and limbless aboard. Even those of us who were ambulant were apologetically offered help. We knew that this ship was among those which had to obey the order to leave us, and accepted the regret that was so obvious in their faces.'

The Germans broadcast the news of the *Tuscaloosa*'s mission to Murmansk: how many men she was repatriating and where she was bound. This precise knowledge of Allied ship movements no longer caused any surprise. Nor was there any great fear that the *Tuscaloosa* would be attacked on her mercy mission, for it was the merchant ships laden with war materials that remained the enemy's prime target. Nevertheless, 'Shads' followed the cruiser and her destroyer escorts across the Barents Sea, and bombers also appeared, though they kept their distance.

So, in this last week of August, with the *Tuscaloosa* gone, we were still stranded impatiently at Archangel, along with hundreds of remaining survivors. Rumours began to circulate about our impending return and we fervently hoped they were genuine. We did not want to remain and be frozen up for the winter, as had happened to more than one Allied ship the previous year.

With the last heat of summer upon the wooden city, the river still flooding and ebbing fast with the tide, the bright cotton frocks of the girls and the insatiable mosquitoes, it required a strong effort of the imagination to picture the scene blanketed in snow and ice, the river a frozen sheet of ice across which people walked. But the sight of skis and sleighs left lying about, the immensely thick jackets and trousers worn as working dress, the double thickness of walls and windows of all the buildings, and the way in which the people's faces clouded over when they spoke of the coming 'vinter', made us realise that the smiling face of summer must soon give way to the hard, grim and bitter visage of the Arctic winter.

Another constant reminder came from the orphaned children living among the logs on the quay, who begged and wheedled every spare piece of woollen clothing from us. Some of these children were 'adopted' by the ships, fed and clothed by them. The *Lord Austin* had two, Nina and Freddie – at least he told us this was his name. They were bright, intelligent children but much older in mind than their English counterparts.

Nina was a very composed and self-possessed little girl with a look in her dark eyes that made you feel she was always laughing at you. Freddie was talkative. 'Comerad Pa-ule, you have the woolly for Freddie – scarf, cap, sock, jersey?' 'But it's too hot for woollies, Freddie.' 'Da, da, but ven the vinter he comes … Brrrrr!' He would stamp his feet and huddle up, shivering. He was difficult to resist until we found that he had already obtained enough woollens to clothe about ten children for the 'vinter'.

Nina and Freddie were fed by our crew and given baths in the engine room when the Chief was absent. Alf, one of the stokers, became their foster father. The skipper refused to allow them to sleep aboard so we used to smuggle them over after dark. We all became very attached to them.

The *Dianella* 'adopted' a seven year old called Woolfga. They renamed him Vodka, made him a little petty officer's suit with the proper badges, and gave him a hammock and a bosun's whistle so he could go around the corvette gleefully piping the routine. He always ate with the crew. Before we left, the crew of the *Dianella* made many efforts to adopt Vodka officially, but in vain.

By the end of August morale reached its lowest point. Sports and practically all activities had long collapsed. Even tombola, a saving grace, which had been played from ship to ship, came to an end when the supplies of tombola tickets ran out. Everything had lost its shine. Visits to Archangel had long stopped and there were fewer calls to the Intourist Club in the local village, the 'Welcome Inn' where officers and ratings drank together with no distinction of rank. Tempers had shortened and needed the merest spark to explode.

Then on 28 August, a date few men there were likely to forget, a minesweeper near us flashed the electrifying signal: 'Come over if you want your mail!' There was none of the usual struggle to find a boat's crew. On the *Lord Austin*, as on all ships that day, hours were spent reading and re-reading the first letters to reach us since we left Iceland, and we blessed the girls' school that had adopted our little ship, for they had sent us a parcel of 2,000 cigarettes. Ashore there were some touching, poignant scenes as the survivors also received their mail: some of the frostbitten eagerly crawled for it on their hands and knees.

At last some supplies of food and NAAFI goods were circulated, and as the food improved, however slightly, so did the men's spirits. Then, finally, the best news of all came: our return convoy, QP 14, would soon be under way, for PQ 18 had sailed from Loch Ewe in Scotland on 2 September – with an aircraft carrier among its heavy escorts.

The escort ships did some quick stocktaking and pooled their resources of stores and ammunition: some depth charges to that ship, some four-inch shells to the other, a few tins of milk and beef and a bag or two of rice changed hands.

For the hungry coal-burning trawlers it was time for a massive coal-up, and a bizarre one it turned out to be, with none of the crews dirtying their hands. Sturdy Amazons armed with shovels came aboard and trimmed the coal in the bunkers as it shot down the long chutes. Our chivalrous skipper sent a working party to help, but it was quickly made clear we were not wanted: the laughing women just pinched the Chief's backside and got on with the job. On the *Lord Middleton* they had quite an argument before it was made clear that the girls had been ordered to trim the coal: they had been sent from camp to work the ship for an extra couple of roubles. So the *Lord Middleton*'s men let the girls get on with it – and rustled up a pot of soup for them. They were so hungry they looked as if they might eat the pots and spoons too.

The Russian coal was very poor stuff, almost dust and earth, and there were grave doubts whether it would keep the trawlers going at a decent enough speed to keep up with the convoy, but we were all determined to get the ships through even if it meant doing shift work down the stokehold. The alternative, it was rumoured, was for the trawlers to be left to freeze into the ice for the winter and for us to be drafted into the Russian Army to fight on the Murmansk front. We would get those ships home if we had to get out and push!

Final confirmation that we would be making the journey came when the *Lord Austin* was ordered to take on her quota of survivors: each ship in the return convoy had to carry a certain number. Many American seamen complained bitterly about returning in the small naval vessels, arguing that according to their articles they should be repatriated in a large liner or cruiser. They were bluntly told that they could take it or leave it: if they decided to stay they might have to remain till next spring. They took it. A great number of merchant men, both British and American, flatly refused to return in the merchant ships, so all the naval escorts were well loaded. Our quota was 15 men.

Amid great secrecy the *Lord Austin* picked up her survivors at 3 a.m. from a deserted quayside. It was hard to part from Nina and Freddie but it had to be done, and they were in tears when they left. They and all the other adopted orphans went off to tell their friends about it. Consequently the whole of Archangel very soon knew that we were about to depart. So much for secrecy.

The ships' officers held a grand farewell party and got gloriously tight: one captain nearly followed the steward into the river when returning aboard.

Sailing date was 13 September. The previous day a rating from *La Malouine* broke his leg playing football and was treated on board the *Zamalek*. Surgeon Lieut. McCallum said, 'He was put in a plaster and a walking metal calliper splint applied to make him mobile. I told him it would keep him upright in the water anyhow, and he wryly replied, "Yes, but at what depth?"

The *Zamalek*'s last passenger aboard was an American seaman from the *Samuel Chase*. He had swum ashore as soon as his ship arrived in Russia and had been detained in a mental hospital. For the return convoy he was sent over to the *Northern Gem*, but before she reached the point-of-convoy assembly he had twice tried to jump over the side of the trawler. He had to be restrained and carried below by force. He would neither eat nor drink, and thought anyone offering him food was trying to poison him. If the *Northern Gem* experienced action they could ill afford a rating to watch the man, so they asked for his transfer to one of the other ships. He was taken to the *Zamalek*, where, surprisingly, he rallied and proved a great help on board.

The Walrus that the *Palomares* had towed half way across the Barents Sea was left behind at Archangel. Its radar set was removed and it was finally abandoned – but not before our Russian hosts had laid strong claim to it, however, as part compensation for our having failed to deliver 87 of the Spitfires expected from PQ 17. Another more enterprising group of Russians offered to buy it.

As the *Lord Austin* drew away from the quayside at Maimaksa a Russian rowing boat slowly passed us. It was struggling against the fast flowing tide, a woman at the oars while two men reclined in the stern. 'Do svidania, Russia!'

Chapter 11

The Final Toll

Sunday 13 September. It was a day of cold and wind and drizzle, the first hard touch of winter upon it. But for us it was a good day, as we steamed from Archangel after our two-month-long enforced stay. Not even the prospect of bitter weather and more fierce battles with the Luftwaffe and U-boats in the next two weeks could mar our eager anticipation of home leave – for those who lived to enjoy it. Better to face the risk than to lie and rot in what had become a wooden prison.

QP 14's 16 merchant ships included surviving vessels from PQ 17 together with others that had been awaiting a return convoy. They were mostly sailing light, though several carried exchange cargoes – and wood! Surprisingly, one British ship, the *Ocean Voice*, had women and children among her passengers, the families of a Russian trade delegation to Britain. Only Russian women would normally have contemplated making such a dangerous journey – and only Russian men let them.

The *Ocean Voice* had been the commodore's ship of PQ 16. On that convoy enemy bombs had torn a great hole in her side, but her crew had doused the fires and fought through. Now she was trim again and once more chosen as the lead ship, with Commodore Dowding aboard. As it progressed the convoy settled into two columns, the *Ocean Voice* leading one and our friends on the *Ocean Freedom* leading the other, with Capt. Walker as vice commodore.

Most of the other PQ 17 escorts were with us again: the 'ack-ack' ships, the corvettes, our sister trawlers and the two rescue ships. There were, besides, two destroyers and three minesweepers new to us. The number of escorts equalled the number of merchantmen, and soon we expected to have many more when warships from the approaching convoy PQ 18 would transfer to us after seeing their charges safely on the last lap to Russia.

The White Sea was unpleasantly choppy and the coal piled up on the *Lord Austin's* decks shifted dangerously. As we steamed north into the Barents Sea our only enemy was the weather. After our long spell of Russian summer it was hard to be flung back into severe Arctic conditions once more, and even harder for some of the lightly loaded merchantmen tossing high in the water.

It seemed strange that these harsh waters could produce such an awe-inspiring spectacle as the aurora borealis or northern lights. The first hesitating white fingers would come groping over the horizon, then like giant searchlights stretch and stretch up in the sky; smaller branches grew out from them and criss-crossed each other until their beams cut up the whole of the heavens into geometrical designs, sometimes achieving a display of the most marvellous colours. Many sailors were fascinated by the sight during the long night watches.

The *Winston Salem* ran into trouble during a snowstorm and the aurora borealis on our first night out of the White Sea. After her rough grounding on Novaya Zemlya she was low, literally floating on her tank tops, and during the northern lights her magnetic compass actually spun – she had no gyro – and she lost the convoy. All her master could do was to aim north and attempt to follow the stragglers' route along the edge of the ice fields.

Soon afterwards the ancient coal-burning *Ironclad* was lagging badly. Escorts went back and fussed round her continually, but it was no use: she could not make any more knots. The convoy would slow down for an hour or two, then go on again at its normal speed and leave the lagging ship astern. At last it was decided that she must be left and a minesweeper was detailed off to be her own special escort.

For the rest of us the first three days were fairly uneventful. Through the sub-zero weather, with its gales, snowstorms and black fog, we did at least have the company of some friendly aircraft, first RAF Hurricanes and then Russian seaplanes and Catalinas. Now and then a Junkers 88 appeared, shadowing us from afar, but gave no trouble and flew off after gunfire from the escorts.

For the *Pozarica*'s company, 15 September was a bleak day. On this day, in the bitter weather, the poor devils drank the last of their rum supply. We were lucky that our own stock, admittedly a weird mixture of rum and vodka, with care looked like lasting the journey.

The first of our troubles concerned our batch of survivors. When they found themselves included in the watch bill – the stokers to the stokehold, the seamen to the lookout and wheel – a deputation was sent to explain to our skipper that, under their articles, they were to be transported home as passengers. The skipper refused to see the deputation, informing them that under his own articles, in this ship every able-bodied man had to lend a hand in some way. When they then sent him a message refusing to do any watches, the reply was brief and blunt: 'No watches, no meals.'

At this the belligerent 'strike leader' washed his hands of the whole business, declaring that no one was going to make him work against his will. He turned into his hammock, where he remained on the pretext of being ill. Of course, he got his food.

Our other 14 'guests', six of them coloured men, were a mixed bunch. Only three had been to sea before and two were cowboys who had never even seen the sea before PQ 17. A burly stoker who had served since the days of sail looked upon his fellows with undisguised contempt. He would sit round the fire with our crew and say loudly, within hearing of the others, 'Of course, they're just a bunch of cream puffs, this lot. I wouldn't have them sailing with me at any price. I like men – not puffs. But these are cream puffs, all right.'

Another old hand among them was a ship's carpenter; he became their new leader and spokesman. He could do any sort of job well and was willing to lend a hand anywhere above or below decks. He handled his crowd with tact and understanding and we found him a good companion in the mess or on watch. He combined an unruffled good temper with a sense of humour.

One of the lighter moments during this quiet period came when some of the escorts began passing messages, firing them across by Costin gun or similar line-throwing apparatus. A minesweeper came up close on our starboard beam and fired her gun. The line was carried by the wind and caught round the firing lanyard of one of the PAC rockets on our bridge. The rocket, still tightly encased in its canvas covering, was triggered off. It shifted drunkenly out of its mounting and, belching flame and smoke, sailed horizontally straight for the sweeper. There were two sailors on her after gun platform: their mouths opened wide as this flaming comet bore down on them, landing plumb on the platform among all the ready-to-use shells. In an instant the two men were furiously ditching everything – rocket, shells, burning canvas – and almost themselves.

An officer who took charge of the firefighting called across to us in one of those tired, naval sort of voices, 'Your aim is damn good, old boy!'

After all this, however, it turned out that the message was not for us: it was addressed to the *Poppy*. Our skipper grabbed his loud-hailer and bawled at the other ship, 'I'm afraid you've given us the wrong message. We've got *Poppy*'s copy and *Poppy* must have our copy. We will send back *Poppy*'s copy for *Poppy* and *Poppy* will give you our copy. Stand by for *Poppy*'s copy!' He had to repeat this twice until he was saying, 'Copy's *Poppy*.' It was hysterically funny.

On 16 September, our fourth day out, the convoy, now far up in the Barents Sea, ploughed on through heavy snowstorms and rolling banks of fog. We passed many huge icebergs. We were due to meet our large escorts after they detached from PQ 18 the next morning, and sure enough, at midnight, a white rocket was seen in the distance. In the early hours of the 17th they joined us, a formidable force led by Rear Admiral Robert Burnett in the cruiser *Scylla*. There were 17 destroyers, which gave us a total of almost 40 warships escorting the remaining 14 merchantmen.

But we had no eyes for the destroyers or the rest. It was another vessel in that immense force that every man on QP 14 strained to see. Suddenly there she was, just over the horizon, looking exactly like a pudding basin: the aircraft carrier *Avenger*. Ugly she might be, this small carrier – the wags remarked that you had only to put a couple of taps on her and you had a bath – but to men chased, bombed and torpedoed the length and breadth of the Barents Sea, the sight of her was pure joy.

It was fascinating to watch the little black 'beetles' crawling along her deck. They seemed so slow from a distance that you felt they would tip over into the sea. But no, each plane rose resolutely into the air, circled the mother ship, and set course southwards on patrol. It was odd to see them signalling to the carrier: the flash of its Aldis lamp seemed bigger than the planes themselves. It looked like a big twinkling star.

These reconnaissance planes were reliable old string-bag Swordfish biplanes, but huddled together on the stern of the 'pudding basin' was a wicked looking collection of fighters: they were Sea Hurricanes, specially designed for aircraft-carrier use. It was the first time many of us had seen anything resembling a Hurricane or Spitfire sea-borne, and it gave us a feeling of tremendous confidence. The *Avenger* took up station right in the centre of the convoy, another tactical departure, which gave her maximum protection from torpedoes. But it was nerve-racking for the ships near to her when, in a terrific burst of speed, she turned into the wind to fly off her planes.

We had already had a number of U-boat alarms and depth charges had been dropped. The effect of these depth-charge explosions on our survivors on the *Lord Austin* was alarming: most leapt immediately from their bunks in a state of near panic. There were similar scenes in other escort vessels and on the *Zamalek* every action-stations alarm created a special problem. The ship's hospital was full of sick members of the Dutch crew from the *Paulus Potter*, many suffering badly from frostbite and still losing toes and fingers. They were all huge men, and all had to be carried up on deck when an alarm sounded – and carried back down afterwards.

The temperature dropped steadily and heavy snow continued to fall. We now had two fleet-oilers with us, who spent their time refuelling the warships that had come all the way from the UK without touching land. One of the oilers was an old friend of PQ 17, the *Gray Ranger*, which had earlier been forced to turn back when damaged by ice.

The convoy now kept up a fairly good speed of around eight knots and eventually we were in the region of Bear Island, scene of the big attack on our outward run. The Swordfish, continually scouting for U-boats, could not stop us from being found by a shadowing Blohm and Voss. Destroyers in the area had a few bangs at it, but, prudently, it kept just outside range. It was joined by two more, and for hours they dogged us. The *Avenger* flew off more planes and a game of hide-and-seek developed. It was strange to see our planes on one side of the convoy and the enemy's on the other. These 'Shads' were very wary, however: every time the carrier's planes went after them they carried out a great sweep to the opposite side of the convoy. The sight of these skirmishing enemy planes was an eye-opener for a member of a Russian delegation being carried on the *Ayrshire*. He had been supremely convinced that there was really no war going on outside the Soviet Union and that all planes were 'Americansky'. Still there was no substantial air attack, and the shadowing enemy planes left.

Next morning, 19 September, the sun shone for the first time for many days. Ahead, reflected in its rays, we saw what at first appeared to be another large iceberg, but it was land: Spitzbergen. That morning, too, one of our lost merchantmen unexpectedly returned to the fold. The *Winston Salem* had cracked on alone alongside the polar ice edge and, during the black of night, had run right across our convoy. Now, as we steamed along Spitzbergen's coastline, another fleet-oiler came out to join us, bringing extra fuel.

Still keeping close to the coast, the convoy turned northward. This was a ruse to deceive the enemy and to put more miles between us and the North Cape airfields. After some hours we turned southwest again and were on our last long lap to Iceland. The U-boats were still being kept at bay by the outer escorts and the 'Shads' had not reappeared. Hopes were high that we would now shepherd all the ships safely home.

Next day, 20 September, was Sunday again – and another Black Sunday it turned out to be. Just before 5.30 a.m. watchers on the *Ayrshire* saw what seemed to be waves breaking on an oddly disturbed sea. They were puzzling over the curious looking waves when a series of explosions rocked the minesweeper *Leda*, which was steaming astern of the convoy. She had been torpedoed and was very quickly in serious trouble.

The *Northern Gem*, steaming two miles astern of the convoy, was stationed about one and a half miles on the *Leda*'s port beam. When a muffled explosion was heard and flames were seen belching from the *Leda*'s funnel, the skipper, Lieutenant W P O Mullender, immediately rang 'Full Ahead'.

'I brought the *Northern Gem* hard-a-starboard,' he said, 'intending to put her alongside *Leda*'s starboard, weather side. When we got within 250 yards of the sweeper I could see many of her company scrambling to the forecastle head: she was well afire amidships and threatened to break in two. I ordered my crew to get our port boat inboard so that we didn't smash it as we went alongside – I thought we might well be in need of it before we got home.

'Then, on looking back at *Leda*, I saw an officer dive overboard to swim to us. By hell, he was getting along! But it was the worst thing he could have done, as suddenly other men started jumping and sliding into the sea off her fore-deck and leaping through the torpedo hole in her side. I had to stop *Northern Gem* 50 yards off the sweeper's bow or we would have drowned them between the two ships.

'I ordered our boat lowered to pick the men up out of the water, but it was a hell of a job to hold them as by this time they were covered with oil which had poured from the torpedoed ship. Other survivors were all around on rafts and clinging to our side nets.

'A trawler which steamed down between us and *Leda* ran over six men on a raft, one of them I think being *Leda*'s doctor. I saw all six men go under the trawler's bottom. *Leda* turned turtle and the last I saw of her captain he was sitting on the ship's bottom, or what was left of it. I think he was saved.

'A destroyer steamed over and ordered me to leave the men in the water and get back to the convoy. I told her to go to hell. Her captain was right in one respect, because if we, too, had been torpedoed while we lay there many more men would have died, but in the circumstances such a chance had to be taken. If only *Leda*'s company had waited until we had got alongside no doubt we could have saved more.' As it was, the *Northern Gem* pulled 70 men from the sea, but others were doomed.

Aboard the *Ayrshire*, which had no scramble nets or rope ladders, Sub Lieutenant John Aylard and others hung over the ship's side with someone holding their feet, grabbing the hands of men in the sea and trying to pull them on board. Because there was oil everywhere in many cases the struggling men's hands slipped from their grasp and the men were swept away and drowned. Cruelly, among them were six survivors of the *River Afton*, which the *Leda* had been bringing home. Others saved from the sea died shortly after rescue. It was a savage blow.

Ominously, the shadowing enemy aircraft were now in the sky again and throughout the rest of the day there were U-boat and aircraft alarms. The *Avenger*'s planes were up all the time, but still those vultures hovered on the horizon. Shortly after 5 p.m. the *Lord Austin* shivered and trembled as if a depth charge had exploded beneath the surface of the sea. We were keeping station on the convoy's starboard quarter and looked across to the ships about a mile away. We saw a giant waterspout rising into the air by the bow of PQ 17's *Silver Sword*. She was silver in colour and name and her decks were loaded with logs. As we stared at each other wondering what was happening, the *Lord Austin* shivered again and a second waterspout leapt up near amidships on the *Silver Sword*.

'Can they be bombing her?' someone asked, glancing skywards. Before he had finished speaking there was a third shudder and a great red glow appeared at the *Silver Sword*'s stern. Suddenly we knew the answer: torpedoes again. She had been 'tinfished' three times. She still seemed to be steaming tranquilly along and for a moment we thought she was not seriously harmed. Then she slowly lost way. Two escorts made for her and soon all three ships were left far astern.

The three torpedoes had smashed the crew's quarters on the *Silver Sword*, both forward and aft. There would have been a grave loss of life but for the fact that practically all hands were amidships for their evening meal. One man in the quarters aft was fatally injured, dying during the night after rescue. The merchantman, her propeller blown off but still not sinking, was shelled and sunk by an escort.

After this second attack the U-boat hunt was on with a vengeance. There were two hours of crashes and rumbles, then suddenly the *Somali*, one of the hunting destroyers, was brought up dead in her tracks by a torpedo. It smacked into her engine room, killing five men and injuring others. She lay in a pall of smoke, rescuers quickly around her. Her damage was crippling but not fatal and it was decided to try to take her in tow. The *Lord Middleton* went alongside to help.

Asdic operator Arthur Jones recalled: 'We started taking off any easily removable stores and personal belongings that could be got at by her crew, then everything moveable, such as shells, ammunition boxes and depth charges – deprimed, we hoped – were seized and flung over the side in an effort to lighten her. We were alongside her for about 20 minutes when suddenly one of the aft engine-room hatches was flung open and out came one of the engine-room crew. Whether he was injured I don't know, as he went over to the other side and boarded another rescue ship which had pulled alongside.'

A skeleton crew was left on board the *Somali* and she was taken in tow by a sister ship, the *Ashanti*, with three more destroyers forming an escort. Ironically, the torpedo should have been the *Ashanti*'s, as she had just changed stations with the *Somali* before the attack.

Nerves were now stretched taut. Three ships torpedoed in a day without any warning from the asdics. The final blow was that our sheet anchor, the aircraft carrier, with her attendant destroyers, had withdrawn in the middle of the U-boat hunt, as had the cruiser *Scylla*. Once again we had that horrible feeling that we were being deserted in our hour of need. The comments in many of the remaining ships were caustic.

We did not know then the reason for the withdrawal: that the *Avenger*'s Swordfish pilots, constantly on the go since the start of PQ 18, were just about at the end of their tether. As we were now beyond the danger point of massed air attack, it was felt they could be rested and the valuable carrier removed from the area of U-boat attack around the slow-moving convoy. It could also have been inviting fate for the cruiser to remain as a U-boat target.

However, these decisions by Admiral Burnett could not be appreciated at the time. All we and our long-suffering survivors could see was the sight of the heavy ships once again vanishing rapidly over the horizon.

Admiral Burnett transferred to one of the remaining destroyers. He had asked for air cover from Coastal Command, and we now watched the sky for the expected arrival of friendly planes. As darkness fell, the tension increased. In the dark especially it was not a pleasant feeling to know that you were being hunted by a U-boat pack.

Morning, 21 September, and we were still being dogged by the 'Shads'. Then a single Catalina arrived. It flew in, contacted the commodore by lamp, and went off on anti-submarine patrol. Two hours later it returned across the front of the convoy, slowly losing altitude, and landed on the water about a mile ahead. It was soon obvious that it was sinking. The tail rose and its crew of five scrambled out on to the wing. They were hurriedly taken off by a boat sent out by a destroyer. We learned that the Catalina had sighted and attacked a U-boat, only to be hit herself. So much for our air cover.

Soon afterwards – 11.15 a.m. – a periscope crossed only 200 yards from the *Pozarica*'s bows. The depth charges thumped all day until darkness came again. The convoy made way at a slow five knots, with the *Somali* struggling along astern, under tow. The situation could not last, nor did it.

Dawn on 22 September broke with a calm sea and a clear sky – clear even of 'Shads'. One of the destroyers left the convoy, taking Admiral Burnett off to rejoin the *Scylla*. Scarcely had she gone when on the *Lord Austin*, shortly after 6 a.m., we felt the familiar shudder. All eyes turned instantly towards the main body of ships. A waterspout was rising beside a big merchantman. In quick succession five more vibrations were felt, the eruptions of water rising so fast that we could not distinguish which ships were being attacked.

The action bell rang and some of our survivors shot out of the mess-deck hatch like demons in a pantomime. One of the 'ack-ack' ships put on a sprint and raced up the line, but we feared her twin had received one of the 'fish'. It would be damnable luck, now that we were so near our destination, if these two stalwarts did not get home together. It was not the 'ack-ack' after all, however. It was her closest neighbour, the *Ocean Voice*, leading the port column. Once again Commodore Dowding felt his ship explode beneath him.

A U-boat well out on the starboard bow had fired at the convoy. The *Ocean Freedom*, leading the starboard column, was just slightly astern of position, so that the first torpedo streaked across her bow and shot over to the *Ocean Voice*, leaping from the water and striking the ship's bow with a tremendous flash and explosion. Three days out one of the Russian wives on the *Ocean Voice* had had a baby: when the torpedo struck the baby was hurriedly put in a suitcase for safety. Then a second torpedo struck, also near the bow. It made the passengers' temporary accommodation collapse – and the suitcase was lost. Several survivors afterwards said they saw the baby floating in and out through the hole torn in the *Ocean Voice*. The ship did not sink but was entirely disabled. The *Zamalek* steamed over to the rescue.

Meanwhile other torpedoes had hit the *Gray Ranger* and the American *Bellingham*. The *Palomares* had a narrow escape as the *Gray Ranger* was hit. The officer of the watch, sensing an emergency, rang down for full speed ahead. As the 'ack-ack' ship picked up speed a torpedo scraped under her stern so close that the men in the engine room heard the noise it made. The *Gray Ranger* was struck aft: the torpedo tore through her buoyancy tanks into her engine room, killing three men. Three deck ratings were also lost: in the explosion a figure looking like a film dummy cartwheeled into the air from the bridge.

Then the *Bellingham* reeled from an explosion. Her great bulk shivered and her stern began to settle. We were quickly signalled to stand by her. Boats and rafts were already pulling away from the sinking ship and the sea was dotted with floating wreckage. We stopped engines and the survivors made a beeline for us. In a few moments we were helping them over the side. 'Thanks, fellers,' one of them said. 'Say, this is becoming quite a habit with me. It's my fifth time since we left Iceland.'

Luckily none of them was injured and only one man was reported missing. While we were helping them aboard and hauling up the very welcome boxes of food they grabbed before leaving, the *Bellingham* rose high above us, half the huge ship thrusting up out of the water at an angle of 60 degrees. It was an awe-inspiring sight from such close range. There was a certain majesty and grandeur about this monster in her death throes. Two or three minutes later she had gone, leaving behind a vortex of whirling wreckage and burning calcium flares: the funeral pyre of the last luckless PQ 17 merchantman to die.

Our rescue work lasted about half an hour. With engines stopped, the convoy disappearing ahead and the unseen U-boats near at hand, we were the perfect target. It was the longest half-hour we could ever remember.

When the *Ocean Voice* was hit Capt. Walker, vice commodore on the *Ocean Freedom*, took over as lead ship of the convoy. 'I can still see Commodore Dowding shaking his fist at me from the bridge as I broke my commodore's pennant,' he said.

The *Zamalek* picked up most of the Russians, and the women and children: the crowded rescue ship rigged up special accommodation for the latter. Apart from the distressed mother who had lost her baby, and another woman with a fractured leg, injuries were slight. The *Ocean Voice*'s crew were taken off by the minesweeper *Seagull*, in which Commodore Dowding finished his passage at the tail end of the convoy.

Capt. Walker remembered: 'Later the Commodore made a couple of attempts to board us from the *Seagull*, but the sea was too rough. I reckon it could have been done had I broken formation and hove-to, but he wouldn't have that – thinking of the ships rather than his own gratification, I guess.' The *Ocean Voice* was sunk by one of the escorts.

The *Gray Ranger*'s engine room was extensively damaged and flooded. Her survivors were quickly ordered to abandon ship. The majority got away by the port motorboat and were picked up by the *Northern Gem*. A few others were rescued by the *Rathlin*. A junior engineer who had jumped overboard from the tanker's stern was thrown a line by one of the rescue vessels. Fortunately it caught him by the wrist, but the ship was unable to stop and pulled him a full mile and a half through the water before managing to drag him aboard half drowned.

He was only 20 years old – not many older men would have survived that terrible ordeal in the icy sea.

The *Gray Ranger* was almost out of oil but she could not be towed. It was not a good idea to chance leaving her for the Germans, so she, too, was finished off by an escort. She was built so sturdily that it took 30 minutes of shelling to sink her.

And then it was all over. When no more attacks came we on the *Lord Austin* turned to looking after our 50-odd new survivors and their pets, a cat and a husky puppy. The desperate problems of sleeping and feeding everyone came up again, though the *Northern Gem* was in a far worse position than we were. Carrying men from the *Leda*, the *Gray Ranger* and now a quota from the *Bellingham* as well, they had scarcely room to turn, and their meagre rations of corned beef, biscuits and tea shrank alarmingly before they reached port, despite a small extra supply begged from a destroyer. And then there was the *Rathlin*. She now had some 200 men aboard besides her crew. With many of the survivors suffering from nervous shock and refusing to go below deck, she was in a highly dangerous condition, jam-packed like an excursion steamer on a river.

For the remainder of that day and into the night, as two Focke-Wulf Condors arrived to shadow us, the convoy steamed doggedly on. Action stations came again at dawn. We zig-zagged furiously for two hours, still with a Condor shadowing us. Where were our planes? As we neared the safety of our own minefields, however, there were no further attacks. In the afternoon, after rolling in a heavy swell, we sighted Iceland. Plans had been changed, however, and most ships were now to run for Loch Ewe.

For the rest of that day and the next, an angry sea took over where the U-boats had left off. A blizzard enveloped us and the wind increased to gale force. During its height, on the *Lord Austin*, we had to swing the smallboats in-board. Steering became almost impossible.

'Sing out when you're on,' came No. 1's voice from the bridge. 'She's swinging 20 degrees either side,' the helmsman replied. 'Then sing out as she whizzes past,' was the dry comment.

In the blinding gale we feared for the crowded *Rathlin*, rolling over almost to her beam-ends. She left us to call at Seydisfjord for emergency supplies, then followed on. The long-suffering vessel *Winston Salem* dropped astern with rudder trouble.

Every ship took an alarming battering from that storm. The *Dianella* suffered her worst moment of the entire voyage. Kenneth Richards recalled: 'We caught a sea on the port side and heeled over. I was on my seat in the bridge hut, and what angle we were at I couldn't say, but I was in a position looking down at the sea and it seemed like an eternity. The voice of the First Officer was heard calling to the helmsman: "Whatever you do, don't touch the wheel!" The scuppers on the starboard side had stuck and the waist was full of water, but somehow she righted herself, and thank God she did.'

The gale abated and there was a sudden new calm. We passed schools of porpoises and floating mines; belatedly, here and there in the sky, Fortresses, Sunderlands and Whitleys appeared. The destroyers left us and we were picked up by a coastal escort. A signal came to Capt. Walker: 'To *Ocean Freedom* from *Seagull*: lead on and take them home. Sorry not to be with you at the end. Pass to all ships well done. Dowding.'

We sighted the Butt of Lewis. Over the radio the BBC informed us that our return convoy had 'arrived safely'. Behind us, however, there was a final tragedy. The *Somali* had struggled along painfully slowly under tow from the *Ashanti*, constantly pumping out the sea that threatened to flood her. Her skeleton crew of 80 men kept her going, and though her boats had been destroyed there were enough rafts for them all in an emergency. Then the gale came – and in the darkness of the night, the end of her tortuous journey. Fortunately, as the towing became more dangerous, all hands had been ordered to stay above deck.

Arthur Jones of the *Lord Middleton* recounted: 'Her forward light was seen to be behaving queerly, see-sawing to and fro at a mad angle, then suddenly the tow-line parted and at the same time there was a great noise of rending metal as the destroyer broke in half and the two ends of the ship fell apart. She went down very quickly. With the heavy sea that was running our skipper decided to lay off astern, knowing that the men we saw jumping overboard would be swept down towards us. We were able to rescue a few, but owing to the fast waters others were swept right past us and so to their deaths. I'm afraid the poor souls had no chance at all.'

Among those miraculously dragged from the sea was the *Somali*'s captain, who was floating unconscious when he was found by the searching *Ashanti*. More than 40 men from the *Somali* died, including some who were hauled from the freezing water too late to survive. Among them was her chief yeoman of signals, who died on the *Lord Middleton* shortly after he was rescued. He was buried at sea off Seydisfjord, almost at journey's end.

26 September 1942. We berthed at Loch Ewe. The *Winston Salem* limped in the following day and we heard later that the *Ironclad* had managed to get to Spitzbergen, afterwards coming on to the UK. So the bald figures were: two British and five American ships were the only surviving merchantmen of PQ 17. These and the two rescue ships survived. The two battered and holed Russian tankers made it to Archangel. What a sorry tale to tell.

For the 1,000 survivors we brought home (some men died on the journey) there was one more short voyage, by mailboat, to a civic reception and lunch in Glasgow. Many enjoyed comfortable billets until they were fit to join other ships and the Americans ready to make passage home across the Atlantic.

All the men had to button their lips, however. Official security. Despite heavy German propaganda and a hundred twisted rumours, there was no communiqué, no statement, nothing. The real story spread to many parts of the world, however, as the survivors went home. The bitterness was carried home to Britain and the USA: a charge of desertion by the Royal Navy following a panic order from the Admiralty unparalleled in the history of the sea.

We took home our memories. For a long time afterwards, every time he closed his eyes, Surgeon Lieut. McCallum of the *Zamalek* saw a Blohm and Voss circling the convoy low on the horizon. It was an experience common to many of us. When Chief Engineer Dawson of the same ship landed he had lost two stone in weight and looked like a scarecrow. He could never get the noise of the bombs and the cries of those being rescued out of his ears. Every night from that year on Gunner Herbert Wharmby of the *Ocean Freedom* said a prayer, thanking God he had been saved.

Aboard the *Palomares*, as she steamed down to Belfast, the ship's company heard over the radio that another convoy had fought its way through to Russia, thanks to the help of the RAF. It was said that when the men on the mess decks heard it, they let out bellows of rage that could be heard the length and breadth of the ship.

It was to be a lasting anger – shared by us all.

Chapter 12

Whose Fault?

Even after the catastrophe, PQ 17 might have slipped into history as another tragic episode of the war. It might have been seen as the worst convoy disaster the Allies suffered, but one from which lessons could be quickly learned. Its destruction might have been avenged as more convoys went on to battle their way through to Russia.

This was not the case, however. Instead, a blanket of secrecy was spread over PQ 17's fate – and the blunder that brought it about.

On the day we berthed at Loch Ewe – 26 September 1942 – we read in the morning papers a very long and glowing Admiralty communiqué detailing PQ 18's great battle, in which 40 enemy planes were destroyed but the majority of ships arrived safely at their destination. At the end of the communiqué there were four short paragraphs noting the passage of QP 14. These recorded 'some losses among the ships' and briefly announced the sinking of HMS *Leda* and HMS *Somali*.

There was nothing about PQ 17. Nor had there been any mention of the convoy in our absence, other than the appearance of a few photographs released to the newspapers on 4 August. These were scenes of the battle with the torpedo bombers on Independence Day exactly a month before, described as 'one of the biggest convoy battles at sea' by a 'huge United Nations convoy'.

An example of the censored reports accompanying the photographs was this from the *Daily Herald*: 'These dramatic pictures show a German air attack by torpedo planes on a convoy to Russia. The ships were taking the Arctic route early last month, when darkness never really sets in, and the visibility helped the enemy. But in spite of repeated attacks, the convoy, with its badly needed war cargoes, got through.'

Yet when this was published, German statements about the mass sinkings, naming individual ships, had already been well circulated among the neutral nations. So had some of the many propaganda pictures taken by the enemy planes and U-boats, showing sinking ships and hapless survivors.

In America on the same day, 4 August, *Life* magazine published a large spread of photographs of the Independence Day battle taken by a staff man who had travelled in the USS *Wainwright*. The ship was unnamed but was described as 'one of the US warships guarding the great train of United Nations ships'. It appeared that *Life* was not as heavily censored as the British newspapers.

It reported: 'The Germans broadcast first that they had sunk a US cruiser and 28 merchant ships in the "greatest catastrophe" of the sea war. They claimed planes had destroyed 122,000 tons; U-boats another 70,000 tons. Their next claim added four more cargo vessels; their next, three more. On

July 9, the Russians announced that the convoy had "arrived safely in a Russian Arctic port". It had taken losses, but it had delivered a huge mass of American and British planes, tanks, guns, food, medicine and wartime tools to the hard-pressed Russians. It had done its part in the long delivery line from factory to the fighting front.'

Actual Allied losses had not yet been announced, *Life* added, but they were 'certainly a great deal smaller than the extravagant claims of the Germans'.

The Admiralty, however, remained silent. A few months later, in the spring of 1943, Lord Winster, a naval officer, caused a stir. In the House of Lords he demanded a statement about what he described as 'the worst voyage in the world'.

The *Daily Express* reported next day: 'Lord Winster disclosed that in one convoy to Arctic Russia we lost 34 out of 38 ships. He was apparently referring to the worst Allied convoy disaster of the war, at the beginning of last July. The enemy claimed annihilation of an entire convoy carrying more than 250,000 tons of planes, tanks, munitions and food. Official German reports claimed that 19 merchant ships were destroyed by bombers and nine by U-boats off Spitzbergen. All the other ships were said to be destroyed 'in a pursuit battle' a day or two later as they neared their destination in the Barents Sea.

'What happened was that after incessant air attack and severe losses on July 2, the convoy turned north – evading a German battle squadron, including the *Tirpitz* – and was again attacked by bombers as it neared Archangel. U-boats finished off damaged stragglers. Only four merchant ships survived.'

The facts about the convoy were now well and truly in the public domain, but still the Admiralty maintained its silence. A few months later, Admiral of the Fleet Sir Dudley Pound, First Sea Lord and Chief of the Naval Staff, resigned because of illness. He died the same year. The conduct of the convoy had ultimately been his responsibility, but even on his death there was no mention of PQ 17.

The official silence continued for two more years, until February 1945, when the Swedish-American exchange ship, the *Gripsholm*, arrived in New York with the first group of American merchant seamen to come home after spending up to three years in a German prison camp. Among them were 25 survivors of PQ 17. They had bitter memories of the loss of their ships, which, they told the welcoming city, had occurred when a heavy naval escort, including destroyers and cruisers, had abandoned them to the mercy of enemy planes and U-boats, lured off in a wild goose chase after German battleships. Men from the *Carlton* and the *Honomu* were especially bitter. They poured out stories of their ordeal to an astounded city gathering. All but four of the 38 merchant ships were sunk, the seamen said. Some heatedly charged the Royal Navy with cowardice: 'The Limey Navy just turned and ran.'

The US newspapers led with these shock reports about the convoy, which had been predominantly American. The US Navy Department declined to comment, so the spotlight fell on the Admiralty. *The New York Times* checked and reported: 'The story was ignored officially by the Admiralty but naval officers described it unofficially as "arrant nonsense ... In a case like that, the practice when attacked has been to disperse the convoy while escort vessels try to break up the attack," officers pointed out.'

For two days, while resentment boiled, the Admiralty did nothing. Then, 'in order to correct erroneous reports recently circulated', it issued a statement. This consisted of a brief account of the movements of the battle fleet, cruisers and escorts. It gave the correct number of ships in the convoy and those lost, but incorrectly stated that five of them were sunk in the Independence Day battle. It did not dwell on the 'scatter' order but said that 'for several hours' after the battle with the torpedo bombers, 'the convoy proceeded on its way without further interference. Later, when in a position due north of the North Cape, an attack by the enemy surface ships seemed imminent and the convoy was ordered to scatter. The six destroyers joined the First Cruiser Squadron to form a balanced striking force. An anxious 24 hours followed, but no surface attack developed on the scattered ships, this project apparently having been abandoned as a result of the dispersion'.

The last observation may be considered something of a classic, since in those 24 hours, as a result of attacks by planes and U-boats, 14 ships were already at the bottom of the sea or quickly heading there.

In conclusion the statement emphasised: 'During the past 42 months our Russian ally has safely received no less than 91.6 per cent of the vast amount of war supplies shipped by the northern route, the great proportion of which have been conveyed under British escort.'

The New York Times, in common with other American newspapers, repeated the statement without comment, observing in passing: 'Out of the dark past, now fading in a brighter light, the British Admiralty reveals some shocking figures … Only now do we realise what dreadful losses we were taking then.'

Then again, silence. Nearly two more years went by with still not the slightest admission of an error in the 'conduct' of the convoy. Then in October 1946, the Russian newspaper *Red Fleet*, official organ of the Soviet naval forces, published two hard-hitting articles written by Captain of the Second Rank V Andreyev, of the Soviet Navy. Entitled 'Lessons of One Convoy', they severely criticised the Admiralty and openly condemned the order to scatter as unnecessary.

Capt. Andreyev said: 'The main motive for the dispersal apparently was the confusion of the English command, exaggerated fear of the German ships, fear of "losses" in battleships which supposedly "could have" taken place.' There was a tradition, said the captain, that ships under escort must be defended. 'In this case the tradition was disregarded, and as a result, after dispersal, when the transports were defenceless, the convoy suffered its heaviest losses.' The order to scatter was given 'when the enemy ships supposedly threatening it were 300 miles away'.

In addition, Capt. Andreyev said the Admiralty did not take the organisation of the convoy 'seriously enough'. Its departure was widely known in Reykjavik and enabled the enemy to prepare his attack. It was insufficiently defended and should have had an aircraft carrier (the captain of the *Donbass* had spoken of seeing only one British plane, the Walrus). Capt. Andreyev said there was 'irresponsibility and panic' among British and American merchant crews, and ships were deserted after suffering only 'negligible damage'.

Capt. Andreyev went into a wealth of detail, and although most of his assertions were not soundly based – he blamed the 'scatter' order on the convoy commodore and the escort commander – he had certainly done his homework. He gave the correct number of ships and sinkings; the dismal total of merchantmen that eventually reached Archangel – 11, including the two damaged Russian tankers – and cited the reply given to the master of the holed *Azerbaijan* when he appealed to a destroyer for help: 'Convoy will not reform. Save yourselves independently. Advise keep to north as far as ice permits. Good luck.'

The fullest disclosure of Capt. Andreyev's articles was made by *The New York Times*. Uproar followed in Britain. Mr Anthony Eden, the wartime Foreign Secretary, publicly declared: 'Any fair-minded ally would have taken the Admiralty's detailed statement issued last year into account in passing judgement on this most daring and hazardous operation. It has, in fact, been completely ignored … It seems to me, to say the least of it, ungracious that our ally should single out the fate of one convoy for remonstrance.'

In the House of Commons, Members of Parliament voiced 'the burning indignation felt by all Britons' over Andreyev's 'outrageous' statements. The Secretary to the Admiralty, Mr John Dugdale, said the account had been read with considerable feeling since it impugned 'not merely the naval tactics of the convoy but also the courage of the British and American seamen who took part in it'. He assured MPs that a further Admiralty statement would be given publicity not only in Britain but abroad.

This statement, reiterating the outstanding success of the 40 Arctic convoys, explained that it would have been inviting disaster for escorts to detach and stand by disabled ships. The only course in the circumstances was to take off the crews and sink the vessels. As for the 'scatter' order, the statement repeated that north of the North Cape 'an attack by surface vessels seemed imminent'. 'The convoy was too far to the eastward for Admiral Tovey's battle fleet to give support, so the Admiralty ordered the convoy to scatter and the cruisers and destroyers to withdraw to form a balanced striking force to divert the enemy: this is the recognised form of defence in such extreme circumstances. In any event, the action of the escort and the scattering of the convoy achieved its primary object, and the enemy heavy ships withdrew and thereby the convoy avoided annihilation.'

Incredibly, according to this account, the action was successful. The truth, they say, is the first casualty of war: this observation is one for historians to examine. However, a fulsome retraction of Capt. Andreyev's account appeared in *Pravda* a day later. The Soviet State and public opinion appreciated the skill and 'indisputable courage' of the United States and British navies in convoy work, it said, 'and this appreciation found concrete expression in the decoration of

British and American sailors'. Capt. Andreyev's articles were 'clearly unsuccessful'. He had chosen the wrong approach: instead of studying the experience of many operations, he had made 'a generalisation on the basis of one isolated operation, and that an unsuccessful one'.

Red Fleet also published *Pravda*'s rebuke in full, but said that foreign commentators had exploited the captain's statement 'for the purposes of an anti-Soviet campaign'.

And that was that. The matter was left there for another four years, until in October 1950 the Admiralty finally released Admiral Tovey's despatches on the Russian convoys, for publication as a supplement to the *London Gazette*. The press pounced on them, for they presented a very different picture from what had gone before.

They revealed how the Commander in Chief Home Fleet had repeatedly asked for better escorts, and for a reduction of the convoys in the early summer until the ice barrier had receded north. They told of his many requests to the Russians for help over the last part of the journey, requests that had met with almost negligible response, the Russians calling for still greater efforts while doing little to help. Promised Russian bombing attacks on the Norwegian airfields had not materialised. Every other page of the despatches held some brief reference to the lack of co-operation from the Kremlin.

And, at last, there were some details of what the press now described as 'the notorious PQ 17 disaster', a story on which, the *Daily Express* said, 'for eight years Admiral Tovey has kept silence, though accused in Parliament of withdrawing the destroyer escort from the convoy to protect his battle squadron'.

The battle fleet's movements were at last made crystal clear. It had cruised to the west in an area bounded roughly by Jan Mayen, Spitzbergen and Bear Island, where Admiral Tovey considered the *Tirpitz* would be most likely to attack. When naval intelligence suggested earlier that the enemy surface raiders planned to attack east of Bear Island, the Commander in Chief had suggested to the Admiralty that on reaching the longitude of 1Q E, the convoy should turn back for 12 to 18 hours (if the *Tirpitz* did sail) to lure the enemy back into his range. This suggestion was not approved. Therefore he could do no more than patrol his own area.

Following the report on 3 July that the *Tirpitz* and the *Hipper* had left Trondheim, Admiral Hamilton decided to continue sailing his cruiser force east of Bear Island. The same day, when air reconnaissance showed that the ice barrier had receded north, the Admiralty suggested to the *Keppel* that the convoy should pass at least 50 miles north of Bear Island. However, Cdr. Broome preferred to stay in low visibility on the original route and make ground eastwards. Admiral Hamilton, deciding that a more northerly route was necessary, then closed the convoy and ordered Cdr. Broome to alter course to pass 70 miles north of Bear Island, and later to open 400 miles from the enemy airfields.

At noon on 4 July, the Admiralty gave Admiral Hamilton permission to take his cruisers beyond 25 degrees E if the occasion demanded, or unless contrary orders were received from the C in C, Admiral Tovey.

Admiral Tovey said: 'This was a reversal of the policy agreed between the Admiralty and myself. As no information I had justified this change, I ordered Hamilton to withdraw when the convoy was east of 25 degrees E or earlier, unless the Admiralty could assure him that the *Tirpitz* would not be met.'

Seven hours later the Admiralty signalled Admiral Hamilton that further information was expected shortly and he was to stay with the convoy pending further instructions. Then, two hours later, came the three fateful signals, all sent over the C in C's head.

The last signal was sent as a correction of the technical wording from 'disperse' to 'scatter', but this was not known at the time. So it was taken by Admiral Hamilton and Cdr. Broome to mean that the *Tirpitz* was chasing – hence Cdr. Broome's action in turning his destroyers to the fight.

At 5 p.m. on 5 July, the Russian submarine the *Red Star* reported that the *Tirpitz* and her consorts were outward bound from the North Cape. Three and a half hours later she was reported by another submarine, but soon afterwards the enemy ships abandoned their enterprise and returned to harbour 'for reasons not known'.

During the night of 5/6 July, the Admiralty signalled Admiral Tovey three times, suggesting that if the battle fleet was sighted steaming east it might make the *Tirpitz* reluctant to go as far as the convoy. The *Red Star* might have damaged her and there would be a chance for the planes of the *Victorious* to attack her.

Admiral Tovey thought this unlikely, but at 6.45 a.m. on 6 July, his destroyers having refuelled, he did alter course back to the north-east. An hour later an enemy plane passed over above the clouds: he tried to attract its attention with gunfire and fighters, but without success. Later that morning he was joined by the cruiser force, and as the weather was unfavourable for air reconnaissance he reversed to the south-west and the ships returned to harbour.

There it was, all concisely explained. But who was responsible for the Admiralty orders clashing with and overruling those of its commander in chief? Whose final decision caused the three fatal signals to be sent? Whose order scattered the convoy, and on what grounds?

Admiral Tovey would not comment to questioning newspapermen. 'There are a great many things that I could say,' he said. 'But perhaps I had better not.'

The official silence continued for seven more years. Then, in 1957, 15 long years after that melancholy Fourth of July, years during which the bitterness had spread and rooted, the truth finally emerged. In the second volume of *The War At Sea* (HMSO, 954–61) the official naval historian, Captain S W Roskill, revealed that the man responsible for repeatedly overruling Admiral Tovey and giving the crucial order to scatter was the First Sea Lord, Admiral of the Fleet Sir Dudley Pound.

So, for the first time, it was admitted, officially and publicly, that the order was a grievous error and should never have been made.

The men of the convoy scarcely knew the name of the First Sea Lord. Unlike the leaders of the other two services, he remained a vague, shadowy figure, masked by the authority of the Admiralty, despite the fact that he had been the First Sea Lord since the outbreak of war.

What kind of man was he? He was 64, with a naval record that included distinguished service in the Battle of Jutland in the First World War. Yet he never became well known among Royal Navy personnel. One of the very few attempts to compile a portrait of him was made by a *Daily Mail* writer just before the First Sea Lord's death, on Trafalgar Day, 1943, shortly after the death of his wife.

'Night after night this man, who held down Britain's most exacting job during the four most exacting years history has produced, would telephone his wife. "I am sorry," he would say, "but I shall not be able to get home." "I understand," Lady Pound would reply.

'The Pounds lived in London, in a six-guineas-a-week furnished flat in Hornton Street, Kensington W8. After war was declared, however, Sir Dudley kept what amounted to a 24-hour watch at the Admiralty. Fifty yards from his large, bare office, hung with charts, was an equally bare bedroom, its cream-coloured walls relieved only with green-painted woodwork. An austere iron bedstead and straw mattress were the only pieces of furniture to indicate the room's use. Even the mahogany chest of drawers was covered in rolled-up signal pads and an assortment of books ranging from the Navy List to signal codes.

'In these monkish surroundings Sir Dudley Pound was always on duty. An action in the darkness of the Channel would mean he had to be called from bed. The fortunes of a convoy for Archangel would keep him as busy by night as by day. In his dressing gown he would go to his office to plunge into vital consultations, urgent telephone calls, and decisions which finished only with the final dictation of the signals of instruction. On other nights he would retire to his bedroom fully dressed, knowing that in an hour or two he would have to return to the duties from which no man could relieve him.

'When Lady Pound's health began to fail he tried to get back to his flat in the evenings. But only on an average of four times a year did he manage to get home. So he set aside his lunch hour to be with her. He never went out to lunch – always he journeyed to the Kensington flat on the second floor. He could never stay longer than just an hour. Then he turned back to his work again.'

Sir Dudley had been bitterly criticised in the Commons late in 1940 for the way in which the Admiralty was conducting its higher operations. It was not the only time he was under fire, but he weathered the storm created by his opponents and was generally credited with getting the Royal Navy through the dark early days of the war. His failing, as testified by officers who worked closely with him, was a tendency to retain too much personal control and not delegate powers sufficiently to his commanders. In the words of the Navy's official historian: '… he was too inclined to try and control squadrons and fleets either from the bridge of his flagship or from Whitehall'. His intervention in the conduct of fleet operations was 'excessive'.

The Admiralty was strongly opposed to sending PQ 17 on its mission in round-the-clock Arctic daylight. When naval intelligence reported the enemy's intention to launch an all-out assault on the convoy with planes, U-boats and surface vessels, losses were almost certain to be heavy, and Sir Dudley believed the biggest threat to be that of attack by the *Tirpitz* and her consorts. He had some two weeks to dwell on this before the convoy sailed.

It transpired that his order for the ships to scatter was not only a very carefully considered personal order, but a fully premeditated one. Vice Admiral B B Schofield, who worked on the organisation of the Russian convoys, made this perfectly clear in his book *The Russian Convoys* (Batsford, 1964), which brilliantly covered the operations of all the convoys and the strategies of the opposing sides.

Admiral Schofield revealed: 'When Admiral Tovey learned that PQ 17, like the previous convoy, was to consist of 35 ships, he suggested to the First Sea Lord that it should be run in two sections, as he still adhered to his opinion that large convoys were undesirable. It was during an unrecorded telephone conversation between them on this point that Admiral Tovey first learned that Admiral Pound had it in mind to order the convoy to scatter should it be assailed in the Barents Sea by a powerful German surface force which included the *Tirpitz*. The order to a convoy to scatter is an accepted naval principle in ocean warfare where a group of merchant ships is attacked by an enemy surface force greatly superior to that escorting it. It had been used successfully when a 37-ship convoy escorted only by the armed merchant cruiser *Jervis Bay* was attacked by the pocket battleship *Scheer* in mid-Atlantic, but the circumstances were entirely different in the Barents Sea, where lack of sea room caused by the pack ice to the north prevented ships from escaping out of range of German shore-based aircraft. Moreover, experience had shown that mutual support was essential in the face of both air and U-boat attack, so that from every point of view Admiral Pound's suggestion came as a profound shock to Admiral Tovey.'

On 3 July the report came through that the *Tirpitz* and the *Hipper* had left Trondheim. Though bad weather hampered further reconnaissance, the Admiralty was practically certain, late on 4 July, that the pair had sailed up to join the *Scheer* at Altenfjord, near the North Cape, and perhaps even then were sailing north-east to attack the convoy. Admiral Tovey's battle fleet, some 350 miles to the rear, could have been ordered to steam eastwards to the convoy, but apart from the time lag, that move would have pitted its single aircraft carrier against an overwhelming mass of German planes. As for the cruisers, these were considered no match for the enemy battleships.

Admiral Schofield wrote: 'It is evident that the threat of attack by the *Tirpitz* was uppermost in the mind of the First Sea Lord. Bad weather might save the convoy from air attack, the perpetual daylight was a hindrance to the U-boats, but only fog could prevent an attack by the surface ships. As already mentioned, he had turned the situation over in his mind long before it actually happened, and reached the conclusion that scattering the convoy was, in the circumstances, the right solution. Although the general feeling of the conference over which he was now presiding was against such action, the arguments advanced were not such as to cause him to change his opinion. When everyone present had had his say, he closed his eyes for a moment while he made up his mind, then, turning to the Director of the Signal Division, he said, "Tell the cruisers to withdraw to the west at high speed, and the convoy to disperse." In the whole of his long and distinguished career Admiral Pound could never have been called upon to make a more fateful decision.'

In fact, at the moment the signal was sent, in the late evening of 4 July, the *Tirpitz* and the others were still in harbour at Altenfjord. They did not sail till noon the next day. It is now commonly admitted that the 'scatter' order was premature. Why Admiral Pound acted so precipitously on the limited intelligence at hand, without waiting for further confirmation of the *Tirpitz's* movements, is doubly puzzling, for clearly the moment the merchant ships scattered, they were prey for enemy planes and U-boats. There were bound to be rapid, heavy losses. Why deliberately imperil them before the danger from the enemy surface ships was more firmly established? Intelligence, as every serviceman knows, is an important aid to operations, but never a deciding factor – and certainly not while any doubt remains. The reported view of Vice Admiral Sir Norman Denning, one of the founders of the Naval Intelligence Division, is salutary here.

The *Sunday Telegraph* of August 1965 stated: 'It was Denning who developed the technique of tracking and identifying the German surface raiders sent to various parts of the world, in a manner which led to the destruction of most of them, including the *Graf Spee*. If his advice had been taken, the disastrous order from Sir Dudley Pound to the Russia-bound convoy PQ 17 – to scatter before imminent U-boat and surface attack – would not have gone out.'

It did go out, however, setting off a tragic chain reaction that could not have been halted. All ships acted expressly to orders, and in the case of the escorts, always according to correct naval procedure.

One of the most poignant features found during research for this book was the agony the men of the destroyers bore through the years. It went much further than their initial anger at the smears of 'cowardice' and 'betrayal' to which they were subjected. Turning away from the convoy, as they had to, went right against the grain. Their every instinct was to protect the merchantmen, and, in fact, as they turned to face the enemy expected on the horizon, this is what they were convinced they were doing. The horror they felt when the harsh reality of the situation became apparent moved men who helped with this book to offer their later war record, that of their ships, and that of the Navy's whole destroyer service as some measure of 'atonement' for that bleak day.

Cdr. Broome (later Captain Broome RN Retd.) crystallised the feelings of everyone in his flotilla when the enemy warships did not, after all, appear. 'Our rapidly increasing distance from the convoy began to infuse unpleasant doubts. Was this situation getting unreal? Were we part of any plan at all? A mathematical fact, striking colder than the freezing Arctic fog, slowly registered that as far as the convoy was concerned, we had passed the point of no return from the fuel angle. From then on, uncertainty nagged and grew, ending in a moment I am not likely to forget, when the first pitiable cry for help came limping through from a merchantman which was being attacked by U-boat and plane. Something had gone hopelessly wrong. A trust we had believed in implicitly had let us down flat. I signalled to the admiral that I was ready and willing to go back, but it was too late.'

As the details of the PQ 17 disaster emerged, various 'inquests' were conducted by people who were not involved. The escort commander, Cdr. Broome, had some blunt comments on these. The authors of this book, which was first published in 1968, wholeheartedly agreed with him.

He said: 'A lot of whitewash and criticism has followed in the wake of this disaster, with the whitewash mainly confined to the end of the story, carrying the top brass. Historians, factual and fictional, still cash in by keeping the pot on the boil, but as one of the few remaining central figures [in 1968] I have never been able to see anything controversial about it. PQ 17 was just another splendid convoy, ploughing along with no claim whatever to history or fiction until those signals arrived from the Admiralty. The order given in the final signal either had to be obeyed or ignored. To my dying regret, I obeyed it. Having done so, it triggered off a sequence of events which, as Admiral Tovey agreed later, were inevitable by accepted naval procedure. Eleven ships reached Archangel. What the results would have been had the order to scatter not been given, no one knows. But with the *Tirpitz* and her consorts then almost regarded as 'sacred cows', the results could hardly have been worse. The responsibility for what actually did happen must therefore for ever rest on the shoulders of the man who gave that order, and his advisers.'

Equally forthright were the views of an officer serving in the *Keppel's* flotilla, Lieutenant W D O'Brien, at the time of this book's publication a vice admiral and Commander Far East Fleet. His ship, the *Offa*, 'very, very nearly' turned and went back to rejoin the convoy.

Admiral O'Brien said: 'I have never been able to rejoice with my American friends on Independence Day, because 4th July is, to me, a day to hang my head in grief for all the men who lost their lives on convoy PQ 17 and in shame at the recollection of one of the bleakest episodes in Royal Naval history, when the warships deserted the merchant ships and left them to their fate. For that, in simple terms, was what we were obliged to do.

'To me, PQ 17 provides the classic lesson, and goodness knows it was not a new lesson, of the dangers that attend a military enterprise when the central authority – in this case the Admiralty – takes over control of the tactical moves of ships from the commanders on the spot. In PQ 17 this error was compounded by the Admiralty passing no information to those commanders on either the intelligence or the reasoning which led to the release of the three dramatic signals.

'I am not, and never have been, in any doubt that these three signals were wrong in principle and wrong in fact. The Commander in Chief Home Fleet was responsible for the planning and passage of PQ 17; Admiral Hamilton, with a US/UK cruiser force of considerable power, was given responsibility by him for covering the convoy against surface attack; Cdr. Broome was likewise charged with the duty of close escort to the convoy. The proper proceeding was to give these senior officers all the intelligence available and leave the tactical decisions to them. They were wholly deprived of this right and placed in the humiliating position of being ordered to desert a convoy without having the information which would allow them to judge whether this horrifying sacrifice was justified or not.

'I do not think I am making this serious judgement wholly with hindsight. There could be no doubt what the fate of the ships of the convoy would be, single defenceless targets on a flat-calm sea in the seemingly eternal daylight. To order this was wholly contrary to the principle, firmly in my mind at that time, that the best defensive posture against all forms of attack, submarine, air or surface, was for a convoy to remain concentrated and for it to be scattered only when under actual attack by overwhelming surface forces.'

The feelings of the men in the cruiser force were as strong as those of the destroyers. Lieutenant Douglas Fairbanks USNR (later Captain Retd.) was an observer aboard the USS *Wichita*. As a member of staff of Rear Admiral Robert C Giffen in the flagship the USS *Washington*, he had been sent to the cruiser on temporary assignment. He was afterwards commissioned to write an official account of the action.

Of the cruisers' withdrawal and the order for the convoy to scatter, Capt. Fairbanks said: 'Our reaction was one of stunned shock. We felt there must have been some error in transmitting the signal.

'The Americans were particularly bitter, cursing the British for what they believed to be running away in the face of a good battle which we had a chance of surviving. We resented leaving the defenceless merchant ships to straggle at nine and ten knots through icy water which we knew from experience would not permit survival for more than a very limited time.

Two of our *Wichita* observation pilots had already died before we could fish them out of the drink. Our anger was made more intense by the philosophic and good-natured spirit in which the merchant ships received the order and saw us turn tail. Only when we were clear of the immediate battle and steaming back in line ahead for Scapa Flow were we able to compare notes with the British cruisers, and found that they were as bitter and angry as we were.

'I recall an exchange of signals between the *London* and the *Wichita* in which we were informed that the Germans had claimed us as sunk and that therefore we must be a ghost ship. Captain Hill replied: "We are so numb we cannot tell but feel positions must be reversed as we have been attending your wake all day."

'In the officers' mess at Scapa, after rather too many beakers, there was much mutual recrimination and many hard words were passed. These were finally resolved in cursing the Admiralty and their inability to judge a tactical situation from a lot of pins on a board more than a thousand miles away. It was considered to be a pusillanimous defeat and a shocking error of judgment.'

The full irony of PQ 17's fate is not even the fact that the *Tirpitz* did not sail until 15 hours after Admiral Pound's order to scatter was given. It is in the later knowledge that had the British and American forces mounted a threatening opposition to her she most certainly would not have left harbour at all. For the Admiralty's concern for its heavy ships was far surpassed by Hitler's own worries about keeping his remaining capital ships intact. He had ordered his naval commanders that the ships were not to be risked even against an equal force, but only when they had definite superiority. Had the Allies known this, the chess game of naval strategy could have been played so very differently.

There are no mysteries about the German plans, which by the time of this book's first publication (1968) had been clarified. A combined attack on the convoy had been agreed. The project was called *Roessel-springer* ('Knight's Move'). The *Tirpitz*, the cruiser *Hipper* and the pocket battleships *Lutzow* and *Scheer*, together with ten destroyers, were to strike out and engage both the close escorts and the convoy – but they were to complete the action before the British battle fleet could intervene. The surface ships were to operate backed by a strong U-boat force and crack air squadrons brought up from Sicily to reinforce the Norwegian and Finnish air bases.

In the event the *Lutzow* grounded while leaving harbour and three destroyers also ran ashore. The *Tirpitz*, the *Hipper*, the *Scheer* and the remaining destroyers did sail from Altenfjord but not until noon on 5 July. Even then, although the enemy was aware of the withdrawal of Admiral Hamilton's cruisers, its heavy ships were only to make a quick strike and run, to avoid a clash with the far-off British battle fleet if it steamed to the attack, or with the planes from its carrier.

The threat from the planes on the *Victorious* was very much on Hitler's mind and largely accounted for his delay in sanctioning the sailing of the *Tirpitz*. In addition, the cruisers the *London* and the *Norfolk* had been reported by German planes as 'aircraft carriers'. In the late evening of 5 July, when the success of the German planes and U-boats became known, the *Tirpitz* was recalled. At 9.30 p.m. she turned back. The two torpedo hits claimed by the *Red Star* were not hits at all and had no bearing on the battleship's withdrawal.

The continuing arguments over the strategy of PQ 17 echoed in wardrooms long after the lifetimes of the men who sailed on the convoy. They are full of 'ifs'. If the convoy had not been prematurely scattered, what would have happened?

The British thought Admiral Tovey's battle fleet could only take on an enemy fleet in open sea, where the Germans had no land-based air support. The loss of the *Prince of Wales* and the *Repulse* had shown that determined planes alone could sink capital ships, so it was considered folly to risk heavy force against heavy force when the enemy had the advantage of several hundred land-based planes and the U-boats. Only if the *Tirpitz* force came west and passed out of range of their air support would the British have the advantage – with two battleships and the planes on the *Victorious*.

Admiral Tovey's two plans, the first to sail the convoy in two parts at intervals, the second to turn the convoy back for 12 to 18 hours to lure the enemy forward to his area, were both rejected by the Admiralty as having serious snags. In the first case the enemy could have attacked each part-convoy as heavily as the whole; in the second, the convoy would have had to steam twice through a very dangerous zone. The Germans were only interested in preventing supplies from reaching Russia; they would not have been foolish enough to follow the convoy back westward into the jaws of the British heavy force, which they knew was somewhere in that area. They could afford to wait until the convoy returned to the Barents Sea.

Admiral Pound's chief concern, if the *Tirpitz* sailed, appeared to be to save valuable warships and let the merchantmen fend for themselves.

The authors do not set themselves up as naval strategists, but the facts are clear. No one knows how the convoy would have fared if it had been dispersed later, when attack really was imminent, though by then, late on 5 July, the ships would have been a day closer both to the Russian coast and to Novaya Zemlya.

There is another major point, however, one made very clear by the great number of naval escort men who contributed to this book. If PQ 17 had gone on as a convoy and the enemy had mounted a series of attacks like that of Independence Day, some ships would have run out of ammunition and others would have run very low, with the inevitable consequence that the merchantmen would have been left undefended just the same. It now seems unlikely that such overwhelming attacks would have been made, but the argument is finely balanced since several of the escorts, on reaching Archangel, were down almost to their last shell. If the fleeing ships had met any of the 'enemy vessels' continually reported by Admiralty signals there would have been a different tale to tell. These curious signals, several of them intercepted by the *Lord Austin*'s limited radio equipment, remain a mystery. None of the 'warships' reported so dramatically was ever seen, though you will remember that on one occasion the *Lord Austin* passed over the exact position of a reported enemy group.

All these considerations, however, do not detract from the main issue, which is that the convoy was scattered prematurely and entirely above the heads of the three commanders at sea. With this firmly established, it is a question of how far commentators will go to heap further blame on a long-dead man.

The second issue concerns the secrecy the Admiralty maintained for years about the operation. This caused almost as much misery as the operation itself, for the admissions of error came too late to repair the hurt caused at the time, and they were not made widely known. Survivors of the convoy, their families and friends, and others not involved with the action remained gripped by it. They repeatedly asked the authors the same plaintive questions. What really happened? And why? Why?

In America particularly, merchant seamen from the convoy saw various articles appear over the years. Within the controversy these aroused, the men observed with sadness how their lost ships were swallowed up in statistics, and their own fate never fully told. They read 'pulp fiction' about ships 'tossing and heaving their way through sheeting blizzards and pitch darkness' in the middle of the Arctic summer, and even stories that described great feats by the enemy.

Such tales were so far removed from reality that they would have been laughable had they not been an insult to those who sailed. The enemy's exuberance at his 'victory' over the scattered merchant vessels is something that stuck in the craw of the surviving crews. One man, twice torpedoed, summed it up: 'They were virtually handed a licence to bomb, torpedo and photograph us, then shoot off home to photograph themselves putting on their medals!'

This, in essence, is true. Seldom can so much film footage have been taken of a single action at sea, all from an enemy standpoint, which reaped such a rich harvest in propaganda. These pictures have, in the years since, provoked many a hollow laugh. For the enemy's action to be taken as any special feat of arms is to border on the ridiculous, considering such incidents as four U-boats stalking one ill-armed merchant ship; a U-boat taking three torpedoes to register a hit on a motionless vessel; combined U-boat and aircraft assaults, in some cases beaten off for hours by a single merchantman; or planes dropping a fantastic number of bombs in a crazy effort to obtain a direct hit. These are scarcely stories of skill and courage. In the major actions, the torpedo-bomber battle of Independence Day alone can be recognised in part as a spirited assault. In part, because although the daring of the squadron leader was unquestioned, the bulk of the other planes could well have done more.

As the *Life* photographer with the USS *Wainwright* commented in his article at the time: 'The Americans watched with interest the way the pilots of the German torpedo planes drove home the attack. Only the squadron leader of a Nazi formation of seven planes dove in through the anti-aircraft fire, and won the admiration of his enemies. The other German pilots veered off, fudged their run and dropped their torpedoes at random. It was a far cry from the way the American and Japanese torpedo planes had been fighting in the Pacific. After two and a half years of it, the Germans seemed to have lost some of their determination.'

The seven hours' bombing of the remnant convoy on its way from Matochkin Strait to the White Sea is an especially dismal statistic for the enemy, one that, for obvious reasons, is thankfully recorded here. In heavy rain and a hail of bombs only two vessels were lost, both of these shelled and sunk by the escorts after damage from near misses. This appalling marksmanship by the enemy bombers was a consistent feature, their inability to hit even a near-defenceless merchantman repeated time and again in the survivors' stories.

As for the U-boats, before 'scatter' they had not sunk a ship or penetrated the escort screen. Even during the attack by torpedo bombers, when the escorts were busy with the planes, they did not move in to attack. The only ships sunk by U-boats were 'sitting-duck' merchantmen without asdics, and it often took three U-boats to sink a ship. No wonder Allied seamen smiled at pictures of the U-boat crews having their medals pinned on. The poor show by the enemy planes and U-boats is an important point to be considered against the Admiralty's reluctance to risk the battle fleet east of Bear Island. Some senior British and American officers who were with the fleet considered that the battleships USS *Washington* and HMS *Duke of York* could well have handled the *Tirpitz* in a showdown.

The plain fact is that by following the 'scatter' order, no ship from PQ 17 should have survived. Had the enemy kept to his original plan and the planes, U-boats and surface craft attacked in a more aggressive manner, PQ 17 would have been totally destroyed, as Lord Haw-Haw prophesied. Admiral Pound asserted that if he had had forces as strong as the enemy's and positions been reversed, he could have stopped all Arctic convoys completely. It was no idle comment.

The finale to PQ 17 is the story of the return convoy. With more determined efforts by the U-boats, two of the surviving American merchantmen went down, along with the lead British ship, a tanker, minesweeper and a destroyer. Six losses, when the merchantmen were outnumbered more than two to one by their escorts.

Admiral O'Brien had strong words to say about QP 14: 'I have always had one major criticism of its conduct – applicable to PQ 18 and QP 14. A special screening formation was produced for the escorts and this formation was stuck to without alteration from the start of PQ 18 to the end of QP 14. I thought it more suitable for a fleet than a convoy, i.e. a formation with a greater speed of advance than eight knots, but I expect this is arguable. What is not arguable, to my mind, is that when under continuous enemy surveillance (as we were) one must employ a flexible system of screening which can be, and should be, varied at frequent intervals. This was never done, and the pattern of sinkings by submarine attack indicated clearly that the Germans worked out a method of penetrating this screen and proceeded to do so with dreadful regularity. One must not help the U-boat. How can one help him more than by presenting him with exactly the same screen formation day after day?

'I remember feeling much sympathy with the ships who found themselves at the rear of the convoy because, it seemed to me, they were the next victims of the inevitable attacks being successfully launched from the quarters of the convoy. And very often they were.'

Looking back at PQ 17 from a standpoint many years hence, one cannot help feeling that it was doomed from the start, and that, sadly, the nagging presentiments of the time were tragically played out. It was a fiasco. Despite the many small miracles – it was remarkable that the actual loss of life was so small – the remnants of the great United Nations convoy to save Stalingrad got through in the end, but with a puny load of supplies. In spite of this failure and the long, long wait for the next convoy, the Russians did not collapse. Not only did they hold out during this time but before long they drove the enemy back. For us it was the final irony.

How different PQ 18 was, with the 'Woolworth' carrier, cruiser cover and plenty of fighting destroyers all the way. With film and newsreels, the whole operation was well publicised. From then on, convoys would have much-needed air cover. So maybe PQ 17 did not sail in vain.

And the *Lord Austin*? After QP 14 she joined Western Approaches Command at Liverpool for a short spell of escort duties. Then the old Admiral, Commander in Chief Northern Ireland, on the verge of tears, told her company she was required for Arctic service again. But not from Iceland this time. Convoys were now sailing from Loch Ewe, because German agents were active in Iceland.

The *Lord Austin* sailed with a convoy in the spring of 1943, in some of the worst weather encountered on the Russian run. Fierce gales and mountainous seas swamped the accompanying *Lord Middleton* and she had to turn back. Enemy activity was negligible, however, and the convoy reached Murmansk without mishap. The *Lord Austin* stayed in Russia for some months, working with minesweepers, then went back to the UK for more escort duties.

Shortly after D-Day she escorted a convoy to Normandy. She was making an asdic patrol round the anchorage off the French coast when she set off an acoustic mine. Several ships had already passed over it unscathed, but it broke her at once. She sank quickly, taking some of her company with her.

Such was the sad end of the gallant little trawler, one of the only two British warships to be sunk during that operation.

'My word, you won't arf cop it. What have you been doing? Fishing?'

Abbreviations

NAAFI	Navy, Army and Air Force Institutes
Retd.	Retired
RFA	Royal Fleet Auxiliary
RN	Royal Navy
RNR	Royal Naval Reserve
RNVR	Royal Naval Volunteer Reserve
USN	United States Navy
USNR	United States Naval Reserve
USS	United States Ship

Acknowledgments

The authors are grateful to the following merchant survivors and naval veterans of PQ 17 who unstintingly gave their time to help in the making of this book, often providing diaries and papers together with their first-hand reports. Names of ships are given alphabetically, with the rank the men held at the time. Decorations are those awarded for service on the convoy.

AMERICAN MERCHANTMEN
The *Bellingham*: A/B Harold D Lunt.
The *Christopher Newport*: Lieutenant (JG) Peter M Coy USNR, Armed Guard Officer.
El Capitan: Lieutenant (JG) Louis D Marks USNR, Armed Guard Officer.
The *Exford*: Oiler Lionel W Smith.
The *Hoosier*: First Assistant Engineer Willard L Davis.

The *John Witherspoon*: A/B Ferocious O'Flaherty (with many thanks for permission to refer to and quote from his book *Abandoned Convoy*).

The *Olopana*: Gunner Edward Hennessey BEM.

The P*ankraft*: Radioman J E Blackwell USN.

The *Peter Kerr*: Second Mate William P Connolly.

The *Silver Sword*: Second Mate John Behnken.

The *Washington*: Captain Julius Richter.

The authors would also like to acknowledge the response and help of: Mrs Anne T Hill (the *Pan Atlantic*); Gunner Arthur McDonald Jr (the *Washington*); Oiler W C Stackhouse (the *Alcoa Ranger*).

The authors also acknowledge the invaluable assistance of the US Navy Department (Captain F Kent Loomis USN Retd., Assistant Director of Naval History) in providing official survivor reports of the following ships: the *Alcoa Ranger*, the *Carlton*, the *Daniel Morgan*, *El Capitan*, the *Honomu*, the *John Witherspoon*, the *Pankraft*, the *Washington* and the *William Hooper*.

BRITISH MERCHANTMEN

The *Bolton Castle*: Cook George Duncan; Chief Cook J Leonard Osmundsen; Gunner Charles H West.

The *Earlston*: Lance Bombardier Richard F Crossley; Stoker A J Robinson; Cadet A V Watt BEM LM.

The *Empire Byron*: Carpenter Frederick Cooper DSM; A/B Walter B Shepherd.

The *Empire Tide*: Chief Officer George E Leech DSC; Boatswain C L Medhurst DSM; Engineer Officer George Robinson; Fireman E V Williams.

The *Hartlebury*: Gunner Arthur Carter.

The *Ocean Freedom*: Acting L/S Gunner Jim A Gordon RN DSM; Captain William Walker DSO; Gunner Herbert A Wharmby.

The *River Afton*: A/B Adam J O'Hagan; A/B W N Marsh.

DUTCH MERCHANTMAN
The *Paulus Potter*: Gunner David J Richards.

RESCUE SHIPS
The *Rathlin*: Junior Officer Ernest M Bentley.
The *Zaafaran*: P/O (Sick Bay) L A Bryant; Carpenter James Ramsay.
The *Zamalek*: Chief Engineer A S Dawson DSC; Surgeon Lieutenant N H R McCallum RNVR.

BRITISH TANKERS (RFA)
The *Aldersdale*: Chief Engineer W J Brown DSC; Captain Archibald Hobson DSC; Third Officer Henry W Phillips; Gunner Thomas W Urwin.
The *Gray Ranger*: Chief Engineer D L S Hood DSC.

BRITISH CLOSE ESCORTS
The *Ayrshire*: Sub Lieutenant John F Aylard RNVR; Lieutenant Richard W H Elsden RNVR.
The *Dianella*: A/B Kenneth J Richards.
The *Halcyon*: Telegraphist J A Hart; Stoker S Isam; Sub Lieutenant James McDowall RNVR; P/O J T C Welch.
La Malouine: Sub Lieutenant F H Petter RNVR.
The *Lord Austin:* T/O Telegraphist Hugh Davey; Signalman Gordon Hooper; Leading Seaman Arthur W Mallett; Signalman Jim Morris; Telegraphist Johnny Rose; Lieutenant E Leslie Wathen DSC RNR Commanding.
The *Lord Middleton*: A/B (SDO) Arthur Jones; O/D Murdo MacGregor; Chief Engineer John P Mair; Stoker Alex Milne.
The *Northern Gem*: Coxswain S A Kerslake; Skipper Lieutenant W P O Mullender DSC RNR.

The *Palomares*: Signalman Douglas Blarney; Sub Lieutenant (SP) Leslie Clements RNVR; Leading Telegraphist Maurice Davies; Signalman J B Taylor.

The *Poppy*: Lieutenant John Beardmore RNVR; Sub Lieutenant Denis C Brooke RNVR; Leading Stoker Reginald Lantsberry; O/D H V Pittman.

The *Pozarica*: A/B Walter Edgley; O/D Charles Gooch; A/B (ST) William S Mayne; CPO (QRI) Peter Reid; A/B A G Webster.

The *Salamander*: Stoker Thomas McClements; Stoker G Moore.

Also: Asdic Rating Alex Atmore (the *Britomart*); John G Galley (the *Pozarica*); A/B Jim Harber (the *Pozarica*); Radar Operator Glyn A Hughes (the *Pozarica*); Stoker E Jeffries (the *Britomart*); Coder R C Kimberley (the *Palomares*); Arthur E Lay-Flurrie (the *Pozarica*); P/O Arthur H Norton (the *Britomart*); R J Smith (the *Palomares*).

DESTROYERS

The *Fury*: O/D (CW) Norman V Smith.

The *Keppel*: A/B A E Davies; P/O Frederick Wicks RN; A/B Harold Williams.

The *Leamington*: A/B Oswald Tranter.

The *Ledbury*: Stoker P/O G H Smith.

The *Offa*: Chief Bosun's Mate Danny A R Daniels; Signalman Richard Hodgett; First Lieutenant W D O'Brien RN.

The *Wilton*: Sub Lieutenant Michael R Collins RN.

The authors acknowledge the kind permission of Captain Jack Broome DSC and A M Heath and Co. Ltd to quote from his article 'I am Ready and Willing to Go Back', featured in *Freedom's Battle*, Vol. 1, *The War At Sea 1939–45*, Hutchinson, 1964.

They also express their deep appreciation of the valuable help and comments of Vice Admiral W D O'Brien CB DSC, Commander Far East Fleet.

US/UK CRUISER FORCE
HMS *London*: Telegraphist C E Blakeborough; C P O Herbert G Bull RN; A/B D Murray.
USS W*ainwright*: P/O John W Crawford; Signalman First Class Merlin J Ewing.
USS *Wichita*: Lieutenant Douglas Fairbanks USNR; Signalman G Edward Young.
The authors thank Captain Douglas Fairbanks USNR Retd. for his kind help and permission to use comments from *Knight Errant* by Brian Connell (Hodder and Stoughton, 1955).

OTHER US/UK WARSHIPS
HMS *Avenger*: A/B John A Annand.
HMS *Somali*: Stoker First Class A Bailey.
USS *Washington*: Lieutenant (JG) Daniel W Jones USNR.
The authors thank Vice Admiral B B Schofield for his very helpful interest in this book and for permission to quote from *The Russian Convoys* (Batsford, 1964).
They also record the kind co-operation of more than 80 US newspapers and 40 UK newspapers, together with maritime unions and organisations of both countries, all of whom played a part in the long search for ships and men. The authors also acknowledge the efforts of a host of helpful correspondents, especially, in America: Howard Bethell (Brooklyn, New York); Frank H Cressey (Portland, Maine); Marc Enright (New York); Charles Hollisian (Cambridge, Mass.); Robert Kissel (Cincinnati, Ohio); John F Laird, Ex-Commander USNR (Colorado); Robert L Mahar (Randolph, Mass.); George Edward Stanley (Memphis, Texas).
And not least, for all her hard work, Mrs Mary Vaughan (California).
The lines from the song 'Jingle, Jangle, Jingle' (composer Joseph J Lilley; lyrics Frank Loesser) are quoted by kind permission of Chappell and Co. Ltd.

Maps

Route of PQ17 up to 'Scatter'

Route of Lord Austin *after 'Scatter'*